FROM TEXTILE MILLS TO TAXI RANKS

DAMES
Dansk Center for Migration
og Etniske Studier

From Textile Mills to Taxi Ranks
Experiences of migration, labour and social change

VIRINDER S. KALRA
Sociology, University of Leicester

Ashgate
Aldershot • Burlington USA • Singapore • Sydney

© Virinder S. Kalra 2000

All rights reserved. No part of this publication may be reproduced, stored in a retrieval system, or transmitted in any form or by any means, electronic, mechanical, photocopying, recording or otherwise without the prior permission of the publisher.

Published by
Ashgate Publishing Ltd
Gower House
Croft Road
Aldershot
Hants GU11 3HR
England

Ashgate Publishing Company
131 Main Street
Burlington
Vermont 05401
USA

Ashgate website: http://www.ashgate.com

British Library Cataloguing in Publication Data
Kalra, Virinder S.
   From textile mills to taxi ranks : experiences of
   migration, labour and social change. - (Research in
   migration and ethnic relations series)
   1.South Asians - Great Britain - Social conditions 2.South
   Asians - Great Britain - Economic conditions 3.Great
   Britain - Social conditions - 20th century
   I.Title
   305.8'95'041

Library of Congress Catalog Card Number: 99-85924

ISBN 1 84014 865 9

Printed and bound by Athenaeum Press, Ltd.,
Gateshead, Tyne & Wear.

Contents

Figures and Tables ix

Acknowledgements x

Introduction 1
    The Story 1
    The Explanation 3
    Organisation of the Book 5

1   Constructing Labour 8
    Introduction 8
    Class and Ethnicity 11
    Ethnicity and Class 16
    Overlapping Perspectives 22
    Enmeshing Formations 24

2   Methodology 32
    Introduction 32
    Ethnicity and the Labelling of Groups 33
    Developing a New Terminology 39
    Reflexive Approaches 42
    Identifying a Field and a Sample 45
    Ethical Issues 49

Applying Methods *50*

3   Migration and Repercussion **52**

Introduction *52*

Migration Theory *53*

Early Migration *55*

Rural Context: Geography, Agriculture and Society *58*

Historical Conduits *60*

Mass Migration *63*

Political History Post-1947 .... *64*

Mangla Dam and its Impact on Migration *65*

Consequences of Mass Migration on Mirpur's Economy and Society ... *69*

Mirham and Oldpur *73*

4   Textile Tours **76**

Introduction *76*

Lancashire, the Indian Sub-continent and Cotton Textiles *77*

Decline of the Textile Industry in England *80*

King Cotton - Oldham *83*

Labour in Lancashire and Oldham *88*

Migrant Labour *92*

Routing Mills *98*

5   Of Mills and Men **101**

Introduction *101*

Routes to Oldham *103*

Routes to a Job *107*

Organising Mill Work *111*

The Night-shift in a Mill *113*

    Mills and Men *116*

6 Of Men and Mills **119**

    Eid and Trips to (Azad) Kashmir/Pakistan *119*
    Union Membership and Participation *122*
    Interaction and Relationship at Work *126*
    Decline of Mills *131*
    Factors for Redundancy *132*

7 Redundant not Despondent **138**

    Introduction *138*
    Initial Responses to Unemployment *139*
    Changes in Life Organisation *145*
    Family Commitments *150*
    Moral Change - Ways of Explaining the World *154*
    Work to Non-Work *157*

8 Take-Away Lives **160**

    Introduction *160*
    South Asian Entrepreneurship *161*
    After the Mills *163*
    Take-aways *166*
    The Maharaba *169*
    Relationships at Work *173*
    Self-employment or Survival ? *176*

9 From Textile Mills to Taxi Ranks **179**

    Introduction *179*
    Taxi Drivers and Taxi Rank Owners *180*

    Cabbing Work *186*
    Risky Business *191*
    From Taxi Ranks to...........? *194*

10   Beyond Labour? **196**
    Introduction *196*
    Explanations *197*
    Narratives *201*
    Audiences *205*

Appendix I **207**
    Profile Of Oldham's (Azad) Kashmiri/Pakistani Population *207*
        Population 207
        Economic Activity 208
        Unemployment Data - by Age 210
    Economic Profile of Oldham *211*

Bibliography **212**

Index **230**

Figures and Tables

Figures

Figure 3.1 Indian Sub - Continent 57
Figure 3.2 Punjab, Jammu and Kashmir and Azad Jammu and Kashmir .. 57
Figure 3.3 (Azad) Kashmir and Region 60
Figure 3.4 Mirpur District and Region 61
Figure 4.1 Textile Types of the North of England 78
Figure 4.2 Gandhi with Mill Workers in Blackburn 79
Figure 4.3 Cotton Yarn Output by Year: 1950 - 1970 81
Figure 4.4 Employment in Spinning by Year : 1950 - 1970 81
Figure 4.5 North and North West England 84
Figure 4.6 Number of Mills in Oldham: 1794 - 1990 85
Figure 4.7 Workforce in Major Cotton Mill Companies: 1975 - 1983 87
Figure 4.8 Employment by Gender in the Cotton Mills of 90
  Oldham:1861 - 1921
Figure 5.1 North and North West England 106
Figure AI.1 Relative Population of Minorities - Oldham, 1995 207
Figure AI.2 South Asian Concentration by Ward - 1991 208
Figure AI.3 Economic Activity of Pakistani and White
  Population in Oldham 1991 209
Figure AI.4 Economic Inactivity of Pakistani and
  White Population in Oldham 1991 209
Figure AI.5 Unemployment by Age - Oldham 1991 210

Tables

Table AI.1 Population of Oldham by Ethnic Group: 1981, 1986
  and 1991, 1995 207
Table AI.2 Economic Status of Pakistani Population:
  Oldham 1991 - 1995 208
Table AI.3 Unemployment by Age Range in
  Oldham's Pakistani Population 1992 210
Table AI.4 Employment Change in the NorthWest 1971 - 1980 211
Table AI.5 Employment Change in Oldham by Industry 1984 - 1993 211

Acknowledgements

Thanks to those who gave me birth and sustenance; mom and dad. Moving to my current support, the first and last, Tej. This particular story could not have been told if it were not for the financial support of 'The British Cotton Growers Workers Welfare Fund' and the insightful appointment made by Dr Roger Ballard. In chronological order, but with equal thanks on many levels for multiple inputs, helps, and supports. To Raminder, Chris Pinney and Kitt Davis, for encouraging me on this misguided route. For initial meaning and motivation to the Panjab Research Group especially Ustad Darshan Singh Tatla, and to Gurharpal, Pritam, and Shinder. To Tariq, Shams, Adaalat, Mottu, Lalla, Raja, Tanveer and Cheema for food for my thoughts and my belly, inspiration and nights out. For making fieldwork sane: Shams, Mahme, Nighat, Rifat, the kids and the rest of that family (in its entirety). To Sanjay and John for providing much needed alternative academic work. For intellectually and socially listening to me moan and for putting up with me for five years, a special thanks to Sean. For giving any meaning to the academic exercise and returning the edge: Nilo, Kabir (and Shahina), Tarsem, Nusrat, Bilu, Manjit and kids.

This book was partially written during a period of employment at Oldham Council and there is a long list of those who were around and provided ongoing help and information. Thanks to: Pasha, Julie, Chris H. and Chris P., Paul and Bruce, to Brian for another insightful appointment, and to Sarah for coping and Ed for lunches. The rest of the Policy Unit, especially Van, Dorotheeaa and Eileen (spooky) for putting up with all the grief. Outside of that gang, this book would not have been written without the on-going and continual support and co-operation of the many *kakas* and *babas* whose stories form the basis of the narrative.

Introduction

The Story

> Millionaires or beggars ? I wish the media would make up its mind.......Are we the scum of the earth, or have we really become the 'new Jews' (as someone recently described us)?....
> The truth is, you can't stereotype us......
> At the end of the day, I'm afraid we'll be whatever the media want us to be, when it suits them most.... (Eastern Eye, 21/6/96: p 9)

This quote is from the weekly British Asian newspaper *Eastern Eye*. The commentator, Thuyafel Ahmed, was responding to a recent academic report on Britain's 'ethnic minorities' derived from data in the 1991 Census. [1] Ahmed, expresses a concern about the socio-economic position of Asians in Britain and how this comes to be represented in the media, as either economically successful or deprived. In this book I share Ahmed's wish that the 'media would make up their mind,' but apply it to the field of academic research on minorities in Britain. The occupational and economic status of racialised and ethnicised groups has attracted a great deal of research since the arrival of post-war migrants. Academic studies have, historically, focused on 'British-Asians as beggars and not millionaires' where deprivation and disadvantage have been the key terms in their description. Recently, however, there has been a shift in perspective with an increasing emphasis on minority success rather than failure. This issue has divided academic opinion in much the same way as Ahmed concludes for the media, with some hailing 'Asians as the new Jews' and others emphasising continuing deprivation and discrimination. By offering a historically grounded analysis, which details patterns of migration and settlement through the lens of income generation and employment, this book illustrates that it is not possible to simply 'stereotype' minorities in terms of success and failure.

Contemporary academic studies on economic activity and South Asians in Britain have concentrated on self-employment and entrepreneurial business development. [2] As Cater and Jones point out: 'Over the past decade or so, Asians have acquired an unshakeable reputation as entrepreneurs, a group whose future is that of the new Jews'

(1988: 182). Given this emphasis, it would not be too difficult to forget that the mass of South Asians came to Britain to work in her declining manufacturing industries. Any move into self-employment by South Asians can therefore be usefully seen in the light of the historical transformations in the economy of Britain. The shift from a predominantly manufacturing economic base to one where services, in their many manifestations, constitute the dominant sector has resulted in far reaching and multiple social changes. These transformations have been keenly felt in the old industrial heartland of Britain, those places which, in the post-war years, have become settler areas for South Asian migrants. From textile mills to taxi ranks, is not only a metonym for the shift to a service sector economy but also literally presents a shift in place of work for many (Azad) Kashmiris/Pakistanis men in the North of England.

This book is not a traditional ethnography about a group of people who are variously labelled as Pakistani, Kashmiri, Black, Muslims, yet it recognises the influence of that genre of writing.[3] It is about a group of people who have emotional, spiritual and material ties to the geographical district of Mirpur in the politically disputed territory of (Azad) Kashmir. It is not representative of those people who labelled themselves Pakistani in the 1991 census, nor is it meant to serve as a morsel of cultural difference for the avaricious appetite of post-modern consumer culture, though no doubt it will become entwined in that particular net. What is presented is an exploration of the way in which the old-fashioned, though nevertheless still substantive, issues of employment, work, income generation and economic status affect and are effected by a racialised group of people, who often closely related, now live for most of the time, in the town of Oldham in the North West of England. Simultaneously, it is also a history of the demise of the textile industry in Oldham and the structural changes in the economy of that town, the North West region and Britain as a whole.

The issues of income generation, employment and unemployment as they relate to the working lives of a section of the Mirpuri/Pakistani 'community', now settled in Oldham, form the core narratives of this book. Stories of workers and industry, of home and abroad, of dreams and realities merge and entwine in the practices of everyday life. For purposes of clarity there are three broad processes under consideration: migration, labour/work and the effects of economic change. Migration from Mirpur has been a long-standing means of providing income for the residents of what was a peripheral area of the British empire and subsequently a disputed territory of independent Pakistan. In the 1960s, the demand for labour in the cotton textile mills of the North West of England attracted large numbers of South Asian male migrant labour. A combination of factors result in migration, such that from the mid-sixties up to the early eighties there was an increasing concentration of (Azad) Kashmiri/Pakistani male labour in the textile industry - both cotton and woollen- of the North of England. For many of these men their lives were consumed by working, saving, and more working, occasionally relieved by trips to (Azad) Kashmir/Pakistan. Throughout the 1970s and 1980s women and children were joining their husbands, and long-term settlements were formed in towns like Oldham throughout the North-West of England.

It is not surprising that the recession of the early eighties had a devastating impact on this section of the labour force. Many of the Mirpuri/(Azad) Kashmiri men, who spent most of their lives employed in the mills, when made redundant in the 1980s, could not secure further formal employment. In the subsequent period there has been a transformation in the socio-economic profile of Mirpuri/(Azad) Kashmiri men in towns like Oldham. While unemployment is the single most significant economic factor affecting the population as a whole, the occupational profile of those in employment has also changed. There is a small salience of cotton textile work, with an increasing concentration of Mirpuri/(Azad) Kashmiri workers in the mills that remain. However, there has also been an increasing diversity in the make-up of the workforce. Taxi driving, shops, market trading and the catering trade have all become areas of employment concentration for ex-mill workers. These shifts into self-employment and particularly the service sector by Mirpuri/(Azad) Kashmiri men reflect the wider transformations in the British economy. These changes have altered social relations amongst male and kin folk, in ways which correspond to the demise of other industrially based social groupings. However, the negative consequences of industrial decline have been offset by renewed commitments to family and religion.[4] Indeed the way in which Mirpuri/(Azad) Kashmiri men manage, negotiate, circumvent and overcome the multiple contexts that they find themselves in is a central part of the narrative running through this book.

The Explanation

A concern with the issues of disadvantage and discrimination has come to dominate British academic discourse on South Asian minorities, particularly in relation to the labour market. A perspective has developed where the socio-economic position of Black workers in Britain is reduced to that of either an underclass or a class fraction (Rex and Moore 1967;

Miles 1982). The question of cultural difference and 'ethnic' self organisation is dismissed as either irrelevant or an ideology masking true class relations (Miles and Phizacklea 1980). An abundance of statistical and quantitative data illustrating the effects of racial disadvantage in the labour market is provided as evidence for this position of disadvantage. Similarly, qualitative studies have tended to focus on the negative views of management and white workers, about the presence of 'immigrants' (see Fevre 1984; Duffield 1988), rather than the perspectives of the migrants themselves.

On the other hand, ethnographic literature relating to 'ethnic' minorities in Britain has tended to focus on the social and moral implications of migration, rather than the practical implications of changing work practices (see Watson 1977; Shaw 1988; Werbner 1990; Ballard 1994). Issues relating to income generation have tended to be encompassed within a framework emphasising continuity with place of migration. The main concern here is on the deployment of 'ethnic' resources to resist and circumnavigate structures of exclusion. These resources stem from the ties of kin and religion which can be used for the furtherance of group aims. Contemporary South Asian business success is, therefore, a result of the advantageous deployment of 'ethnic' resources. Ethnographic studies of South Asian business populations has provided the qualitative backing to these generalisations. Further quantitative evidence for this approach has been recently provided by the analysis of results from the 1991 Census, which has revealed higher levels of self-employment amongst South Asians when compared to other 'ethnic' groups (Iganski and Payne 1996; Peach 1996).

This book attempts to weave a path between, through and around these two distinct theoretical approaches to the study of minority economic status. Two levels of criticism can be levelled at both perspectives. Firstly, both have remained remarkably consistent in their portrayal of South Asian minorities in the last thirty years. On the one hand, Black workers socio-economic status is a result of structural deprivation and, on the other, the result of cultural choices. In each case, little account has been taken of the effect of historical transformations from industrial work to service sector employment on minority economic status. Similarly, theories relating to the 1960s which refer to a predominantly male, overseas born, employed population are not necessarily going to apply to British-born, unemployed, women in the 1990s. Secondly, the main focus for both sets of writers is to explain differences between the white population and the minority population based upon differences of 'race' or 'ethnicity'. Other fissures along lines of class, gender or age are therefore not considered at all or are made secondary.

To develop a theoretical framework which reflects the ethnographic sections of this book, it is necessary to first move away from polemical positions, such as structuralist and culturalist. In this way, the ethnographic chapters utilise both structuralist and culturalist approaches. However, in order to overcome the divide between structure and agency present in these works, it is useful to address recent research by Avtar Brah (1993, 1996). In these studies, Brah develops a framework which accounts for the 'enmeshing' nature of structure and culture, the multiple determinants of socio-economic position and the necessity of an historical appreciation of colonialism and migration. Applying Brah's approach to my specific project, I illustrate how the focus on the workplace presented in this book differs from and develops on the themes laid out in her framework. The main tenets of the perspective, I put forward, are illustrated by reference to the remaining chapters in the book.

Organisation of the Book

Chapter One begins by reviewing the theoretical literature pertaining to minorities and socio-economic status. This is divided in terms of those accounts which emphasise class over ethnicity and vice-versa. My own theoretical perspective is offered via a development of Brah's work. In Chapter Two, I outline the particular methods which I used in developing my theoretical approach during fieldwork. Central to my methodology is the construction of a set of analytical categories which act as guides to the narratives presented in the ethnographic chapters. A practical examination of choice of fieldwork, difficulties in access and the thorny question of translation are also briefly touched upon. Both the theoretical and methodology chapters provide a set of basic analytical tools which are applied to varying degrees in the subsequent chapters.

Chapters Three and Four trace the reasons for mass migration from Mirpur and the factors for labour demand in the textile industry in the North West of England. Both of these chapters serve as background and setting for the ethnographic chapters which follow. In Chapter Three, I review the literature on migration from Mirpur and contend that insufficient attention has been paid, by previous academic accounts to the political causes of migration from the region. The social and economic impact of migration on Mirpur is explored in light of Ballard's (1987) comments that migration is not a one-off occurrence but an on-going process which results in both Mirpur and Oldham becoming a single field of interaction. Chapter Four takes up the other side of the story and begins by considering the development of the textile industry in Oldham and the North West in general. Historically, the industry attracted migrant labour, and this chapter traces the history of the various types of workers who came to the town. This culminates in the arrival of the South Asian migrants with whom continuities and disjunctions with previous migrant and women workers are traced.

In Chapters Five, Six and Seven the gain and loss of employment in the mills by Mirpuri/Pakistani workers is explored. Central to the ethnographic tract is the role of the extended kinship network; the *biraderi* as an alternative to formal welfare provision. In Chapter Five, the process by which the Mirpuri/(Azad) Kashmiri men found their way to Oldham, obtained jobs and organised their every day living in and out of work is outlined. The mills as the dominant agent of social change in the lives of the male workers is shown repeatedly in this Chapter. From type of work, to control of time and pay, the mill hierarchy and industrial working time imposes itself on the migrants. In contrast to this, Chapter Six focuses on relationships at work and sites of resistance. In particular, the mobilisation of the Mirpuri/(Azad) Kashmiri males workers around issues of Eid and extended holidays highlights their agency in the face of harsh structural constraints. It is in the meshing of the needs of the men and the needs of management that the working practices of the late 1960s and 1970s are best understood. In Chapter Seven, the subsequent loss of employment in the textile mills is examined in terms of opportunities for other employment in Oldham and (Azad) Kashmir. The means by which many Mirpuri men coped with long-term unemployment in terms of renewed commitment to *biraderi* and religion is also illustrated. Chapters Five, Six and Seven are primarily concerned with the life histories and processes of incorporation of male migrants into the textile mills. The next two chapters take up the story of their male offspring and their employment

The concentration of (Azad) Kashmiri men in the taxi, retail and restaurant businesses is investigated in some ethnographic detail in Chapters Eight and Nine. A comparison of working in the mills and working in business is framed by the general debate about the reasons for high levels of Asian self-employment. The concept of risk, as a means of understanding the changing relationship of these male workers to their environment is also examined. Indeed, these two chapters are concerned with the contemporary labour market in Oldham and provide a sad indictment of the state of the sons of mill workers. The conclusion summarises some of the main themes covered in the book and highlights some of the insights that the empirical sections can provide to a theoretical understanding of the labour market status of racialised groups.

---

[1] The report referred to was *Ethnicity in the 1991 Census Volume Two, The Ethnic Minority Populations of Great Britain*, C. Peach (ed.) (1996).

[2] See Modood et al (1996) for a useful review of the literature on Asian businesses and self-employment.

[3] Black with a capital B reflects all racialised groups. Black with a small 'b' refers to African and African-Caribbean groupings only.

[4] See Table two in Appendix I for a full breakdown of economic activity of the Pakistani population from the 1991 Census.

1 Constructing Labour

Introduction

The relationship between the labour market and South Asian settlers in Britain has been an area of political and academic concern since the first wave of mass migration in the early sixties. Occupational concentration of Black workers in the lower skill levels of industry throughout the 1960s and 1970s warranted concern and academic explanation, as has the contemporary large proportionate number of South Asians in business and self-employment. In order to assess, explain and understand the impact which employment in the textile mills, unemployment and a shift into taxi ranks by Mirpuri/Pakistani workers has had, it is necessary to review the literature that has theorised about these issues and to construct a framework which is most appropriate to the ethnographic chapters. [1] When considering the history of the labour market position of South Asian settlers, it is possible to view the literature in what can be crudely called British race and ethnic relations, in two competing frames of explanation. Anthias (1992) labels these perspectives 'structuralist' and 'British ethnic school'. For the purpose of clarity, and as a useful heuristic device, in this chapter and throughout the book I follow Anthias' use of the term 'structuralist' but prefer 'culturalist' to 'British ethnic school'. [2] While these generic terms gloss over many subtle differences between authors, they are legitimate in terms of the polemic nature of the debate engaged in by writers of both schools (see Dahya 1974 vs Rex and Moore 1967 and CCCS 1982 vs Saifullah Khan 1977).

Central to structuralist standpoints is the notion that the operation of capital determines the economic status of Black workers in Britain (Miles 1982). Therefore, the initial concentration of Black workers in manual and semi-skilled occupations was a result of the needs of capital for cheap labour (Duffield 1988). The socio-economic position of Black workers in Britain, at that time, is explained in terms of an 'underclass' or of a class fraction (Rex 1969; Miles 1982). After the decline of industrial manufacturing, the subsequent high rates of unemployment and uneven distribution across the spectrum of occupations of Black workers is also deemed a result of structural constraints; such as limited access to new jobs and low availability of training (Ohri and Faruqui 1988). Contemporary high rates of Asian self-employment are therefore seen as a response to the lack of access to formal employment and other economic resources (Aldrich et al 1981). Despite the historical changes in the class make-up of South Asian settlers and the changing structure of the British economy, throughout the structuralist literature stress is placed on locating and describing disadvantage and exclusion from the norms of British society (Ballard 1992). Evidence for this perspective is provided by a large body of statistical and quantitative data which compares the socio-economic position of the white population to that of the racialised minorities. In qualitative terms the focus that develops from the structuralist viewpoint is on how white management and workers develop practices and policies which exclude Black workers (Fevre 1984; Duffield 1988).

In contrast to the structuralists, the culturalists give primacy to group solidarity, arguing that South Asians have set themselves goals separate from those of the majority society. The fact that they are not fully participating in British society is considered a 'strategy of resistance' (Ballard 1992), rather than a result of discrimination. The occupational position of South Asian migrants was, therefore, a result of them following these objectives, taking work that required little long-term commitment and paid relatively well. From the time of industrial occupation to present day self-employment, South Asian settlers pursued these 'culturally' inspired goals relying on their own resources. Therefore, in general terms, culturalists theorise ethnicity in terms of the mobilisation of symbolic and material resources to particular ends (Wallman 1979). Ethnic resources consist of solidarities based on ties of religion and kin and can be utilised for the furtherance of collective group aims (Werbner 1990). The emphasis here is on the deployment of 'ethnic' resources to resist and circumnavigate structures of exclusion (Ballard 1992). Evidence for this point of view comes from detailed ethnographic studies of particular minority communities (Dahya 1970; Anwar 1979; Werbner 1990), rather than statistics. However, this situation has changed somewhat with the results of the 1991 census and more recent surveys providing more detailed information about the increasing economic mobility of certain South Asian groupings (Iganski and Payne 1996; Peach 1996).

Given the mutual concern with the economic status of black/South Asian settlers, there should be a marked degree of overlap at the juncture between the structuralist and culturalist schools. However, this is often not the case where mutual polemical criticism, rather than constructive engagement, is more often the outcome of theoretical encounters.[3] In this book I attempt to weave a path between these two distinct theoretical approaches to the study of minority economic activity, illustrating some common assumptions of both approaches and using this as a base to develop my own framework. The structuralist and culturalist schools have remained remarkably consistent in their portrayal of South Asian minorities over the last thirty years. On the one hand, arguing that from industrial manufacturing to present day self-employment, the socio-economic status of minorities has been determined by barriers to their participation and on the other hand, arguing that minorities have remained true to their original aims on arrival and that these determine their pursuit of self-employment. In each case the historical transformations from industrial work to service sector employment and the ramifications of these kinds of shifts are not considered sufficient to alter the original thesis. Therefore, theories relating to the fully employed, industrially located male migrant population of the 1960s are assumed to apply to women engaged in homeworking in the 1990s. My second main criticism of both structuralists and culturalists stems from the fact that both schools rely on singular determinants, be it 'race' or 'ethnicity,' to determine the economic status of minorities. In so doing a reduction comes into play, which makes differences of gender or class secondary to those resulting from 'ethnicity' or 'race'.

Developing a perspective which can account for the specificity of the ethnographic study requires an interaction between ethnography and theory in order to establish which analytical tools best advance the understanding of a particular set of social and economic circumstances. This approach requires a move away from polemical positions, such as structuralist and culturalist, to an analysis which more closely reflects ethnographic work. In this way, my ethnography utilises the work of both structuralists and culturalists. In so doing, I develop a standpoint which can account for the historical change from textile mills to taxi ranks with an explicit recognition of the multi-determinant nature of social action. Brah's (1993, 1996) recent theoretical intervention on South Asian employment issues develops on a study carried out on the labour market position of young South Asian Muslim women (Brah and Shaw 1992). Brah (1993, 1996) argues that to understand the labour market position of these young women requires a framework which can overcome the divide between structure and culture, address the multiply determinant nature of social action and also account for a historical appreciation of colonialism and migration. An adaptation of Brah's theoretical outline to take into account the crucial specificity of work place, be it textile mills, taxi-ranks or take-aways, forms the final section of the chapter.

Class and Ethnicity

Structuralist explanations of the occupational position and general socio-economic status of South Asian migrants and their offspring can be divided into theoretical and empirical sections. The theoretical thrust attempts to develop a relationship between race/ethnicity and class, while the empirical corollary investigates, exposes and demonstrates the impact of discrimination on racialised groups. Drawing on Marxist interpretations of society, the theoretical terrain traversed by structuralist writers reflects changing theorisation within general Marxist theory. In reviewing the various theories of the relationship between race and class, Anthias (1992) notes four distinct approaches (Miles 1982; Solomos 1986; Gilroy 1987). In the review presented here, I only consider two, exemplified by the writing of Miles and Rex. This involves a review of the notions of 'underclass', unfree labour as developed by Rex and the contrary idea of 'class fraction' developed by Miles. I then criticise their theoretical positions from the position of Gilroy (1987), who argues that racialised groups can operate in a manner autonomous of class structures.

One of the more theoretically consistent positions developed to explain the specific socio-economic status of Black migrants on their arrival in Britain is presented in terms of the requirements of capitalism - via the demands of the mode of production - and as a category of labour. In these accounts, the specificity of the migrants' various historical and social conditions are secondary to their situation within the class structure. This point of view is best outlined by Castles and Kosack's (1973) study of immigrants in Europe :

> In this work we shall describe other similarities, such as subordinate position on the labour market.....widespread prejudice, and discrimination from the indigenous populations...These similarities, we contend, make it necessary to regard immigrant workers and their families in all the four *countries as having the same function irrespective of their original backgrounds.* Immigrants should be looked at not in terms of their specific group characteristics - ethnic, social and cultural - but in terms of their actual social position (Castles and Kosack 1973: 5 my emphasis).

Theoretical perspectives of this kind have informed empirical work on industrial location of Black migrants. Allen et al (1977) and Fevre (1984) focus on the Bradford woollen textile industry while Duffield (1988) considers the foundries of the West Midlands. Both Fevre and Duffield are more interested in the attitudes of management and unions, respectively, than that of the Black workers themselves. Fevre's (1984) work on the woollen textile industry in Bradford is detailed and well informed. In the opening pages, Fevre states his intentions to focus on the industry rather than the Black workers:

> Nor will we spend much time discussing Black workers themselves since we will be more interested in their employers....it would be indefensible for a White researcher to turn the 'Blacks' into an object of study (Fevre 1984: ix).

In pursuing this point Fevre puts forward an argument that is strongly against any perspective that relates characteristics of workers to their socio-economic position, a theme which is expanded on in a later section. In a similar vein Duffield (1988) considers the position of Black (Indian) workers in the foundries of the Midlands. Duffield's main focus is on the role (or lack of role) of the unions in the support of Black workers in the Midlands in the late 1950s. His interest in Indian workers is in terms of their role in resisting the imposition of certain work practices on them. Both of these studies offer useful, historical detail about the workings of British industry in the 1950s and 1960s. The theoretical debates in which they engage offer new insights into the methods by which Black workers were excluded or included in certain British industries. However, they offer little illustration of the actual experiences of the Black workers in the industrial setting.

Miles (1982) develops Castles and Kosack's approach by questioning the usefulness of differentiating various groups of workers in terms of racial categories and then attributing significance to these differences. From his standpoint, "'race' is nothing more than an ideological effect, a phenomenal form masking real economic relationships analogous to a mirage" (Gilroy 1987: 22). For Miles, the task is:

> ... to explain, inter alia, why the category of 'race relations' came to be used to categorise a certain group of social relations which, once examined from a different perspective, cannot be shown to be essentially distinct from any other social relations (Miles 1982: 16).

Miles is, therefore, interested in the phenomenon of racism and how it is produced as a part of the struggle between capital and labour in the form of migrant labour. He is keen to emphasise that there is nothing unique about the migration of Black immigrants that warrants a separate analysis in terms of race. He portrays this by reference to the similar treatment of other migrant groups, such as the Irish and Jews, in other historical periods. Miles (1982), in fact, lays great emphasis on cultural differences between migrant groups but only in the sense that these 'differences' are a blockage to pan-migrant unity. He maintains that there is no possibility of 'race' forming a unifying political force and actually that to promote this type of organisation is harmful for the possibility of finding unity with the white working class (Miles 1982). [4] Miles repeats the move made by Castles and Kosack (1973) which erases the importance of the migrants' history from the model of analysis, thereby not taking into account their independent agency. Before considering this point in greater detail, it is necessary to consider the parallel debate about the socio-economic position of Black immigrants forwarded by Rex.

Perhaps the most influential proponent of a race relations school in British sociology is John Rex. As his work spans the last thirty years his theoretical concerns have shifted on a number of occasions. However, his early research is significant for the influence it exerted on empirical studies of discrimination in employment. [5] Writing in the late 1960s and early 1970s, Rex developed two related concepts to explain the housing and labour market position of what he termed 'colonial migrants', that of unfree labour and the underclass. The socio-economic position of 'colonial migrants' in British society is structured by their antecedent status as unfree labour in the colonised country. 'In the new context, discrimination against the worker is achieved by the production of negative imagery of the colonial worker' (Rex 1973: 154-156). Racism is therefore the medium through which the exploitation of labour required by the economic system is rationalised and reinforced. The new workers are seen as unwelcome competitors rather than fellow workers by the indigenous working class and are therefore discriminated against. This discrimination occurs primarily in terms of restricted access to certain central resources - housing, education and employment. Rex argues that because of the intense forms of discrimination and disadvantage which 'colonial migrants' face:

> ...instead of identifying with working class culture, community or politics they formed their own organisations and became in effect a separate underprivileged class (Rex and Tomlinson 1979: 275).

Even though Rex employs the term under*class,* he is not using the term class in the Marxist sense of a relationship to the mode of production. Rather, class is used in the Weberian sense of a stratum of society. Writing at a time where there was full employment of Black workers in various industries, Rex is not concerned with employment discrimination. His main concern is in the field of housing and political representation (1967, 1978). In Rex's view, society is hierarchically stratified according to the degree to which groups have access to essential resources. Each of these groups are therefore in competition over these resources which are perceived as scarce and finite.[6] Both the idea of 'unfree labour' and the 'underclass' have been criticised from a range of viewpoints (Bourne 1980; Gilroy 1987; Anthias 1994), but for present purposes the critique of the underclass by Miles (1982) is the most useful. By defining migrants as part of an underclass, not related to the forces of capital and production but in terms of access to resources, Rex places racialised minorities outside the formal class system.[7] In so doing, Miles states that:

> Rex necessarily rules out the possibility of analysing and finding important economic, political and ideological continuities in the position of the 'colonial immigrant' and the 'indigenous' working class (Miles 1982: 37).

An analysis which begins by considering the class position in terms of relationship to productive forces would find that in terms of relationship to the mode of production Black and white workers are actually in the same structural location. Black workers should therefore not be considered as an 'underclass' but a stratum of the working class (Miles 1982). Furthermore, Miles and Phizacklea (1980) argue that the presence of Black and white workers in the trade unions and labour movements can lead to common struggle, but that this class unity is separate from forms of 'ethnic' organisation. Miles (1982) goes so far as to contend that there is a complete discontinuity between the interests of the Black middle class and working class.

Miles' analysis is more useful for the period of mass industrial employment of Black workers than that offered by Rex, as it offers the possibility of continuities with the experiences of other workers. However, it has two main shortcomings. Firstly, Miles' standpoint conflates migrant labour with racialised group and then to a single class fraction (Anthias 1992). This slippage incurs serious effects, primarily in its inability to take into account the fifty percent British-born population who are not technically migrants but also in the assumption of class heterogeneity within the migrant population. This latter point is especially significant given the changes in the class make-up of the South Asian minorities in the last thirty years with the shift into self-employment (Srinivasan 1995). The second and perhaps most significant problem with Miles' work, for the purposes of this book, is the differentiation he posits between 'ethnic' and 'class' mobilisation. Gilroy (1987) maintains that this distinction does not match with the history of Black struggles in Britain; where anti-racist movements, particularly in the field of education, have united both Black professionals and working class.[8] Werbner (1991a) also illustrates, in the case of Pakistanis, how elites and workers united over the Rushdie affair.[9] As later chapters will show, it was precisely those times when 'ethnic' organisation and class struggle intersected that mobilisations occurred most successfully in the textile mills. For example, extended holidays, sickness benefits and injury compensations were issues that resulted in action from South Asian workers, but were of interest to all workers in the mills.

Contemporary studies of South Asian business further reflect an emphasis on the role of structural hindrances in economic activity despite shifts in class position. For instance, one of the major explanations of Asian entry into self-employment is the result of the need to avoid racial discrimination and the resulting confinement to low status jobs in the labour market (Aldrich et al 1982; Ram 1992). Experiences of racism in the wider labour market are an additional factor in pushing some members of ethnic minorities into self-employment. Hence, their entry into self-employment is seen as a 'damage limitation' exercise to avoid unemployment (Aldrich et al 1984). Further evidence to support this view is provided by Ward and Jenkins (1984). In their survey of Asian businesses they argue that self-employment is an 'economic dead-end' with long hours of work and generally low returns. Taking the lead from the structuralist school, South Asians go from being an 'underclass' or 'class fraction' to a 'lumpen-bourgeoisie'. This outlook is neatly summed up by McEvoy:

> ... the socio-economic position of Asians in Britain will not be decided by the resources of the Asian communities themselves: it will be determined by the opportunities afforded by the host society (McEvoy 1982: 10).

Despite the transition from working class to petite bourgeoisie positions in British society (in terms of relationship to means of production), there is still a necessity to take into account the minority status or 'difference' from a perceived white class system.

Ethnicity and Class

Class is also a concern for those who have studied Britain's minorities from an anthropological perspective and who have not been overtly concerned with macro processes. The volume *Ethnicity at Work* edited by Wallman (1979) attempts to develop a general theoretical approach to the study of ethnicity and work. Perceptively, Wallman makes the point that two workers in the same factory, in the same job, may eat differently, spend their money differently and relate differently to other people. There is no determinant factor upon social action associated with the mere fact of working. However, it is only when this difference becomes significant and is used to define 'us against them', that ethnicity comes into play (Wallman 1979). Following in the theoretical path trod out by Barth (1969) and Cohen (1974), she maintains that ethnicity is the mobilisation of symbolic and material resources to particular ends. [10] In terms of the work situation, Wallman states that:

> Systems of work may be created or maintained by ethnicity; ethnicity may be a product of the structure of work (Wallman 1979: 10).

Two areas of research emerge from this theoretical outline, on the one hand, an examination of how culture fits into the interstices of formal occupation structures, and on the other, an exploration of employment structures and the spaces in which ethnicity is or is not significant. In arguing for the equivalence of both types of analysis, Wallman maintains consistency with her general argument about the formation of social boundaries. For instance, in this volume she argues that ethnic and work based identities are two sides of the same conceptual coin. The 'group oriented groups' are those normally called 'ethnic' while 'the task oriented groups' are those pursuing a particular job, occupation or livelihood' (1979: 7). [11] However, by positing an equivalence between systems of work created by workers' actions and those created by the force of the work structure, Wallman, as with other culturalist writers, side-steps crucial issues of power differentials (Jenkins 1986). This omission on Wallman's part is best depicted by the reasons she forwards for occupational concentration of ethnic groups.

Wallman (1979) makes the salient point that the main issue of concern is to explain why there is a concentration of 'ethnic' groups in certain jobs at certain times in particular places. Countering the structuralist school, she argues, that these: 'ethnic concentrations are only rarely the effects of explicit job restrictions or of formal *apartheid* rules (1979: 1). In attempting to generate a general theory of this kind, Wallman's perspective suffers from a lack of evidence in support of the general claims. For example, an informal form of 'apartheid' was in operation in many British industries at the time of arrival of Black workers, which restricted the scope of their employment. Yet, for Wallman, the role of 'culture'/characteristics in determining occupation and labour market position is central:

> Conversely they will not see, will not accept, will not succeed in the opportunity offered if it is not appropriate to their choice of work or their cultural experience (Wallman 1979: 14).

This point is further developed on by Brooks and Singh in the same volume:

> It consisted of groups of workers with their own distinctive traditions and their own ethnic identities, which in turn influenced their occupational and industrial distribution (Brooks and Singh 1979: 110).

Anthias (1992) criticises this view in terms of its theorisation of ethnicity. She states:

> Ethnicity has become defined as a static cultural property that informs actors' choices, rather than as a dynamic relation to particular socio-economic and political structures (Anthias 1992: 15). [12]

In attempting to put forward a general theory, Wallman's perspective is unable to accommodate the detailed examinations of work histories of Black workers in Britain. For example, she states that one of the issues to understand is the way in which 'ethnic workers' are *not* confined to one level in an industry, whereas for the case of Black workers they were concentrated in certain industries and specific sections therein. Nevertheless, more specific studies of South Asian/Pakistani workers in Britain develop the themes laid out by Wallman emphasising cultural choice and the role of ethnic workgroups whilst playing down the effect of structural constraint.

Moving on from industrial employment to self-employment, Werbner takes up Wallman's mantle, developing a theoretically sophisticated approach. Werbner (1990) argues that the gifts given by Pakistani women are converted to commodities by the business deals made by their husbands. In this way women contribute to the household income (Werbner 1990). The issue of gift-giving, as sealing alliances amongst *biraderi* members and outsiders, is an interesting continuity with the work of Brooks and Singh (1979) who describe the system of gift-giving in the industrial setting. [13] In both cases the underlying premise is the subsuming of the economic by the cultural. Economic exchange, in terms of commodities, is predicated on the cultural exchange in terms of gifts. In the process, other relationships such as those between boss and worker are diminished (Miles 1993).[14]

In terms of general theories relating to the labour market position of racialised minorities writers from the culturalist school have not been too insightful. However, when focusing on specific processes that relate to sections of the South Asian population, Dahya, Anwar and Werbner have each contributed to the development of two key concepts. These are 'chain migration' and the 'myth of return'. The migration process is described by Dahya (1974) in terms of chains, where one migrant arrives in England, and then calls other members of his immediate family, then extended kin and ultimately others in his area to join him. In effect, a chain of migrants is set up, each linked to the other, through *biraderi* or friendship relations. 'Chain migration' is central to the explanation given for the creation of 'ethnic' workgroups and therefore the concentration of Pakistani workers in particular industries. Anwar (1979) describes the process for the textile mills of Rochdale:

> The Pakistani emigration to Britain was organised and depended on a system of migration and patronage which made it selective and confined to some kin groups in a few villages in a few areas.....
> It was found during the field work that many relatives were working together in certain firms on certain shifts in certain departments....
> ....Pakistanis used their *biraderi* and kinship networks to obtain jobs and worked with their fellow country men (Anwar 1979: 107).

The concentration of workers in one industry is therefore a logical extension of the process of chain migration to chains of workers. One worker secures a job and introduces his relatives and friends as vacancies arise. Werbner (1990) has further developed this notion to take on board the movement into self-employment and business that many Pakistanis in Manchester have taken. In her book, *The Migration Process*, she describes the process by which:

> Pakistani entrepreneurship thus tended during its formative years to take

the form of entrepreneurial chains, with the consequent creation of clusters of migrants from the same areas of origin in particular sections of the trade (Werbner 1990: 23).

Crucial to the creation and maintenance of these chains is the role of the broker. It is this person who facilitates the migration process in terms of finding housing and employment for the new migrant. Brooks and Singh (1979) offer a sophisticated account of the reasons for the emergence of the broker or pivot, as they call it. The role of the pivot is to act as a mediator between the management of the factory/workplace and the workers. This person is often related in multiple ways to the workers, through kinship, friendship as well as being a fellow worker. Brooks and Singh do acknowledge the role of discrimination in aiding the creation of the pivot. They appreciate that fact that, if South Asian workers could gain employment in a wider range of places then the power of the brokers would be lost. Nonetheless, in their study a greater emphasis is laid on the significance of 'cultural' baggage than indicated structural constraints. In particular the notions of Punjabi society as hierarchical, with 'gift-giving' as a norm which therefore facilitates the 'natural' development of brokers as these relationships are sustained through the process of 'gift-giving' and reciprocation.

Chain migration serves to elucidate the process by which certain concentrations of South Asian/Mirpuri workers were created in certain industries. In addition, the notion of the 'myth of return' is deemed to explain why workers stay in a certain occupational level and their general attitudes towards work. The notion of the 'myth of return' simply relates the idea that migrants perceive themselves as resident in the 'host' country for a limited period of time, after which they will return to their 'home' country. This ideal of return becomes a myth when the actuality of the return becomes increasingly distant and therefore comes to act as an ideology or a charter for determining behaviour of migrants towards various aspects of their lives (Dahya 1974). This notion was popularised by Anwar (1979), but appears in various forms throughout the vast majority of the literature on Pakistanis and minorities. As early as the work of Rose, there is the argument that Pakistanis are, 'acquiescent, wanting nothing more than to work and return to their country of origin, further they are not particularly aware of or resentful of discrimination' (Rose et al 1969: 169). Werbner twenty years on makes a similar claim: 'They engage very little in open protest; they avoid confrontational situations' (Werbner 1990: 7). The 'myth of return' orients the migrant toward the 'home' society and therefore the significant social and moral framework is not in England but in Pakistan, which therefore explains their behaviour in the 'host' country (Ballard 1994). This general argument has specific manifestations in terms of the field of employment and work. The 'myth of return' implies that the type of work engaged in by the migrants is unimportant relative to the wages being received (Dahya 1970). There is the implication of a lack of commitment to the workplace and a general avoidance of conflict, as the workers see themselves as temporary. [15]

At the same time, other scholars, from an industrial sociology background have come to similar conclusions as the previous authors about the general attitudes of migrant workers. However, in contrast, these authors do not rely on the conceptualisation of 'cultural' difference in terms of kin groups but rely on a notion of the general disposition of migrants or the dual labour market theory. [16] In either case, worker motivation becomes a central way to explain why Pakistani workers are in low-skilled, low-pay jobs and do not show opposition in the workplace. The motives of the worker are towards another society as Worsley states:

> ...the insecurity of their residence and their vulnerability to deportation, their habits of deference and lack of a collective identity and praxis of self-assertion relevant to their current situation - their orientations, in any case, to another society altogether - makes them malleable and compliant (Worsley 1976 :136).

In a similar vein, Bonacich (1972) maintains that immigrants will put up with unattractive work if it is temporary and they have an alternative life to return to. More specifically, the migrant worker may be interested in improving status elsewhere and consequently be willing to submit to lower wages and longer hours. In this respect they came close to the ideal-typical 'target workers': 'someone who goes abroad to earn as much money as possible, as quickly as possible, in order to return home' (Bohning, 1972: 62). Black workers are assumed to lack the cultural and political resources with which to adapt to the customs of the industrial workforce, in a similar manner to women's domestic responsibilities lowering their expectations of waged work (Wainright 1978; Fevre 1984). Rimmer develops this point, arguing that immigrant workers have 'different cultural values and patterns of behaviour' (Rimmer 1972: 12), from the white working class, which means that they are unable to fit in with the established patterns of industrial working. In these instances, it should be noted that culture is not taken as something that has aided Pakistanis, but rather is perceived of as a hindrance.

These self-same features which are used to explain the fact that the Pakistanis are more likely to put up with bad working and pay conditions in terms of industrial employment are converted into reasons for their success in business, as illustrated by Werbner:

> Being in the society but - as strangers - 'not of it' they are freed from their hosts' frame of reference, and thus able to pursue a way of living which is, in the Pakistani case, particularly supportive of entrepreneurs (Werbner 1984: 167).

Werbner argues that it is a cultural heritage which stresses thrift, deferred gratification, industriousness and self-reliance that are critical factors in understanding Pakistani business success (Werbner 1990). This view of Asian self-employment is supported by recent research in Oxford (Srinivasan 1995) and Warwickshire (Basu 1995). In both of these cases Asian businesses' development was seen more in terms of a positive choice to enter into business rather than a response to discrimination and blocked economic activity. Asian businesses develop and grow because they are able to utilise the structures of mutual help and support that kinship networks generate. Modood, Virdee and Metcalf (1996) go so far as to cite the role of 'chain migration' in developing support networks for business activity.

The association of 'Pakistani/South Asian culture' with business success implies an essentialised notion of 'culture' which can be utilised by entrepreneurs. However, the factors outlined above as characteristic of 'South Asian culture' also appear in other contexts. Bechhofer and Elliot state that the petty bourgeoisie has certain basic values attributable to that class: 'Economic individualism, belief in the importance of private property as a measure of security, independence, success and upward mobility, the myth of individual success' (Bechhofer and Elliot 1976: 76). These same characteristics are cited by Dahya (1974) and Anwar (1979) as features of Pakistani 'culture'. [17] Referring to a group's 'culture' in this way can lead to an esssentialism which can result in statements from such unlikely quarters as Rex:

> There is a complex and unresolved sociological problem as to why Islam encourages commercial motives. We do not pretend to have resolved this........the Pakistani, even though he may be a peasant with no experience of the city, takes quite *naturally* to commercial ventures (Rex 1967: 165,

my emphasis). [18]

Further, given the Weberian outlook associated with Rex it is interesting to note how the notion of the 'myth of return' resonates with that of the 'Protestant work ethic'. Willingness to succumb to the ideal of deferred gratification, austere living conditions, and the ability to work inordinately long hours with a high level of acquiescence are all attributes given to the Protestant working class (Joyce 1980). These factors show a remarkable degree of parity with those ascribed to migrants in general and Pakistanis in particular. [19]

Overlapping Perspectives

> We know it is theory that determines what we can observe and how we interpret it (Wallman 1979: 8).

From the position outlined by Castles and Kosack (1973), where the role of culture is unimportant in determining the economic status of migrants, to the subsuming of the economic by the cultural in Werbner's (1990) work, there is a great deal of analytical ground. Banks has recently reasoned that these are two types of projects that are mutually exclusive:

> That is, Castles and Kosack and Watson and his contributors have different research agendas, are interested in different issues and collect differing kinds of data (Banks 1996: 110).

Despite Bank's assertion, the theoretical debate concerning structural determinism and cultural creativity has, in fact, many overlaps. In order to weave a path between these two positions the specific role of culture in determining the economic position of migrants is illustrated here by the debate invoked in the influential collection *The Empire Strikes Back* (CCCS 1982) which, in the main, criticises the culturalists but also strikes parallels with contemporary culturalist writings on the reasons for contemporary Asian economic success. The second area of concern is the ahistorical nature of many of the accounts and this is again best exemplified by reference to the contemporary debate on South Asian employment where there is remarkable continuity in the viewpoints of both the culturalist and the structuralist schools, with the former emphasising 'ethnic resources' and the latter barriers to employment.

When considering the impact of culture on socio-economic status, the issue at stake is not whether workers' motivations and cultural resources have a part to play in determining occupational position and subsequent attitudes to work, but rather whether these factors can be seen as positive or negative. Polar perspectives have developed which either diminish or dismiss the importance of 'ethnic resources' and worker characteristics or tend to over emphasise and valorise the significance of these factors. This debate is illustrated, in the *The Empire Strikes Back* (CCCS 1982). Beginning with the critique of the culturalist position presented by Lawrence:

> They do not 'choose' to live in inadequate housing any more than they 'choose' to do 'shit-work'........
> The shift from a 'social deprivation' to a 'culturalist' problematic has entailed a closer scrutiny of the family/kinship systems............
> This makes it possible to argue that the cultural 'obstructions' to 'fuller participation' in society are reproduced within black families by black people themselves (Lawrence 1982: 116).

Yet, in the same volume 'culture' is not completely rejected. For example, Parmar writes:

> Despite the force of racist stereotypes Asian women do not experience the racism from which they suffer in a passive way. They have developed their own forms of resistance, articulate their own ideas about British society, and rely on their own historical cultural traditions as a means of support (Parmar 1982: 39).

This position on resistance is almost the blueprint for the programme Ballard (1992) endorses ten years on:

> Thus it is precisely the capacity to be morally, spiritually and linguistically deviant that accounts for the extraordinary effectiveness of Britain's 'migrant minorities' - be they white or non-white- strategies of resistance (Ballard 1992: 7).

Despite these shared concerns, there would be little agreement between the authors over what that 'resistance' actually consisted of, what it was articulated against and in which contexts it occurred. Parmar again criticises the culturalists' perspective:

The emphasis in the work of Khan and others is on the Asian communities themselves, rather than on the economic, political and ideological structures which reproduces Asian women as a specific class category. The hazards of this approach are that it becomes easy to blame cultural, religious and communal factors for the subordinate positions which Asian women occupy in the British social structure (Parmar 1982: 262).

At the same time, even Parmar is arguing for the acknowledgement of some sort of cultural difference which is rooted in:

.....a rich and varied tradition of resistance and struggle and the forms these struggles take are culturally, racially and gender specific (Parmar 1982: 264).

In the to-ing and fro-ing of this debate what emerges is a necessity to acknowledge that once the question of 'culture' enters into the debate, it is not value free but takes on certain manifestations in given contexts. Banks (1996) perceptively notes the fact that 'culture' has been inadequately discussed by most of the theorists of minorities in Britain, either considering it as unimportant or viewing it in an instrumental and static manner. Often ethnicity has come to stand for cultural difference and that in turn has become a matter of describing, dress, ritual and kinship patterns. To avoid these pitfalls, it is necessary to develop a perspective which can account for the enmeshing of structure and culture and the multi-determinant nature of social action.

Enmeshing Formations

To move on from these points of critique there is a need to develop an account for the historical change from textile mills to taxi ranks with an explicit recognition of the multi-determinant nature of social action. Neither class nor ethnicity are therefore the sole factors determining occupational status and shift. The work of Brah (1993) is most useful, in this sense, as she develops a sophisticated framework which accounts for the 'enmeshing' nature of structure and culture, the multiple determinants of socio-economic position and the necessity of a historical appreciation of colonialism and migration. Applying Brah's perspective to my specific project, I note the need to broaden the scope of the theoretical terrain.

Developing a framework which can account for the specificity of the ethnographic study requires an interaction between ethnography and theory in order to establish which analytical tools best advance the understanding of a particular set of situations. This requires a move away from the polemical positions presented earlier towards an analysis which more closely reflects the ethnographic work. In this regard the recent studies by Brah on the role of South Asian Muslim women in the British labour market provides a useful starting point. [20] Brah begins her analysis by developing a notion of culture which is far more sophisticated than that offered by previous scholars on South Asian minorities in Britain:

> It will be evident from the above that there is no suggestion of a binary divide between culture and structure. A concept of culture that is evoked here does not reference a fixed array of customs, values and traditions. But rather, culture is conceptualised as a process; a nexus of intersecting significations; a terrain on which social meanings are produced, appropriated, disrupted and contested. Cultural specificities remain important but they are construed as fluid modalities, as shifting boundaries that mediate structures and relations of power. Hence, structure and culture are enmeshing formations. The one is not privileged over the other (Brah 1993: 443-444).

This perspective echoes the work of Hall (1992) and West (1994) who argue that 'culture' is itself constitutive of 'structure'. West notes: 'Culture is as much a structure as the economy or politics (West 1994: 19). From this point of view, 'culture' becomes inseparable from ideology, which creates hegemonic structures. Therefore, 'Structures and behaviour are inseparable... institutions and values go hand in hand' (West 1994: 18). Bridging the polemical divide between culturalists and structuralists, this outlook on culture is more akin to post-structuralist accounts (Eade 1996). Structure is not solely determinant of human action, nor is it a monolith that can be circumvented by the 'resources' of ethnic minorities. The focus of study then becomes the way in which structure and culture are articulated. In the context of this book, this is a useful perspective as it can simultaneously account for how the textile mills were changed by the Mirpuri/Pakistani workers therein, as well as how simultaneously working in the mill changed their everyday practices.

Brah (1996) develops this notion of culture to construct a framework which takes into account how 'multiple determinations' come into play when addressing the issues of the labour market position of South Asian Muslim young women. Structural constraints are not monolithic but are construed through differences of race, ethnicity, class and gender. Reiterating Hall (1980), her interests are in the articulation between different forms of social differentiation - class, gender or ethnicity - which are themselves contingent and historically bound. It is the relations between the 'mode of differentiation' and the labour market which are at the centre of Brah's analysis:

> The point is that modes of differentiation such as 'race', class, gender, sexuality, ethnicity, age or disability are at the heart of the constitution, operations and differential effects of labour markets (Brah 1996: 128).

Brah (1996) goes on to outline four areas of research to understand the labour market position of young Muslim women.[21] I have modified and applied them to the present research on male Mirpuri/Pakistani workers. In order to understand the processes involved in the movement from peasant migrant to industrial worker to unemployed/redundant worker to self-employment for male workers, it is necessary to:

- Describe how the category of labour of (Azad) Kashmiri /Pakistani workers comes in to existence and its relationship to the white working class.
- Illustrate how labour markets and particular market niches are constituted by and constitutive of this category of workers.
- Relate changes in the local, national and global economy to the experiences of this category of labour.
- Illustrate how the experiences of (Azad) Kashmiri/Pakistani labour is framed within personal and collective narratives.

To describe how the category of (Azad) Kashmiri /Pakistani labour comes into being requires an analysis which can take into account the history of colonialism and how it affects the migration process. It is these general processes that link the history of the textile industry and indeed the industrial development of Britain with the imperial domination of the Indian sub-continent. Indeed, the creation of the category of Pakistani/ (Azad) Kashmiri racialised labour is profoundly entwined with the historical relationships between Britain and the Indian sub-continent. How this is played out in the specific case of the textile mill industry forms the context in which the category of (Azad) Kashmiri/Pakistani labour becomes significant. Various theories of migration have been deployed to analyse these processes. In Chapter Three the main theories of migration are presented and along with Chapter Four the historical conduits through which migration from Mirpur occurred are examined. Brah's framework, nonetheless reminds us that there is a need to be sensitive to historical change. Migrant labour theory is useful for examining transnational connections but is not so useful when the people in question are no longer migrating or labouring (Cross 1992).

Another dimension to the question of creation of a South Asian labouring class is its relation to the white working class. This needs to be considered in terms of the factors that divide the white working class and the time frame under consideration. There is a need to be aware of Anthias' (1992) observation about the changing class composition over time of both the South Asian and white working classes. From the mill period to working in the service sector, (Azad) Kashmir/Pakistani men's class position changed alongside the general class composition of white people, a point further complicated by gender distinctions. It is also important to analyse how these relationships work out at the individual level, as these interactions often inform general stereotypes that construe wider social differences.

The second main theme relating to labour market and market niches reflects the labour history of (Azad) Kashmiri settlers in Britain. From working on the night-shift in textile mills to a concentration in taxi ranks and take-aways, these workers have occupied and created labour market niches. The creation, control and consequences of the occupancy of these niches brings forth a problematic about agency. At the abstract level of labour market, it is difficult to gauge the extent the agency that South Asian labour exerted over textile mills as a whole. However, at the specific level of workplace struggles and interaction across the management hierarchy a range of complex and interesting aspects of agency can be analysed. This is not the simplistic question of 'choice' as proposed by Wallman, but rather the key question of what impact labour mobilisation has on the work environment, especially when we are dealing with profound racial and gender divides in workforce composition. This question of agency then becomes a useful tool with which to examine the changes in workers lives across labour markets, in the shift from industrial to service sector employment.

The third area of concern is how shifts in the economy are related to the experiences of this category of labour. From textiles mills to taxi ranks is a metonym for the transformation in the British economy from manufacturing to services. However, in Brah and Shaw's (1992) study the labour market is an abstract and monolithic entity wheras this book examines particular places of employment/unemployment within a geographical location over a period of time. Rather than just be concerned with the process of economic change, it is also important to take into account some of the social consequences that have arisen from this. A number of theoretical models have arisen to explain what has been variously called post-fordist, post-industrial and post modern society. Given the limited engagement of this literature with the position of racialised minorities in Britain, it is only in the final ethnographic chapter (9), that reference is made to these shifts. Engaging with Beck's (1992) conceptualisation of risk society, Chapter Nine most fully explores the impact of the shift from industrial to service sector employment. Beck's conceptualisation of the emerging risk society is closely linked with the concept of individualisation and provides an interesting way to compare the (Azad) Kashmiri men's experiences of textile mills and taxi ranks. Inevitably, the workings of the labour market are ultimately exposed to mitigate against the long-term prospects of these migrant workers and their offspring. Indeed, any analysis of the local, national and global economic context in which these Black workers have found themselves provides depressing reading.

It is against these harsh transformations in the global economy that the narratives of the lives of the men presented in this book take shape. Brah's final point is perhaps the most significant to the structure of the chapters that follow. Indeed this book attempts to describe and explore the labour market position of male (Azad) Kashmiri migrants in a local and global context, through personal and collective narratives. The two-way nature of the interaction of the workers with their local work environment in the context of national shifts in the economy forms a crucial background to the stories presented. The way in which changes in work environment, type of work, timings of work and income have an impact on the way that male (Azad) Kashmiri/Pakistani workers organise certain aspects of their lives is considered through the shift from textile mills to taxi ranks. These issues and others emerge from extended interviews with workers and from case studies.

In a similar manner to Brah's work, this book is profoundly gendered. The experiences presented and the narratives offered are solely about men. In this regard there remains an unwritten story of the migration, settlement and labour processes that effected (Azad) Kashmiri women in this same period. The reasons for this asbsence are practical, given fieldwork restraints, as well as empirical: I came across no cases of (Azad) Kashmiri women working in the mills, though this does not mean that this did not happen, especially in other towns.[22] Overall, Brah's framework provides an invaluable structure through which the issues that emerge in the process of migration, labour and beyond can be understood. How these themes come to be constructed as social knowledge and ultimately as text is taken up in the next chapter.

---

[1] I use the term Mirpuri/Pakistani to refer to the population as a whole from that region. When I wish to distinguish between the two groups, I use 'Mirpuri and Pakistani'. A fuller explanation of terminology is given in Chapter Two.
[2] This use of the term culturalist follows more from the CCCS (1982) definition. It is, however, essentially the same group of writers referred to in Anthias (1992).
[3] See Modood (1992) on Cater and Jones (1988) for a recent example.
[4] Gilroy (1987) shows how Miles' theoretical project provides justification for slogans such as 'Black and White Unite and Fight,' much vaunted by organisations such as the Socialist Workers Party and the Anti-Nazi League. A critique of these organisations can be found in the book, *Dis-Orienting Rhythms: The Politics of the New Asian Dance Music* (1996) S. Sharma, J. Hutnyk, and A. Sharma (eds.).
[5] Allen et al (1977) follow Rex by postulating that race and class combine to form a double jeopardy such that Black workers constitute an underclass.
[6] This essentially Weberian perspective is also shared by most of the writers of the culturalist school.
[7] It could also be argued that this puts the population outside any constructions of the British nation. See Gilroy (1987).
[8] This is especially the case on education issues and the anti-racist struggle in general.
[9] Rushdie is another apt example.
[10] Wallman (1979) is explicit about the way in which ethnicity is completely context bound and only emerges when differences become significant and due to structural reasons. She also sees how cultural affiliation can be both positive in the sense of it giving access to employment and negative when the person giving the access happens to be from any other group. Depending on the perceptions of the actors and the constraints and opportunities in which they act, ethnicity may be an essential resource, an utter irrelevance or a crippling liability. Wallman (1979) forwards three summary points on ethnicity:
1. Population not defined by characteristics but by the meaningful contrast to the classifier.
2. Difference is objective between two people, but subjective in its effect.
3. Characteristic is significant whether self imposed or other imposed.
[11] Miles (1982) criticises Wallman because of her focus on cultural difference. He argues that making the focus social boundaries, the problem of distinguishing between what is ethnic and what is not comes to the fore. Any group with a common shared identity then becomes ethnic; feminists, punks, greens, trade union members fall into Wallman's definition.
However, I would argue that this emphasis on social boundaries is not the central problem as it allows for the possibility of exploring more than one identity and does

not prioritise ethnicity or class. The more central concern with this perspective is the equating of several identities, without taking into account wider issues of power differentials within society (Jenkins 1986).

[12] This is reactive ethnicity, resulting from racial oppression, and a part of cultural affirmation. This is grounded in a passive and personal instrumental approach.

[13] This is described in greater detail in a later section.

[14] Miles (1993) criticises Werbner on precisely this point, where he accuses her of not taking into account the fact that the relationship between a Pakistani boss and his worker is the same as that between any boss and worker. Even though Miles' point is a simplification of a complex set of relations, the point worth keeping in mind, and illustrated by my ethnography, is that conflict regardless of the ethnicity of the foreman, was as much a part of the shop floor and workplace as were these descriptions of harmonious merging of different viewpoints.

[15] After public protests about the Rushdie affair, Shaw (1994) has forwarded 'fear of the West' and its corollary 'commitment to Islam' as a similar organising principle to the 'myth of return'.

[16] A popular model in the 1970s to explain the position of Black workers was the dual labour market theory, developed by American theorists and applied to Britain by Bosanquet and Doeringer (1973). In brief, the dual labour market theory posits two types of labour market, the primary and secondary, with Black workers in the low paid, low skilled secondary one. They are there because of low expectations, no political resources to resist, and different/wrong motives (Fevre 1984).

[17] So much for the insoluble differences between Islam and Protestantism.

[18] This also follows from Weber and the notion of the Protestant ethic being more akin to Western capitalism while Islam will be more akin to trade.

[19] In a similar vein, if we consider Shaw's (1994) notion of 'fear of the West,' which she contends now replaces the 'myth of return' as an organising principle for Muslim Pakistanis, we find a similar link to the work ethic of contemporary Britain. Featherstone (1991) notes how post-industrial culture is marked by an individualistic, consumer-centred emphasis on lifestyle at the expense of communal and religious values. It is this shift in values that Shaw highlights as particularly worrying to Muslim parents bringing up their children in Britain.

[20] In this work she develops a framework for the analysis of the position of young Muslim women challenging many of the discourses that create Muslim women as objects of family seclusion and religious pressure.

[21] Brah states '...a study of young Muslim women and the labour market would need to address how the labour of this category of women is:

a) socially constructed
b) represented in discourse
c) is constituted by and is constitutive of labour markets and,
d) is framed within personal narratives and collective histories'
(Brah 1996: 130).

[22] My doctoral dissertation upon which this book is based briefly examines (Azad) Kashmiri/Pakistani women's labour market experiences. Forthcoming work by Nusrat Shaheen, Angela Dale, Edward Fieldhouse and Virinder S Kalra will offer a more informed and nuanced perspective on these issues.

2 Methodology

Introduction

To explore the themes outlined in the previous chapter requires a methodology which can function on three levels: the practical, the epistemological and the ethical. Recent academic trends have significantly increased the concern with methodology in the social sciences and humanities. The simple fact that the tasks of observing, understanding and explaining are not value-free has made plain the constructed nature of academic texts (Clifford and Marcus 1986; Eade 1996). Therefore, the methods by which sociological data is extracted from the practices of everyday life critically impact on the nature of the results presented. As such, the methodology of social research is as much concerned with epistemology as with the methods of data collection. In explaining the various limitations of a particular method and the means by which the social field is divided, the way in which descriptions of events and narratives are construed through the methods of viewing is made transparent. This is not to argue that the only important issue to explore is the method, but rather to appreciate that all representations are contestable and constructed through a process. The important task in setting up social research, then, is to ensure, as far as is possible, that the categories deployed and the techniques used are open to scrutiny and critique.

This chapter begins by reviewing the labelling of minority racialised groups in British academic and to some extent policy discourse. I consider how useful a means of labelling groups 'self-definition' is, given the multiple identifications that are possible for any one group. In pursuing alternative forms of group definition, an analysis is presented of other terms used in representation. Muslim, Mirpuri, (Azad) Kashmiri, Pakistani, Asian and Black are, and have been, used to represent racialised/ethnicised groups in a variety of academic and media discourses. I argue that each of these terms is only capable of describing single, unitary constituencies which underplay divisions of gender and generation. To address this problem I describe the development of an ethnographically derived set of categories, which attempt to incorporate differences of gender, generation and migration.

I then turn to my own position as a researcher, a move which bridges the gap between epistemological and practical issues. My location as a researcher is examined in terms of the multiple identity positions - male, visible Sikh, middle class - I occupy and how these effected my relationships with other academics and the people I interviewed/worked with. I maintain that it is necessary to indicate areas of disconnection as well as connection with people in the field. In the final section I chronicle the means by which I gained access, and chose people to interview. The ethical issues that this kind of research raised are also explored. Research in highly bureaucratised, urban, Britain requires data collection techniques that can be somehow distinguished from the general processes of information accumulation that take place. As a researcher, I am therefore, once again, pre-figured in the social field. However, in this case, ethical issues are raised about the use of social knowledge, especially as the research is on employment issues. [1]

Ethnicity and the Labelling of Groups

The labelling of racialised/ethnicised minority groups by academia, the media, community leaders and members of the groups themselves is neither consistent nor static. Self-definition as with categorisation by others involves a dialectical process of interaction with the state, leaders, members of the group and the media (Werbner 1991a). However, a clear distinction between self-definition by members of minority groups and categorisation by others, has been set up by certain academic writers (Dahya 1970; Saifullah Khan 1977; Ballard 1994). [2] The separation of self-definition and other labelling is problematic because it does not take into account the fluid and changing nature of self-identification nor the process by which identities are forged. There is not sufficient space to detail the contours of this debate. It is sufficient to note the multiple ways in which people define themselves and the dialogic nature of any enunciation of identity. Therefore, the categories Muslim, Mirpuri, Pakistani, Black, South Asian, and (Azad) Kashmiri are all used in the following chapters, sometimes interchangeably but more often, in a specific sense. Taking each term in turn, I briefly review their historical usage and specific utilisation in the rest of the book. Beginning with the term Black, I then move on to Muslim and then to the other terms. In the final part of this section I offer a new terminology, largely derived from fieldwork, which attempts to overcome the shortcomings of the labels previously discussed.

Saifullah Khan (1977) asserts that the assumption that the Pakistani population is homogeneous is to ignore salient and significant 'cultural' differences which can have a marked effect on social policy. She would rather use the term Mirpuri arguing that this is closer to people's own definitions. In a similar manner almost twenty years on, Westwood states:

> In this book I rarely use the term Asian because the women I knew consistently referred to themselves as Indian. In so far as it is their voices that we hear in this book, I have *tried to be faithful to their accounts of themselves* and it is this latter designation I have followed throughout (Westwood 1984: 10 my emphasis).

Both Westwood and Saifullah Khan argue for the self-definition of minority groups as the best means of categorisation, a trait common to most anthropological writings about minorities in Britain. Two problems arise from this focus on self-definition which emanate from the fact that self-definitions are not static but fluid. Firstly, self-identification changes in terms of the context of the conversation; who is being talked to and the nature of the contact. Different identities are forwarded in different situations of space and time - in terms of region, village, caste, *biraderi* and religion. Secondly, and perhaps more significantly, the labels themselves change through time. For instance, the assertion in the last fifteen years of a British Kashmiri identity by people who may have previously called themselves British Pakistani is a pertinent example (Ali et al 1996). Self categorisation can therefore be used as a diversionary device to maintain a coherent sense of a group in the face of multiple identities faced in fieldwork. It is necessary to confront each of the potential labels Muslim, Mirpuri, Pakistani, Black, South Asian, and (Azad) Kashmiri as they are presented in distinct contexts.

The use of the term Black, to describe the commonality of groups who experience racism has, arguably, in contemporary Britain, given way to a myriad of identities emphasising plurality of identity and specificity of oppressions and struggles (Hall 1992). In fact, as highlighted in the theoretical section, very few academic writers - other than Sivanandan (1982) and the Institute of Race Relations group - actually used the term Black in anything other than a technical sense and therefore as opposite to white. In terms of issues around employment, in both structuralist and culturalist studies, there has been a long-standing tendency to split groups into Asian and black - referring to African and Caribbean origin - and further along ethno-nationalist lines, such as Pakistani and Indian.Increasingly, writers such as Gilroy (1987, 1992) locate the term 'black' exclusively within the narrative of the slave experience thereby setting up a 'black' cultural project with specific reference to African, African-Caribbeans and African Americans. Similarly, Modood (1992) has argued that 'Black' is an inappropriate term to describe the experiences of South Asians in Britain. Modood (1992) asserts that the term Asian is more appropriate to describe the experiences of this group of people. Specifying and denying 'black' in these ways leaves a gap in the terminology for those situations where racism unites historically distinct social groupings. This is not only in terms of mobilisation of the groups concerned, but also in terms of an analytical description of the situations in which these groups are constructed as 'other' to white society. Until a new satisfactory terminology is developed, the term Black remains useful to describe that collective constituency which is variously effected by the practices of racial exclusion. [3] For instance, the treatment of all workers in the textile mills of the North West by white management was racialised and gendered. However, the particular ideology through which South Asians as effeminate, and African-Caribbeans as unintelligent was constructed, requires an analysis which can take into account racisms. [4] On a more particular level, this requires considering how religious practices were signifiers for racial practices of exclusion and for the mills, it is necessary to consider the impact of Islam.

Opposition to the effects of exclusion by Black groups may take multiple routes. In recent times, the most predominant has been that around the signifier 'Muslim'. Following from the Honeyford and Rushdie affairs in the 1980s (and numerous other local campaigns around education) Islam and the term 'Muslim' have become widespread categories in public discourse in Britain. Precisely because of these public demonstrations, and the challenges they posed to theorisations of minorities in Britain, there has been a great expansion of interest in Islam. [5] To trace the emergence of a Muslim identity would require a far greater level of analysis than is possible here. However, the fact that 'Muslim' is now a term widely used both as ascription and self-description of people who may have previously used Pakistani or Mirpuri is an apt illustration of the changing nature of self-identification. It is also an example of how the state in particular is unable to respond to the assertion of religious identities. In this book my concern with issues of labour, employment and income generation uniquely impinge on the emergence of the category Muslim. Previous academic constructions of Muslims have tended to focus on the issues of education, changes within the legal system and religious sectarianism (see Lewis 1994). The notable exception is the work of Rafiq (1992) who compares Muslim and non-Muslim businesses in Bradford and disputes whether religious/cultural difference is a significant factor in terms of orientation towards business. He does note that cultural preferences may determine, the type of business that groups will go into, therefore Muslims may avoid business which have dealings with alcohol and non-halal meat (Rafiq 1992). Despite this factor, his overall conclusion is that socio-economic factors such as education and class background play the greatest part in determining business location, size and turnover. Nonetheless the pertinent issue of discrimination against Muslims has meant that the Commission for Racial Equality, in 1996, launched the 'Religious Discrimination - Your Rights' campaign, encouraging minorities to come forward to complain if they feel they have suffered because of their religious beliefs. Interestingly, the only cases that have thus far been taken to court or tribunal have been brought by Muslim plaintiffs. In this book the labels Islam/Muslim are used when specifically referring to those issues or events that are readily associated with an exclusive body of workers: these are holidays for Eid, dietary restriction and the development of institutions such as mosques. This level of specificity is problematic in that it ignores mobilisations by Muslims on other issues such as education, but is accurate in as far as it relates to the influences on employment and labour that are of interest here.

Whereas the terms Black and Muslim refer primarily to political constituencies, the term Asian, in its British usage, has geographical connotations relating to the Indian sub-continent. Brah (1996) has recently traced the emergence of an Asian constituency in Britain through the processes of migration and settlement. However, there is a debate as to whether this is an appropriate term given the diversity of the population included in the category. Srinivasan (1995) argues in favour of studying South Asians as a whole contending that a more specific focus loses sight of common processes effecting and produced by the different groups. She further maintains that when cultural difference is not the area under study then the 'risks involved in over-generalisation are relatively few and that much would be lost by over-specificity' (Srinivasan 1995: 12). Conversely, Ballard has argued that it may be 'dangerously misleading' (Ballard 1990: 219) to apply the blanket term Asian to peoples from such diverse regions as Pakistan, India and Bangladesh. In line with other anthropologists, he proposes that regional, caste and kinship groupings are more illuminating for purposes of sociological analysis. In one sense both authors are correct in the field they are trying to analyse, but by arguing for distinct positions they lose sight of the multiple nature of identifications. It is necessary to be specific about regional and caste affiliations when this is necessary to the subject under analysis. In the following chapters certain processes of migration, labour and employment apply consistently to all South Asians in Oldham. To avoid the problems with popular usage of the term Asian and the fact it invokes problems in terms of its Chinese and far East referentials (Kaur and Kalra 1996), I use the term South Asian in this book.

By far the most common terminology used to describe South Asian minorities are the ethno-national categories, such as Indian and Pakistani. With the inclusion of an 'ethnic' question in the 1991 census, ethno-national labels have become enshrined within public discourse. The label Pakistani, Indian, Bangladeshi in this sense, are the most widely used in local and national state publications and media broadcasts. Subsequent to the 1991 Census, surveys and monitoring forms have followed the same format - in terms of the ethnic question - in order to make longitudinal comparisons. This process has taken place despite the fundamental problem that these terms ascribe people born in Britain in terms of nation states which many may never have visited. Furthermore, the 1991 Census provides a critique of the process of self-labelling defined previously. On the one hand the ethnic question in the 1991 Census can be viewed as a mass exercise in self-definition, as it was the responsibility of the head of household to fill out the form. The results of the census revealed that the majority of people from Pakistan (and implicitly (Azad) Kashmir), or with parental links to the area, ticked the Pakistani box when it came to the issue of ethnicity (Ballard and Kalra 1994). Yet, at the beginning of this section Saifullah Khan argues that the term Mirpuri is closer to people's own definition and Ali et al (1996) highlights the way in which 'Kashmiri' is now becoming a term for self-definition from many young people in Luton. This contradiction between the form of self-definition the Census offers and that forwarded by ethnographers illustrates how the dialectic between state and individuals is often swayed in the favour of who is doing the defining.

Given the weight of statistical data utilising terms such as Indian and Pakistani, in this book the term Pakistani is used to describe macro-economic data about West Punjabis, Pathans and Mirpuris in Oldham. The utilisation of data in this way recognises that unless specific survey work is carried out to distinguish between these groups it is difficult to make statistically meaningful statements about Mirpuris other than by using the term Pakistani. Given this problem, it is possible to appreciate that in

Oldham this group consists of a majority from (Azad) Kashmir. So, while statistics use the term Pakistani there is a qualitative distinction to be made between Pakistani and (Azad) Kashmiri. In much of the academic literature, the term Pakistani is used to refer to people from Mirpur/(Azad) Kashmir, even though the region has, on paper, a semi-autonomous status from Pakistan. One reason for this may be that that Mirpuris have, as Saifullah Khan (1976) and Ballard (1983) note, an 'essentially' Punjabi/Putohari culture, which therefore does not overly distinguish them from Pakistani Punjabis. An additional factor is the fact that the autonomy of the region is more ceremonial and for most practical purposes it is integrated with Pakistan.

Yet there are various reasons, both historical and contemporary, which enable a distinction between (Azad) Kashmiri and Punjabi to be sustained. In the remainder of this book the term Mirpuri and (Azad) Kashmiri are used for two broad reasons. The first point relates to the distinct political histories of (Azad) Kashmir and West Punjab, from the time of colonial rule to the present day. In turn this has differentially affected the development of infrastructural resources in each of the regions which has had an impact on reasons for migration. These points are elaborated in Chapter Three. The second reason for arguing for a separation between Pakistani/Punjabis and (Azad) Kashmiri/Mirpuris is the class disparity between the two groups in Britain. This latter point is illustrated in some detail in the rest of the book, but can also be gauged by a review of the academic fieldwork amongst Pakistanis in Britain. The three main published ethnographies on Pakistanis in Britain, by Anwar (1979), Shaw (1988) and Werbner (1990), have each focused on Punjabis even though Mirpuris are demographically the more predominant group (Ballard 1983). An interesting comparison can be made when considering the Census data on economic status of Pakistanis in the cities of Manchester and Oxford with Oldham and Bradford. Statistically speaking Pakistanis fare relatively better in the former areas than they do in the latter, reflecting the population concentrations of Mirpuris and Punjabis. The class distinction between these two groups forms a central platform through the ethnographic tracts of this book and as such is the central reason for making the distinction between (Azad) Kashmiri and Pakistani.

Whether using the term Muslim or Mirpuri, it is crucial to be clear and transparent when applying a set of labels to a racialised/ethnicised group. The simplistic notion of 'self-definition' can act as a convenient avoidance of explanations as to how categories are attained. In my own fieldwork experience, terms of self-definition varied according to who I was talking to and where and when I was talking to them. Applying different labels to the same group of people throughout the book is therefore an attempt to capture the multiple nature of identification processes that occur in contemporary England. In so doing the dialectical nature of group labelling is revealed, skipping between individual responses, state ascription and local group self-promotion. In spite of this multiple usage of terms, the next section argues that the categories Black, South Asian, Muslim and Mirpuri are themselves analytically inadequate to describe the differences across gender and generation that are crucial for representation of any group of people.

Developing a New Terminology

> The Mirpuri immigrant whom we used as an example is quite capable of seeing himself or herself, as a British citizen, or a member of the working class as he or she is of identifying with a particular biraderi, with Kashmir or with Islam (Rex and Drury 1994: 5 my emphasis).

> In Bradford, for *young Pakistanis* in particular, the issue of identity, whether Pakistani, Mirpuri or Muslim was an impassioned issue....(Samad 1996: 98 my emphasis).

In these quotes, Rex et al and Samad attempt to convey the multiple nature of self-identification in contemporary Britain, in much the same way as I have argued above. However, in order to define their field of study, they are forced to initially privilege a particular identification - in this case either Pakistani or Mirpuri. This is the more profound dilemma of labelling which requires a radical re-think of the process of identification itself. It is not a problem that is fully addressed in this text, as my own starting point is also with a group labelled Mirpuri/Pakistani. To partially overcome this issue, I propose the development of a new terminology, necessarily liminal, but most applicable to my fieldwork experiences. Following Parkin:

> If, for experimental purposes, we abandon the opposition between, for instance, positivism and hermeneutics, universalism and relativism and the macro and the micro and recast our observations in a different, ethnographically extracted dichotomy.......however provisional its status we perhaps loosen the hold of essentialized concepts and draw analytical

observation closer to practice (1995: 161).

By developing a new terminology, I begin to address the problem of the reduction of differences of gender, generation and class to functions of a pre-ordained unchanging ethnicity. [6] Terms such as Mirpuri or Pakistani or South Asian can become containers for a certain kind of cultural baggage which can be applied to a large number of cases, be it in the field of employment, housing or health. Therefore I recognise that the core group of people on whom this theses focuses are in one sense nationally defined by the terms, Pakistani-Mirpuris, but also wish to acknowledge that this group is divided according to age, time of migration and gender.

The terms I have adopted from my fieldwork are *babas, kakas, mangeters*, lads and women. In forwarding these terms, as descriptive tools for analysis, I attempt to overcome the closures and problems of terms such as Pakistani and Mirpuri. Equally important, however, is the recognition that the terms *babas* and *kakas* have developed from fieldwork experience. These terms are therefore the outcome of a dialogic interaction between the interviewees and myself, not a result of objective observation and scientific study. They, therefore, do not have any claim outside of the confines of this text, though they do evoke a response and understanding when used in the field.

Babas, kakas and lads refer exclusively to male groups while the term *mangeter* can refer to either men or women. The focus on men in this book is largely a function of the focus on the textile industry and fieldwork restrictions. [7] The term *baba* is a generic term of respect for an elder male, widely used in the North of the sub-continent. It is often added as a suffix to the name of widely known and respected male elders. In the ethnographic chapters, *babas* refers to those men who came to Britain in the early to mid sixties, who were the primary settlers and have stronger attachments, materially and imagined, to a sense of being Mirpuri/Pakistani. [8] Significantly, all of their education was in (Azad) Kashmir or Pakistan. Similar to the term *baba*, the word *kaka* implies generation as well as gender distinction. However, *kaka* is more flexible in its usage, as it can equally apply to a male of six or sixty years in age as long as the appellant is older. To avoid confusion, in this book the term *kakas* is utilised in a more specific manner, than its more general usage. [9] Therefore, *kakas* are the sons of the *babas*. They came to Britain as children, under the age of sixteen, often with their mothers. They were often left in the jurisdiction of fathers and uncles, as mothers would often only stay in Britain for a short while before returning to (Azad) Kashmir (Ballard 1987). These young men received some schooling in Mirpur and often one to four years in Britain. However, the country of birth is not of concern here. The notable aspect of their upbringing, is that some of their education was in Britain. Both the *kakas* and the *babas* are also defined in terms of their experience of life in the mills. This in itself is quite an inclusive criterion as all of the men I came into contact with had some connection with the mills, either as workers or through friends and relatives who had worked in a mill. In contrast to the *babas* and *kakas*, for many Oldham born young people, the mills are part of a bygone era no longer providing a source of income or even of interest. It is this group who are called 'lads' in this scheme (Willis 1977).[10] They do not form a large part of this study other than as a marginalised group in terms of their labour market position and their relationships with the *kakas* and *babas*.

The schema presented is not intended to make inter-generational difference the source of all change and conflict within Britain's South Asian minorities as has been the case with much previous work (see Shaw 1994). The notion of generational conflict is not borne out by my ethnographic evidence, where the situation of *mangeters* clearly illustrates how a simple splitting of generations cannot explain the particular reasons for their social and economic position. *Mangeters* are very rarely considered as a separate group in analysis of South Asian minorities, because they do not sit comfortably with a 'between two cultures' (Watson 1977) or 'generational conflict' framework. In technical terms, *mangeter* refers to a fiancé, someone who has literally been summoned for marriage. In Britain, this term has come to refer to those people, male or female, who have come to Britain as a result of marriage rather than primary migration. This has been the main source of in-migration to Britain's South Asian groupings since the end of primary migration in the early 1970s. *Mangeters* straddle the older and younger generations. They share the same rural histories as the *babas* where their commitment to the *biraderi* is an obvious example of a shared perception of the world. At the same time their level of skills and qualifications place them in the same job market as many of the sixteen and seventeen year olds who leave school without qualifications in Oldham. Their weak position is further exacerbated by the fact that, as new immigrants, for one year they are effectively at the behest of their wife/husband and her/his family. Any hint of a failed marriage would result in deportation illustrating the role of the state in enforcing certain codes of kinship conduct.[11]

Given sufficient ethnographic material, a similar set of terms to those outlined above could be devised for the female group. Of the categories developed, only *mangeter,* is gender neutral and therefore applicable to both men and women. However, even here male and female *mangeters* are subject to differing life experiences. The reasons for not developing a set of female categories relates to problems of access to women for a male researcher, which are outlined in detail further on, and the focus of the book on textile mill workers. Obviously, by presenting a study of male workers, the issue of gender is illustrated; what is missing is the representation of women's voices. For instance, in chapter eight the issue of homeworking is considered, largely from secondary sources. In presenting my ethnography I attempt to take into account various sub-divisions of category of woman, especially in terms of *mangeters* and young people, but maintain the male-female division as the most significant. Future research needs to take into account the various subdivisions of this gendered category for an accurate picture of the labour market position of female Muslim Mirpuri/Pakistani women to be drawn.

The epistemological problem of outlining and developing appropriate non-essential categories forms the heart of the terminology I have presented. Arguably the terms I have developed can themselves be criticised for creating essential categories. However, in contrast to existing categorisations, I have outlined the method in which the labels I use are formed. In so doing the terms, *baba, kaka, mangeter* and lad, are subject to change and modification. Throughout the remaining chapters I alternate between using combinations of ethno-national labels and the terminology I have developed here. These labellings are strategic and are used to reflect the particular area or issue under study.

Reflexive Approaches

Simeran Man Singh Gell in the September 1996 issue of *Critique of Anthropology* raises several far reaching issues, in this small review article, about the nature of anthropology in general and particularly studies of South Asian migrants in Britain. Gell raises many points, of which the most relevant for present purposes, is her analysis of the relationship between the 'white' social scientist as, assumed, universal and objective, and the South Asian anthropologist. In a previous article, Werbner (1995) has criticised Gell for forwarding descriptions of Muslims which are reflective of the historical antagonism between Muslims and Sikhs. Werbner argues that Gell has not studied Muslims and, as she is a Sikh and Sikhism is her area of expertise, her comments about Muslims are tinged by this. In response to these criticisms, Gell contends that Werbner's line of thought implies that it is only the objective, 'white' anthropologist who can make comments about communities other than their own. Therefore, writers such as Gell and other South Asians studying South Asians in Britain are only qualified to study their own communities. In the light of my visible appearance as a Sikh studying non-Sikhs, Gell's experiences of other 'white' anthropologists resonate with my own encounters.

Part of my fieldwork involved a trip to (Azad) Kashmir. During my preparation for this journey I was accosted by three, white -one male, two female- anthropologists, who took great glee in highlighting the problems I might have as a turban wearing, bearded Sikh going to Kashmir. Often these conversation would invoke partition and the fact that 'Muslims don't like Sikhs you know'. Inevitably these comments would be followed by an account of their own experiences of having a wonderful time during their fieldwork in Pakistan or England with Pakistanis. This latter point would invoke questions about any problems I might have had during my fieldwork with 'Muslims' in Oldham. Throughout these assaults on my being, I did not retort, well you should hear what many of my correspondents have to say about 'white people' because that would merely be reiterating their framework of reference with which I was being presented.

These encounters highlight one of the central problems of the anthropology of minorities in Britain. White, western trained academics and often those non-white scholars also are trained to believe that the knowledge they are extracting is divorced from the historical and contemporary relationship that they, as part of a collectivity, have with the 'natives' (hooks 1991). Colonialism and racism are both prevalent discourses in contemporary Britain. The 'natives' are well aware of how white people have treated them historically and continue to treat them in England. However, this fact is conveniently not mentioned in fieldwork notes, nor in the history of the subject. [12] In its place, attempts are made to emphasise connection between the anthropologist and the object of study. For instance, Werbner (1990) prefaces her study with the recognition that she is a migrant and that this gave her a 'deep affinity' with Manchester Pakistanis. She also forwards herself as an 'Israeli Jew critical of Israel (Werbner 1995: 426). This reflection on self-identity, by Werbner emphasises connection, both being a migrant and critical of Israel, are points of association with

Pakistani/Muslims. However, the other side to this coin is Zionism and racism, which are both obvious points of disconnection.[13] In recognising both points of connection and *disconnection* the fieldworker is able to explore the historical and social background which forms the basis of interaction. In Britain this inevitably involves some discrepancy in terms of class, gender and, of course, 'race'.

The boundaries of the connections that I made with people were forged on the basis of my various subject positions as Sikh, researcher, young, male, Asian, Punjabi speaker. In turn, each of these were potential sites of connection and disconnection. For the most part I was received well both in Oldham and (Azad) Kashmir. Obviously, my relationships were marked by the context of the speech, who I was with and the mode of the conversation. However, as someone who is visibly signified as being a Sikh, this formed the basis of my relationship with most of the *babas* and *kakas* I talked to. My personal history, inscribed on my body, was the access to talking and relating. I was always fully aware of how this factor affected the nature of the conversations that I had. The Khalistani movement and the Kashmir liberation movement provide the means for connection and communication, just as migration to England and working with fellow Sikhs in the mills did in a previous historical period. It was only with the very old men that the question of partition and violence arose. However, this was, most often, quickly brushed over. Most of these *babas* were more interested in gaining some knowledge of contemporary East Punjab. The fact that there is a very small visible Sikh population in Oldham also contributed to the desire to engage with me.

For other groups, particularly council/voluntary sector workers, I was a fellow Asian with whom they related on the basis of being fellow professionals. This group was also the most wary about the nature of my research. For example, the extent to which the findings may be of 'use' to anyone and the fact that social research is politically loaded. However, the most significant aspect of 'disconnection' was due to my identity as a male. It was very difficult to talk to middle-aged and older women, other than those professionals working in the voluntary sector and the local authority. The importance of gender has been previously recognised by most male researchers of South Asian Muslim minorities (Dayha 1970; Anwar 1979; Ballard 1983). In this respect my experiences of fieldwork were no different than those outlined by these authors.

Identifying a Field and a Sample

In the construction of the final text, epistemological concerns become more important than the actual means by which the subject of research is located and data extracted. In this section, I redress the balance by outlining the reasons for choosing Oldham as a site of study and the methods by which I gained the knowledge represented in this text. Critically, these methods depended on the area of research I was interested in and the type of people I was talking to which changed during the duration of my fieldwork. For instance, the majority of the research with the *babas* involved in-depth interviews, whereas I used participant-observation techniques while in take-aways and taxi ranks.

Research on South Asians in Britain has tended to be geographically restricted to the large conurbations of London, the Midlands and the North. Within these Birmingham, and particularly Bradford, have attracted the most attention. In the case of Bradford the town has become almost an icon of 'multicultural' Britain (McLoughlin 1997). [14] In contrast to these studies, the research by Anwar (1979) and Werbner (1990) has focused on Rochdale and Manchester respectively. There is a close focus on the textile industry in Anwar's work and clothing manufacturers in Werbner's work. In the context of finding a town with a high concentration of Pakistanis and a centre of the textile industry, Rochdale may have proved to be the first choice as it would also have built on Anwar's study. However, for reasons which become more apparent during the following chapters, it was also important to consider the size of the (Azad) Kashmiri/Mirpuri population in the town. In Rochdale the majority grouping is Pakistani Punjabi (Anwar 1979). Given the fact that the (Azad) Kashmiri population is larger than the Punjabi Pakistani one, it is surprising that more ethnographic studies have focused on the latter rather than the former. [15]

Smaller towns have tended to be ignored in much work on minorities in Britain, a point made most recently by Srinivasan (1995) who makes a study of Oxford. As the North West is dotted with towns with small populations of Pakistanis, such as Bury, Nelson and Bolton, it seemed appropriate to choose a fieldwork site which reflected the particularity of the region. Oldham fulfils many of the initial criteria of the research in terms of textile history, size of minority population, and proximity to Manchester and Bradford. In fact, Oldham geographically falls in a triangle between Rochdale and Manchester and is relatively close to Bradford. It is, therefore, fairly well placed in between large centres of South Asian/Pakistani settlement. Its location also provides a useful addition to the ethnographies by Anwar and Werbner of nearby Rochdale and Manchester. The Pakistani population is statistically the largest minority in the town of which, on a rough estimate, over eighty percent are from (Azad) Kashmir, more specifically Mirpur. Furthermore, the main source of employment for the South Asian workers who first came to the town was in the textile mills. Oldham was one of the centres of the global textile industry and at its peak was deeply linked to the Indian sub-continent.

My fieldwork began in January 1994 and ended in April 1995 with a trip to (Azad) Kashmir. I do not consider my experiences in (Azad) Kashmir in this account, as the trip was largely a background and fact finding excursion. The literature and material I found there, particularly inform the next chapter. In Oldham I utilised a range of methods to obtain data which are closely related to the area of my concern. For instance, research on the migration process and of working in the mills was carried out with the *babas* mainly utilising in-depth interviews, whereas field work in taxi ranks and take-aways involved participant observation techniques. My fieldwork was, in fact, split in this way with the first half mainly spent locating and interviewing *babas* and the second half engaged in participant-observation.

During my M.Phil., I had developed an interview schedule for interviewing the *babas*. The first issue I faced was that of access. This operated on several levels; geographical, physical, mobility and, most importantly, having the necessary skills to gain access. From an analysis of census data I knew that the Pakistani population was concentrated in two wards of the town. [16] The folk lore model of beginning field work by 'hanging out' or loitering and seeing what happens, in the British setting, can lead to arrest under the loitering laws. Even though this is an extreme example, the idea of relationships developing on an ad hoc basis in an urban environment is not practical. To overcome the limitations of urban research, other fieldworkers have utilised 'gatekeepers' to achieve access to networks of kin and family. In order to begin my research this proved invaluable. I was interested in finding ex-mill workers over the age of fifty who had been unemployed or on long-term sickness for three to five years. Through the work of gatekeepers I was able to locate some members of this group.

I carried out initial interviews with these men without a tape recorder in order to develop a research schedule. My main concern was to obtain narratives about working in the mills of Oldham, reasons for migration from Mirpur and the time at which they were made redundant.

From this small group, I used the 'snowballing' technique to gain access to other men in similar circumstances. Once word had spread about what I was doing, a process of self-selection took place where *babas* who were interested in talking to me would arrange appointments, allow me into their houses to tape interviews. [17] These would often be over three hours long and encompassed a wide range of subjects. Even though I attempted to use a more formalised structure to my interviewing, on answering my questions they would often retort with a question for me or ask for an opinion on other matters. Using the 'snowballing' technique ensured that the people I talked to had some prior knowledge of my research. However, it also had the disadvantage of limiting my research to one sub-group of the *babas*. To compensate for this I also carried out 'opportunistic sampling' in areas where I knew old unemployed men would meet. Welfare rights sessions, held in public places such as schools and community centres proved useful starting points. In these places, I would conduct short formal interviews while the men were waiting to see the advisor. These short meetings often led to arrangements for more in-depth interviews.

Most of the research on the *babas* was carried out with individuals. The only group work carried out happened by default where an interview would be interrupted by friends visiting, and they would then join in the conversation. Otherwise, I attended various public events where *babas* were present, such as funerals and weddings. However, in these contexts the conversations were oriented to contemporary concerns rather than to stories of the past. This is a crucial point in the methodology of this book, as many of the *babas* would begin in the past but quickly move to their concerns about the present. For many of these men their last experience of work in the mills was three to ten years previous to the time of this research. Therefore, the narratives they present need to be carefully considered in terms of their present conditions and concerns.

The fact that I carried out mainly individual interviews is reflected in the text presented in chapters three to seven. The names attached to the quotes in these chapters do not correspond with the people I interviewed. This was to maintain anonymity in a situation. In some cases, I have kept the person's name, but this was only where we had fully discussed the uses to which the research would be put. By and large I assured everybody that the work would be confidential and for this reason most of the names are mixtures from the pool of names of the people I interviewed.

Research on taxi ranks and take-aways was carried out mainly with the *kakas*. In the first place these men were the sons of some of the *babas* I talked to. This was also the group who are currently working in the few mills that are still in operation. These *kakas* were interviewed in order to compare their experiences with the *babas* in the mills. I developed a historical background to employment in taxi ranks and take-aways by carrying out taped interviews with owners. This was followed up by participative-observation in one take-away and taxi rank. Each of the workers were also interviewed during the period of participant-observation. This is reflected in the fact that chapter eight contains more case study sections which are descriptive passages gleaned from my experiences in the take-away. For a general perspective on taxi driving I also interviewed drivers at Hackney cab ranks in the city centre while they were waiting for customers. These were without prior introduction and proved an illuminating contrast to the more in-depth interviews.

During my fieldwork, I also met and talked to young men born in Britain, the lads and *mangeters*. It was not my initial intention to focus on these groups. However, the fact that their experiences were markedly different from that of the *babas* and the *kakas* meant that later on in my fieldwork, I actually began to identify *mangeters* and in fact made this an additional criterion in interviewing. In parallel I also visited a youth club for a period of time to gauge the opinions and experiences of young people. Finally, I interviewed a small group of professional Mirpuri/Pakistani women working in the field of advice work and social services to gauge their opinion of women's experiences of migration and settlement. Chapter Eight reflects the secondary nature of my data sources on the issues of women and homeworking, where there are few direct interviews and a greater focus on research done in other parts of the country.

The majority of the formal interviews were carried out in Punjabi/Putohari. Those that were carried out without a tape-recorder were translated immediately. Notes, from these interviews were written in English, other than where I was unsure of the exact meaning of a word, or its context. In these cases I would note the word/phrase in Punjabi (Gurmukhi) and translate it at a later date. However, the bulk of these interviews were immediately filtered by the process of translation into English and, as such, form the backbone to the recorded material. The taped interviews were translated on transcription. This process often involved more than one translator as there were various contexts and words which were not immediately apparent to me. I was especially supported by my father and friends in Oldham in this process.

Ethical Issues

In urban research, personal, bureaucratic and historical encounters that respondents have experienced oftentimes foreground relationships with them in the field. As previously stated, my position as a visible Sikh and a male, for example, has an effect on the nature of the relationship between interviewer and interviewee. In the context of research in an inner-city, these are areas which are often open to much closer scrutiny from state agencies. This may be as innocuous as housing repair through to surveillance by the police. When one assesses the degree of local and national state intervention in areas designated as 'deprived', it becomes of concern to any research. Many of these areas and their inhabitants have been subject to intense scrutiny by means of surveys and 'community development' input. In fact, it was difficult for many of my correspondents to understand the purpose of my research outside of a clearly designated role within the state apparatus. At the same time members of the local state were dismissive of research that was not clearly aimed at tackling issues of social policy and in a narrow reading of deprivation. [18]

The nature of the study required a demarcation of explicit boundaries about what was to go into my final report and what was not. this was negotiated very early on with the people I worked with in the take-aways, and I have respected those areas which the men preferred not to be made public. My interest in issues of employment, pay and times of working were especially sensitive when it came to research in the area of taxi driving and working in the take-aways. These areas of the economy have long operated on a 'cash' payment basis and as such are open to intense scrutiny from tax and benefit agencies. The process of gaining trust, in this way was always marked with the question 'You're not from the benefits office asking all these questions, are you?'. I overcame many of these difficulties by spending time and developing relationships with various members of the groups I wished to talk to. I was also as explicit as possible about the aims of the project and the extent to which it was for a University degree rather than for the local authority.

In an analysis of the informal economy, such as the one that manifestly exists in Lancashire, the idea of a dole 'spy' is not too far-fetched and may stop people being willing to divest information. Both the questionnaire and the formal interview are used for the gathering of official and commercial data. For example, structured formal interviews occur in a variety of arenas: Social Security office, job interview, social workers visit.

This illustrates the high degree to which relationships are pre-figured when considering an urban field in a highly bureaucratised society.

Applying Methods

From epistemological issues to practical concerns, this methodology chapter covers the main points that I faced during my fieldwork and subsequent construction of this text. Crucially, I have developed a set of categories from the articulation of my fieldwork experiences with theoretical concerns. The divisions in the social field in terms of gender, generation and migration reflect the theoretical construction developed in Chapter One. From these epistemological concerns, the role of myself as fieldworker illustrated some of the core problems with current research into South Asian minorities in Britain. I illustrated how important it is to take into account areas of disconnection as well as connection with the field and fieldwork subjects. Access to the field and the actual way in which the divisions earlier presented required separate techniques for data collection was outlined in the final section.

This methodology chapter is a tool which should be applied to the next ethnographic chapters of the book where interviews and statements about the working lives of the *babas* and the *kakas* are presented in a seamless fashion. The location of the narrators of the quotes are not detailed in those chapters. It is therefore necessary to keep in mind the construction of their place presented in this chapter. Similarly, the huge amount of editing of personal narratives and the selective construction of life stories is not made apparent throughout the book. This is the job of methodology; which should remain a constant reminder of the way in which the various labels used, categories constructed and stories told are liminal and ultimately open to refutation, criticism and change.

---

[1] The recent government campaign to report those people involved in benefit fraud is on example of this.
[2] A group I have referred to as culturalists in Chapter One.
[3] This is also a historical reckoning and one that corroborates with the use of the word *kale* to describe their status as workers within the mills when talking about all of the workers not just *'apne lok'*. In this sense I disagree strongly with Modood who attempts to essentialise the use of the word *kale* by stating the obvious fact that it has different historical roots in the sub-continent. The point is

that during the period of industrial work, the word *kale* was used as a generic description.

[4] Even though I recognise that this definition: constructs a Black identity that is present only as a victim of White society and in the process reduces racism to what White people do to Black people, because they are Black' (Anthias and Davis 1994: 15). This is not true of African and Caribbean mobilisation where black has been and is a significant construct for mobilisation.

[5] The demise of the Soviet Union and the perception of the Islamic 'terrorist' threat from Iran, Iraq and Libya has also contributed to this interest. See Sayyid, B. (1997) *The Fundamental Fear.*

[6] Throughout most of Dahya and Anwar's texts there is the distinct impression that the term Pakistani is being used as synonymous with Pakistani male, which once again raises problems highlighted in the previous section of who is being represented.

[7] In a later section an exploration of the limitations of being a male researcher partially explains the gendered nature of this approach.

[8] *Babas* is a play on the word *baba* as the plural form of the word is *babeh*. There is a rule of thumb with borrowed words that the plural tends to become indigenised.

[9] As *babas* is a play on *baba* so *kakas* is a play on *kaka*. *Kake* would be the correct plural form of the word.

[10] Willis (1977) uses the term 'lads' to describe alienated youth.

[11] The immigration laws on marriage partners are such that any breakdown in the marriage in the first year, results in the immigrant foregoing their right of stay in Britain. A more detailed account of this procedure is given in Chapter Eight.

[12] Contrast Bourne (1980) with Werbner (1987).

[13] This is not to argue that Werbner is a Zionist or a racist, but to illustrate that these are potential points of conflict which are not addressed.

[14] Bradford has also attracted a considerable focus, in terms of the woollen textile industry in the town (Allen et al 1977; Cohen 1978; Fevre 1984).

[15] It is difficult to quantify the relative numbers as they do not appear on census information.

See Anwar (1979), Werbner (1990) and Shaw (1988) for detailed research on Punjabi Pakistanis. Only Ballard (1983, 1987) and Saifullah Khan (1977) have done specific work on Mirpuris/(Azad) Kashmiris.

[16] See Appendix I for a full breakdown.

[17] Those not interested would often be too polite to refuse to my face, but they would usually not be in the house, when I called to carry out the interview. This occurred quite regularly.

[18] I had many interactions with members of the local authority in attempts to gain information. Certain individuals were very helpful, but overall I was seen as another student wasting their time.

3 Migration and Repercussion

Introduction

(Azad) Kashmir in general and Mirpur district in particular has gained significance in contemporary Britain for two reasons. Firstly, a large number of people from the area have migrated to and settled in Britain, and secondly two wars have been fought between India and Pakistan over the Jammu and Kashmir territory of which Mirpur forms a geographical part. The political situation in Jammu and Kashmir and its historical antecedents have been described and analysed in a great deal of detail elsewhere and does not form the central focus of attention here. [1] The primary concern of this chapter is to detail the reasons for migration from Mirpur/(Azad) Kashmir. The trope of migration has come to be synonymous with Mirpur not only in academic writing but also in popular representations of the region both in Britain and Pakistan. This is primarily due to the mass migration which has occurred from the territory in the last thirty years which has resulted in almost one quarter of the population of Mirpur district now residing abroad (Khan et al 1982) rising to over fifty percent in certain areas (Ballard 1985).

Detailed explanations for the high level of migration from Mirpur have been forwarded by, Dahya (1970), Saifullah Khan (1977) and Ballard (1983, 1985). The reasons for migration forwarded by these authors revolve around the concept of 'chain migration', and the historical links between Mirpur and Britain. This chapter develops on the work of these academics, sometimes enhancing at other times contradicting the perspectives they forward. The central argument of this chapter is that previous studies of migration from Mirpur have leant too much towards the working of 'chain migration', to the detriment of structural factors and in contrast this chapter illustrates that migration from Mirpur was a result of a combination of historical, geographical and political causes. Evidence for this perspective is developed by considering migration during the British/Dogra rule period, which began in 1846 and ended in 1947 and the post-partition period to the present day. Beginning with the historical reasons for migration from Mirpur/Kashmir in the pre-partition period, I consider the political and geographical factors which combined to produce migration from the area. I also highlight the economic and political links between (Azad) Kashmir and England, Mirpur and Oldham and show how these are the conduits through which the flow of humans streamed. In the post-partition era, the geo-political considerations focus on the consequences of the Mangla dam project, which resulted in the displacement of tens of thousands of people. In some detail, I outline the effect of the project on subsequent migration from the area. The final part of the chapter considers the ongoing economic and social consequences of the mass migration to Britain and other parts of the world, on Mirpur.

Migration Theory

The topic of migration has generated three main theoretical approaches: world systems theory, push and pull factors, and network theory (Light and Bhachu, 1993) Each of these approaches has been utilised to develop an understanding of the presence of Black migrants in Britain. In the previous chapter, the work of Castles and Kozack (1973) and Miles (1982) illustrates world systems theory, where people move from areas of labour excess to those of labour demand. This movement parallels division between the Third world and the West, where movement is from the former to the latter. The specific locales from which migration takes place are unimportant in this theorisation. Migrants move simply because of the requirements of capital. However, this approach cannot answer specific questions about the details of migration; for instance why is there a concentration of emigration from certain parts of the Indian sub-continent, in particular from sub-regions ? Furthermore, these areas cannot necessarily be defined as those with the greatest excess of labour. In particular, why is Mirpur a prime area of migration and not Jammu which has similar geography and agricultural terrain ? To begin to answer some of these questions we can turn to the second approach, which has been most utilised in academic literature - the push and pull perspective (Light and Bhachu 1993). Here, migration is considered in terms of those factors that 'push' people to migrate - these are often structural such as poverty, flood, famine - and pull factors are those that attract people to the area of emigration. The main point of attraction is the demand for labour. The push-pull approach develops world systems theory because it considers both localities when explaining reasons for migration and emigration respectively. Taking into account local pressures can then explain why some areas become migrant dense and others do not. However, there is a level of determinism in the push-pull theory which assumes that the migrant has no agency, but is pulled and pushed between countries. To reintroduce the concept of migrant agency, network theory has been forwarded as a useful approach (Light and Bhachu 1993).

The central premise of migrant network theory is to illustrate how networks enable people to migrate. Massey argues that migration takes place through sets of interpersonal bonds that: 'link migrants, former migrants and non-migrants in origin and destination areas through the bonds of kinship, friendship and shared community origin' (Massey 1988: 396). Massey further maintains that the network becomes independent of the initial reasons that caused the migration. The main significance of migrant network theory is that it highlights the creation of autonomous social structures that support migration. These support structures reduce the social, economic and emotional costs of immigration. Light and Bhachu (1993) contend that, unlike the world systems and pull/push approaches, migrant network theory is able to deal with both micro and macro aspects of migration. However, by considering the network only as a facilitator, structural changes that may affect the working of the network are slighted. The network is assumed to be unaffected by changes in immigration law or by other political and economic changes.

In the literature on migration from Mirpur, it is Dahya (1974), Saifullah Khan (1977) and Ballard (1983, 1985) who have most vigorously applied the tenets of migration network theory. Three main points develop from this application. Firstly, migration from the region in both pre- and post-partition periods was not a result of poverty forcing people to look for an income, rather 'Pakistanis emigrate not in order to earn a livelihood but to supplement the economic resources of their families of origin...'(Dahya 1974: 82). Therefore, the middle-income land-owners migrate and 'chain migration' is the mechanism by which this migration takes place. This process is independent of structural factors and it is the fact that relatives or friends have already migrated, rather than loss of land or exile, which explains mass migration (Saifullah Khan 1977). The third main point is that migration to Britain was, in specific terms, a result of the historical links between Mirpur and Britain and the long tradition of international migration from the region. These three points are developed in this chapter by a reconsideration of the historical evidence. My main criticism of Dahya, Ballard and Saifullah Khan's perspective is in terms of the emphasis in their narratives on migration as an 'entrepreneurial activity'. In contrast, my focus is on the role of the state and of other structural hindrances. Migration as organised by individuals, in order to enhance their economic well being, underplays structural elements of the migration process, which may constitute push factors. In this chapter I argue that this stress on 'individual choice' is misplaced. The particular case of Mirpur is an apt illustration of how political, social and economic factors combine to produce a situation in which migration is the *only* option. This is not to deny that the actual process by which migration takes place is not *organised* along the principles of 'chain migration' nor the historical factors which constitute a route to Britain, but to give due recognition to the ways in which the migrant network is shaped by structural factors.

Early Migration

According to Dahya (1974) and Ballard (1987), international migration from Mirpur began in the late nineteenth century with men from the region joining merchant ships from Bombay to work in the boiler room as stokers. This tradition of men working out of their home region was enhanced by recruitment to the British Indian army in the 1880s. Dahya (1974) cites the *Punjab District Gazetteer* (1907) as evidence of migration from the Chhachh area of what is now Pakistan and by inference argues that migration from Mirpur was of a similar order; whereas Ballard's (1985, 1987) evidence for this early migration is not made explicit in his work and presumably comes from fieldwork interviews. Nevertheless, for both authors the main reasons for this early migration are related to an excess of male labour in the region due to poor agricultural land. Dahya (1974) also cites primogeniture, the division of land amongst males of succeeding generations as a reason for increased pressure on land. Both authors limit this migration to a particular group of people, the sons of middle-income land owners, rather than a response by all of those who could find work in shipping or the army.

I am in agreement with both authors over the importance of these factors. However, points of disagreement arise over the lack of a role given to the state and the type of people who migrated. Neither Ballard (1983) nor Dahya (1974) sufficiently explore the political factors that gave rise to many of the structural problems that caused this early migration. The consequence of Jammu and Kashmir's status as a Princely state under British rule is not explored by either author, yet this is critical to understanding the push factors for migration. A detailed assessment of the rural economic and social situation in pre-partition Mirpur illustrates that migration was not the result of middle-income land-owners looking to supplement their income, but rather an attempt by all residents to generate a subsistence income. [2]

In 1931 a peasant uprising took place in Mirpur *tehsil* against the imposition of a new land tax by the Maharaja's land revenue department (Rahim 1995). [3] Protests against the tax grew into a general anti-Maharaja movement and later turned into communal riots. In order to suppress this revolt, the British government, on the request of the Maharaja, sent troops to the area. Lord Salisbury reported on the event and also made a general analysis of the social and economic situation in Mirpur. [4] This quote from his findings is of most interest:

> I find that there are a larger sprinkling of returned Indians (*Mirpuris*) from the colonies and shipping lines and ex-soldiers of the British Indian army. They all have very distinct views of their rights (Salisbury 1932:12).

The reasons given by Salisbury for migration from the area were to supplement the meagre income from the sale of *ghee* (clarified butter) and husbandry. The fact that the land could not easily be mortgaged by the *zamindars* (land-owners) limited the cash that could be generated. The only option was to go into debt. Much of the early migrant remittances were used to get out of debt and to actually purchase land outright from *mahajans* (money lenders). [5] Salisbury's report is the only documentary evidence that pertains to migration from Mirpur. The *Jammu and Kashmir Gazetteer* of the time makes only passing reference to the area, as it was a peripheral part of the Maharaja's territory. Making inferences about Mirpur from sources such as the *Rawalpindi Gazetteer* is untenable as the political situation in British-controlled India was markedly different, especially in terms of agricultural taxation. It is this political difference which makes a significant contribution to the reasons for early and subsequent migration from the area. Detailed historical accounts of the Kashmir valley and the Jammu area, compiled mainly by British travellers and army men, are available from the 1800s onwards. [6] These studies make mention of Mirpur town and occasionally Bhimber, however, only in passing. The main contribution made by these historical accounts to an understanding of the area are that by the end of the nineteenth century, Mirpur town was the third largest in the area after Srinagar and Jammu. Despite this lack of specific historical evidence, it is still possible to locate Mirpur within the general political history of Jammu and Kashmir, at least from the time of the Dogra rule which is the period of most interest with

Migration and Repercussion   57

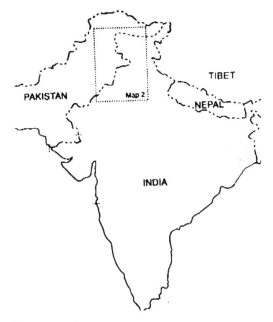

Figure 3.1 Indian Sub-Continent

Figure 3.2 Punjab, Jammu and Kashmir and Azad Jammu and Kashmir

regard to migration. What this history reveals is that Mirpur was a peripheral area of the Kashmir kingdom during colonial rule and, as a disputed territory in post-partition Pakistan, it has suffered a similar fate. The contemporary area of Jammu and Kashmir (JK), divided between India and Pakistan, is largely a construction of boundaries fixed by the British (Figure 3.1 and Figure 3.2). With the annexation of the Punjab in 1846, Jammu and Kashmir came under the jurisdiction of the British Imperial crown. In return for the help he had provided during the Anglo-Sikh wars, the British sold JK to Maharaja Gulab Singh for three hundred thousand pounds. These Princely states were allowed semi-autonomous self-rule and, more significantly, the ability to collect finance as long as they did not interfere with British imperial policy. The type of rule in these states varied enormously. But, in the case of Kashmir, the Maharaja was notorious for exploiting the people and the resources of the state.

The effect of the Maharaja's policies were such that, when compared to British India and even the nearby Rawalpindi and Jhelum, the infrastructural development of the Mirpur region was minimal. The development of a communications network - railways and post - and a comprehensive education system in British India did not fully extend to Kashmir. Infrastructural developments that did take place were mainly in and around the cities of Srinagar and Jammu. The area of present day (Azad) Kashmir was considered a back-water of the state and was treated as such. At the time of partition, there were only two hundred and fifty-four primary schools of which only four were for girls, six high schools and no further or higher education colleges. The physical infrastructure, given the hilly terrain, was worse than the educational, with only one hundred kilometers of road and no rail transport. [7]

Rural Context: Geography, Agriculture and Society

During the period of Dogra rule, the Maharaja was the official owner of almost ninety percent of the land in Jammu and Kashmir. Therefore, the *zamindars* who tilled the land had to pay a rent to the Maharaja, even though the land may have been in the farmer's family for generations previously. It was also difficult for the farmer to mortgage the land because of this situation. Land that was not the property of the Maharaja was in the hands of the British or had been given as a gift by the Maharaja to the predominantly Hindu and Sikh aristocracy. As previously stated, farms were small, the majority being four acres or less, and conditions were such that farming was usually at subsistence level or below. The need for off-farm income was, therefore, a matter of survival for most families. British records from the beginning of the twentieth century, make it quite clear that the circumstance of the average Muslim farmer in Mirpur was not a good one. [8]

In addition to these political obstructions to agricultural development there were also geographical hindrances, primarily the fact that there was little arable farmland in the area. Mirpur consists of foothills of low altitude ranging from about one hundred to two thousand feet. The majority of land available for farming in the Mirpur area is *barani* (rain fed), terraced or flat, which makes for small areas of land under crop. Housing develops near these areas and is therefore widely distributed. The distinction between irrigated- *bar* and rain fed- *barani* is particularly important in terms of the development of agriculture in a region. The lack of irrigation in Mirpur and the north of Pakistan in general has meant that farming has never been more than subsistence. Wheat, maize and millet are the three main crops grown during the agricultural year. However, there is very little horticulture and animal husbandry. Those vegetables that are grown and the livestock that is reared is primarily for household consumption (Khan et al 1982).

The rural context in Mirpur, as elsewhere in the sub-continent, is roughly divided into two major social groupings: those who own land- *zamindars*- and those who provide services for land-owners. Those in the service sector have, traditionally, been further sub-divided on the basis of occupation, such as carpenter, blacksmith and weaver. Similarly, *zamindars* are themselves grouped according to *biraderi* and hierarchically according to the amount of land owned. [9] In my fieldwork experience, the only distinction that was regularly made was between land-owner and *khasbi*, which is nominally a weaver caste. [10] The strength of caste in the region is undermined by various factors, predominant of which is the lack of the large *jagirdars* (land-holdings) of the Punjab plains. The Putohar belt is characterised by small land-holdings with the largest being usually only eight to ten acres. This is further fragmented by land division amongst sons from one generation to the next. The economic basis of caste is therefore undermined as the farmer is not able to support himself, let alone provide work for other occupational groups. The long-standing migration from the area has meant that occupations have become more and more varied and less linked to caste. The procurement of land by someone of a non-land owning caste is also a route to taking on the name and ritual status of someone of a higher caste. Given the predominance of land-owners in the region, the significance of these distinctions is fairly minimal. [11]

The combined effect of political marginality and geographical hindrances to agriculture affected all rural families in Mirpur. At the end of the nineteenth and the beginning of the twentieth century, there were few options for generating income open to people in Mirpur, other than to look further afield. How and why men first travelled from the region is still undetermined (Ballard 1987). However, it is clear that this migration took place through a variety of routes and was closely related to the historical conduits that were created by the British presence in the region.

Historical Conduits

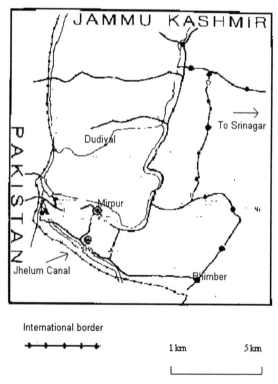

Figure 3.3 (Azad) Kashmir and Region

The present day geographical boundaries of (Azad) Kashmir are provided by the rivers Jhelum and Neelum to the West and the cease fire line to the East (Figure 3.3). Even though Mirpur town is quite close, as the crow flies, to Srinagar, the historical capital of Kashmir, they are separated by mountainous terrain. The historical route between the two areas followed a path through Bhimber by which much trade occurred. Contemporary (Azad) Kashmir comprises of five districts: Bagh, Mirpur, Muzaffarabad, Poonch and Kotli.[12] The final district, Kotli, was carved out of Mirpur in 1975. For present purposes the district of Mirpur and Kotli are of particular interest as they are the most densely populated and it is from these regions that the majority of migration has taken place. These districts also form a continuity with the Putohar foothills and are geographically quite distinct from the mountainous regions of Bagh, Muzzaffarabad and Poonch. District Mirpur is further sub-divided into three *tehsils* - Bhimber, Mirpur and Dudiyal. While these areas have historically been administered by authorities based in Srinagar, Mirpur district forms an economic and social continuity with the Punjab.

It is worth considering this inter-regional relationship in more detail as it pertains to the various routes by which excess male labour from this region found employment in other parts of initially British India and eventually the world. The three *tehsils*, Bhimber, Mirpur and Dudiyal, are closer, in terms of accessibility, to large cities in the Punjab than to each other, as is illustrated in Figure 3.4.[13]

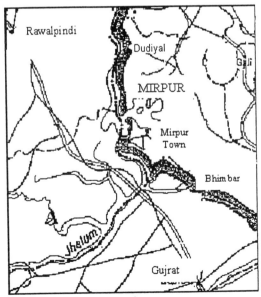

Figure 3.4 Mirpur District and Region

For Mirpur the closest and therefore most significant town is Jhelum, and this has also been the case historically. For Dudiyal the town of Gujjar Khan is the closest centre of commercial activity. Finally, for Bhimber the nearest market town is Gujerat. The fact that these main cities were linked to the rest of the British Empire via road and rail links and, more significantly, were British army and navy recruiting centres, has major implications for migration from Mirpur district. The surrounding major cities of Jhelum, Gujjar Khan, Gujerat and Rawalpindi were the first point of call for the potential migrant. According to Ballard (1986), the earliest source of international exposure came in the form of work in the British merchant navy. Towards the end of the nineteenth and the beginning of the twentieth centuries, Mirpuri men began to work as stokers on steam ships out of Bombay. In this way, many men travelled throughout the colonial world. Precisely how Mirpuri men came by this work is difficult to determine (Ballard 1986). However, given the limited communications in the area and the restriction on potential work as stokers, it is more likely that this route was geographically restricted to the Dudiyal *tehsil*.

The general source of employment with extra-local links during this period was probably the British Indian army and later the Royal Navy.[14] Perhaps the main source of non-rural employment in the whole of the Putohar plateau was the army. At the time of partition of the Indian sub-continent in 1947, seventy seven percent of the Pakistani army was made up of recruits from Rawalpindi, Jhelum, Cambellpur and NWFP (Cohen, 1984:57) Given the fact that, at the time of British rule, the Fourteenth Punjab and the First Punjab regiments were based in Jhelum, the army became a central source of employment of Mirpuri excess male labour. Regimental records also add weight to this conclusion.[5] According to Salisbury (1932), Mirpur district supplied a large number of men for the First World War. Most of the villages of Mirpur *tehsil* had some connections with the British Indian Services. Salisbury (1932) notes how there were many contractors, soldiers, sailors and policemen from British India who had come back to the village after their time of service. The Second World War also saw heavy recruitment to both the army and the Royal Navy from Mirpur, both of which had recruitment centres at Jhelum and Rawalpindi. Given the limited geographical area from which these migrants came, the poor communications and the general geography of the area, it is problematic to draw conclusions about migration from the Mirpur as a whole on the basis of the employment of stokers.

Mass Migration

Saifullah Khan (1977) and Ballard (1983) argue that the long history of migration from Mirpur and the specific connection of stokers on British Merchant Navy ships are the primary reasons for the mass migration of Mirpuris to Britain. Ballard states:

> In the late 1940s and early 1950s an increasing number of seamen left their ships to take industrial jobs on shore, and soon afterwards began actively to call kinsmen and fellow villagers over to join them; it was thus that a process of 'chain migration' began (Ballard 1987:24).

This notion of 'chain migration' then follows from Massey's (1988) point that reasons for migration are independent of structural factors, such as the displacement of persons by the Mangla dam project. Therefore, from Ballard and Saifullah Khan's point of view the migrant network becomes the sole means for migration to the detriment of structural considerations. Saifullah Khan goes as far to say that 'no villager would go without some established contact' (Saifullah Khan 1977: 67). This line of reasoning implies that everybody who migrated from the region was in touch, either through family or extended kinship networks, with everybody else who migrated. As previously stated, experience of work in the Army and the Royal Navy created in Mirpur a historical climate of what can be called, for want of a better term, an environment of migration. Both these factors, however, do not sufficiently account for the mass migration to Britain that occurred in the early 1960s. Rather, the political climate in post-partition (Azad) Kashmir and the building of the Mangla dam have to be taken into account. To illustrate this claim, I consider the post-partition political history of (Azad) Kashmir and the effects this had on migration. More significantly, I present a detailed analysis of the Mangla dam project and relate its effects to the process of migration from the area.

According to Ballard (1986), the earliest source of international exposure, for the people of Mirpur, came in the form of work in the British merchant navy. Ballard (1985) argues that the stokers were the pioneer immigrants who paved the way for the subsequent mass migration to Britain. Certainly, recruits to the merchant navy would have gained experience of Britain through the docks in Liverpool and Plymouth. From this point it is not too hard to imagine men finding work labouring in Britain. The main ethnographic basis for these findings comes from the work of Dahya (1974), who notes how such a group of ex-seamen were first directed from Hull to munitions factories in Bradford in 1941.

The argument forwarded by Dahya, Saifullah Khan and Ballard, poses several problems from both an ethnographic and an analytical point of view. Given the notion of 'chain migration' previously outlined, is it to be assumed that all of the migrants that came to Britain from Mirpur were in some way related to the merchant seamen who left their ships in the 1940s and 1950s ? This assumes that communications in the area were sufficient to allow large networks to form, yet this does not take into account the previously outlined topography of the area, whereby communications of this sort would not have been possible. Similarly, in the previous section it was illustrated how the area where stokers went from was restricted to Dudiyal district. Even, if it is assumed that migration occurred through the merchant seamen, then the question arises as to why mass migration to Britain did not occur earlier, as it had with Indians and African-Caribbeans. In fact, mass migration from Mirpur occurs around the time of the building of the Mangla dam. [16] Perhaps, most problematically, by dismissing the effects of the Mangla dam project, Ballard and Saifullah Khan ignore the widespread effects the dam project had on the general economy of the area, not just in terms of those who were displaced but on those who relied on the area as a central market and economic zone. Crucially, the structural factors that constitute the push factors while present in Saifullah Khan's and Ballard's argument are nevertheless mentioned only in passing and considered as secondary to the working of 'chain migration'.

Political History Post-1947

The partition of the Indian sub-continent in 1947, nominally along religious grounds, led to the division of three regions - the Punjab, Bengal and Kashmir. [17] In each of these cases, partition has subsequently led to a particular configuration of contemporary political instability, which has often ended in violence. [18] The division of Jammu and Kashmir (JK) reflects, particularly well, the unresolved dynamics that partition unleashed. Two wars and a long-term climate of hostility between Pakistan and India are the most overt manifestations of the crisis in JK. These political dynamics, while of great importance, constitute a separate study and have been dealt with in more detail elsewhere. However, it is through partition that the contemporary area known as (Azad) Kashmir is born. Naming takes on a huge significance in the struggle over territory. (Azad)

Kashmir means 'free' or 'independent' Kashmir and is posited against the area of Jammu and Kashmir in India, which in this nomenclature is referred to as 'occupied' Kashmir. [19] However, as Ballard (1991) and Rahim (1995) have noted this *'Azadi'* is only in name. (Azad) Kashmir is treated as a political tool, in relations between Pakistan and India (Samad 1994), and kept under control, in administrative terms, of the Ministry of Kashmir Affairs in Islamabad. [20] The area was not formally recognised in the constitution of Pakistan at the time of partition, and there was no elected assembly or legislative body in the area until 1970. An autonomous government and administration is now elected in the region and is based in Muzaffarabad. However, this forum relies on patronage from the Pakistani government to survive. Given this political climate, it is not surprising that little infrastructural development, in terms of agriculture and educational opportunities, has taken place since 1947.

While land redistribution occurred after partition and the debts owed to Hindu money lenders were cleared, these problems were replaced by new ones. (Azad) Kashmir's neo-colonial status in post-independence Pakistan meant that the issues of educational and agricultural infrastructural creation were still not dealt with. The indeterminate political status of the region has resulted in the refusal of passports for people from AK and no consultation over the building of the Mangla dam. [21] Electrification of villages only began in earnest in the late 1960s and early 1970s. The lack of rail and air links to the area means that communications are limited. Road transport is the only source of haulage. However, due to the hilly terrain this is slow and only practical for small loads. These factors may have been overcome in newly independent Pakistan, given a political will to develop the area. However, in light of the political history of (Azad) Kashmir and its indeterminate status, this did not occur. One of the main responses by Mirpuris to these conditions has been migration in search of employment. Geographical limitations to agriculture associated with political constraints has meant that farming has long been a limited source of income for people in the region.

Mangla Dam and its Impact on Migration

> .... but the effects of this event [building of the Mangla dam], which apparently led to the 'displacement' of 100,000 people, are viewed by her [Saifullah Khan] only in terms of providing an impetus for some to try their luck in Britain. She provides no information that would enable us to

understand why it was built......who made available the funds....There is nothing in her account which makes migration a necessary response to 'displacement' (Lawrence 1982: 112).

This quote forms part of what is a scathing and, perhaps, a slightly unfair criticism of Saifullah Khan's (1977) perspective on the Mangla dam development. The reasons for the construction of the dam and those involved in its construction form part of a political and social history, not yet written in English about the region. In terms of migration, Saifullah Khan (1977) does attempt to contextualise the building of the dam in the general history of the area. However, she dismisses its relevance to the process of migration. A detailed exploration of the dam project and its implications reveal its significance to both the process and means of migration. It is not possible to allocate the migratory effects of the project to the 'entrepreneurial' effort of individuals living in Mirpur. In simple terms, their land was submerged under water which resulted in the creation of a population which needed to be relocated. The historical connection between Britain and Mirpur is obviously important in terms of where Mangla migrants went, but even the necessity of this historical link is drawn into question by the account presented here, as Britain was one of the partner countries in the dam's construction. The historical development of the dam illustrates two broad points. Firstly, there is the recognition of the continuing role of Britain in migration from the area and secondly, one of the primary reasons for migration from the area in the early 1960s was a result of forced displacement caused by the Mangla dam project.

The partition of the Indian sub-continent in 1947 resulted in many problems for the two newly formed countries. The question of river waters was one of the most prominent that arose. The dividing line of partition did not neatly distribute river waters and, in order to resolve this issue, the Indus Water Treaty was signed between India and Pakistan in 1960. In this treaty the building of the Mangla dam is mentioned only as the Jhelum river project, a part of the wider Indus basin project. [22] This avoidance of mentioning Mangla was primarily because of the disputed nature of the (Azad) Kashmir territory (Aloys 1967). To avoid a situation where the dam might become part of an independent Kashmir, the boundaries of (Azad) Kashmir were re-drawn such that the town of Mangla and the dam itself became part of the Punjab and therefore under the direct jurisdiction of the Pakistani government. [23]

The most profound implication of the dam for the people of Mirpur was the submergence of over sixty five thousand acres of land by the

Mangla reservoir (Aloys 1967). This resulted in the immersion of about two hundred villages and of Mirpur town itself. The area submerged formed a natural physical geographical cup, which also contained the regions' best farm land. Estimates of the number of displaced persons caused as a result of the dam vary from between fifty and one hundred thousand. Aloys (1967) in a pro-Mangla report describes these people as 'Mangla-affected persons' which is an accurate, if impersonal, description. He relates that these people were given appropriate reimbursement for their loss. A new Mirpur Town was built on the south of the reservoir and further land compensation was given to the affected persons in Punjab. It is worth taking a closer look at Aloys' claims. The new town of Mirpur began to emerge after 1963, when the area was officially evacuated. Rahim (1995) contends that many people did not leave their houses until the dam waters began to rise in 1967. In either case, Old Mirpur town was fully submerged in 1967. Small land-holders received a minimum cash compensation while larger land-holders, those owning over four acres, were offered land in Lyallpur, Sargodha and Multan districts. Each of these plots being at a considerable distance from Mirpur and, given the socio-political makeup of the country were almost impossible to claim without local contacts in those regions (see Figure 3.2).

Saifullah Khan (1977) has pointed out that it is difficult to assess the patterns of migration that resulted from the flooding of the reservoir. The three possibilities were resettlement within Mirpur, land compensation in Punjab or migration abroad. Given that the population in Old Mirpur, at the time of the evacuation, was approximately nine thousand and by 1971 the new town had a population of thirty-five thousand, it is possible to assume that a proportion of those who lost land settled in the city. [24] If the displaced persons were even fifty thousand in number, the absorption rate of the new town has not been that great. The second possibility of land compensation in other parts of Pakistan is almost impossible to quantify. What is clear is that land was not offered in neighbouring districts as promised, but in the central Punjab where land was available and at great distances from (Azad) Kashmir (See Figure 3.2). Due to land pressure and the fact that the dam project was severely opposed in (Azad) Kashmir, land compensation in other parts of Pakistan was widespread. This land was often sold, as soon as possible, because of the difficulties in farming in a new region with limited knowledge of the locality. Given the limited success of these two options, international migration would appear to be the best alternative.

Academic debate and popular discourse in Britain and Pakistan has emerged which links the Mangla dam to overseas migration, particularly to Britain (Allen 1971; Deakin 1976; Saifullah Khan 1977). The technical support and design team on the Mangla dam was headed by a British company, and even though Britain was not the major financial contributor, it played a crucial role in seeing through the dam's completion. Rahim (1995) and Musa (1994) relate how a deal was made between Ayub Khan - Pakistan's president at the time - and the British government, whereby Mirpuris were given priority in terms of allocation of vouchers to go to Britain as a result of displacement from the dam. Saifullah Khan (1977) also notes how passport offices were opened in Rawalpindi at the time, where previously Lahore had been the nearest centre to Mirpur. Deakin (1970: 46) goes as far as to state that 5000 men were allowed into England as a result of this scheme. The perceived involvement of the British state in encouraging migration parallels the period between 1962-66 when there was indeed a system of vouchers to enter England and a need for labour. [25] A report on migration from the Indian sub-continent by solicitors, resident in areas of major migrant concentration -Jullundur, Mirpur, Sylhet, takes this claim further. They describe how an offer to take persons displaced by the dam to England was made by Dr. David Owen, the Government minister, when he visited the Mangla site. They also go on to state that Queen Elizabeth II declared that workers from the region would be welcomed in the UK, in a speech given in Peshawar at around the same time (Powell 1990). The actual 'facts' behind these claims are not that easy to substantiate (Allen 1971) but what is of interest is that they are made at all.

    This close correlation between the dam and mass migration to Britain does not undermine the process of 'chain migration'. As previously mentioned it emphasises how displaced persons were created rather than how displacement was responded to. The core argument is that two types of migration can be recognised. The small scale movement of men from Mirpur to other parts of Pakistan and abroad which occurred from the end of the nineteenth century up to the mid-to late-1950s and a large scale mass migration which occurred through the 1960s. These two are obviously closely tied and are essentially consequences of the political and agricultural marginality of the people of the area. If it were not for the historical migration, it is unlikely that international migration to Britain would have been the final destination of 'Mangla affected persons'. [26] What is indisputable, however, is the fact that large numbers of people have migrated from Mirpur to Britain. and as a result there have been widespread social, economic and political repercussions in the area.

Consequences of Mass Migration on Mirpur's Economy and Society

In the final section of this chapter, the consequences of mass migration on Mirpur illustrate the reversal of this process and illustrate how the migrant network has structural effects on Mirpur/(Azad) Kashmir. The general patterns of leaving Mirpur for Britain have been explored in detail in the oral narratives presented in various books, usually published by local authorities. [27] In academic writing Saifullah Khan (1977) gives a general introduction to the methods and means of migration from Mirpur. The following two narratives explain with great eloquence the broad model by which men went to Britain.

> At that time I was in Mirpur and in the bad conditions, because of the dam, I made the plans to come to the UK. At the end of 1960 I made my mind to come to the UK. There were no vouchers. There was no difficulty in getting here, no visas. All you needed was a passport which you could only get from Karachi. There were no offices in Rawalpindi or Mirpur. Once you got your passport that was it. My relative sent me the fare and I arrived in England in March 1961 (Iqbal Rahim).

Post-voucher migration was hindered by the need for an address in Pakistan due to the indeterminate status of (Azad) Kashmir.

> Well to get to England would take five to six thousand rupees, to get the ticket and the passport and everything together. Now I did not have that much. There was one of my elders, *Chacha* (uncle) Faquir Mohammed, *tekhedar* (Azad) Kashmir. They had a shop, car spare parts, and I worked with them for a year. At the time the Mangla Dam was being built and by 1962 the voucher system had started. *Chacha* applied for my voucher. They sent a form and registered me in London in the Labour Ministry. *Allah dee karam*, it was in my fate to come to this country. After four months I got my visa in Lahore, got a passport and got a voucher. There were some men in Mirpur who charged to do this. They made my passport, first from Lahore then from the Kashmiri ministry in Rawalpindi. Then after two weeks I came to England (Tariq Khan).

This use of agents to secure passports and visas was commonplace and not all experiences of them were as positive as the above account. At various times, passports would not turn up, or tickets would be cancelled at the last minute. Despite these tribulations, large numbers of men migrated between 1962 and 1966 under the voucher scheme. This was followed by migration of dependants, primarily sons, who would be able to work and therefore not be a burden on their fathers. However, immigration legislation in Britain ensured a closing window of opportunity for migration. The impact on the economy of Mirpur from British and Gulf emigrant remittances was substantive and far-reaching.

In order to fully explore the consequences of mass migration on the economy of Mirpur, it is important to recognise continuities with previous periods and types of migration from the region. The state of agriculture is an apt starting point to investigate the economic impact of migration. As previously stated, Mirpur was historically not able to provide sufficient food for the people who lived there. A study carried out in 1982 by the Punjab Economic Research Institute outlines three reasons for the lack of development of the agricultural sector: 'lack of irrigation water, poor physical and institutional infrastructure and large scale emigration of able-bodied males to Europe and Gulf states in search of more remunerative employment' (Khan 1982: 25). The migration of able-bodied men has meant that there is now substantial under-usage of land. So even though, as in the 1930s, men used their remittances to buy land, this was not put to agricultural use. Ballard goes as far to say that, 'agricultural activity has not been stimulated by migration: on the contrary it has been depressed' (Ballard 1987:32). A combination of negligible support by the government, low agricultural prices and contentiously, the low status of agricultural work has resulted in it becoming less of an option for residents and returnee migrants alike. There is no incentive for families who are part of the immigration boom to engage in intensive farming, as food can be readily and cheaply imported from neighbouring Punjab. The only real activity, on the agricultural front, is by those people who have migrated to the area from other parts of Pakistan or are refugees from Jammu and Kashmir.

If agriculture has not been a point of investment for emigrant remittances then how has the money been utilised ? Ballard (1985) outlines two main areas, property speculation and retail outlets. These are closely linked because houses and shops are often in a single building and both require land to be built on. A general trend with migrants from the Indian sub-continent is to invest initially in property and land (Ballard 1983). This is to be expected given that these are fixed and secure assets in what are highly volatile and fluctuating economies. A tour of Mirpuri villages reveals padlocks on large gates on even larger households is one of the dominant images that. Migrant remittances resulted in a huge house-building boom in the 1970s and these properties which are now often empty are used by refugees from Jammu and Kashmir. The property boom had spin-offs for the brick-making industry and for construction labour. But more significantly has resulted in property/land speculation. Ballard (1985) outlines how land prices rose as relatively wealthy returnees began to acquire land in their villages. This soon turned into speculative procurement not only in Mirpur, but also in Islamabad, Jhelum and Rawalpindi .[28] The property market is particularly exaggerated in Mirpur, both in terms of price and availability. There are certain reasons for this state of affairs, most interesting of which are the political constraints imposed on the market. In theory, only people who are registered as being born in (Azad) Kashmir or with two generations resident in the state are allowed to buy land there. [29] Given the demand for land from emigrant returnees, an internal market is created in which wider inflationary and economic pressures do not feature. In a sense, those competing in this market are working in 'virtual' pounds, as it is that currency which determines the inflated prices. For instance, a one acre plot of land, set just off the ring road around the Mangla lake cost Rs 3500 in 1968 and was being sold for three point eight million rupees in 1995. Even accounting for inflation, this is an enormous increase in value.

A cursory tour of villages around the Mangla lake - Akaalgarh, Chakswari, Ghasguma - reveals two dominant features of village life: Large houses, often occupying two to three *kanals* and what at first appear to be empty garages, on closer inspection are actually empty retail units. In an economy whose main function is to provide services, food, cloth, fuel, household materials, a retail outlet is the most logical and easiest form of business in which to invest. The development of shopping in almost every village of the region and the presence of a duty free shop in Mirpur town are the witnesses to this consumer revolution. On the flip side there are an ubiquitous number of empty and half- built shop fronts. This is not unexpected given the limited size of the retail market and the large number of people who have capital to enter it. [30] Other than production of bricks, the main areas of business growth, are the transport and hoteling/restaurant sector. The lack of train and air facilities combined with minimal state transport has made private vehicular transport essential. Large numbers of returnee migrants landing at Islamabad or Lahore are an obvious source of business for these companies. The Mangla dam has also led to an increase in the necessity of road transport. [31] The second area of growth is in the hoteling and restaurant business. The lack of agricultural and other sources of employment in the region combined with a source of income means that boredom and lack of entertainment are two increasingly prominent facets of life. Hotels in Mirpur town and in nearby Jhelum serve to fill the gaps and provide a useful meeting place. These establishments also serve as zones of entertainment for returnees who, bored with village life, go to nearby towns to spend their money.

An emphasis on business opportunities provides a migrant-centric view of Mirpur. The jobs most sought after in the region, as elsewhere in the sub-continent, are those with the government. These provide employment with a security of tenure and a relatively reasonable level of pay. In (Azad) Kashmir, only (Azad) Kashmiris are allowed to hold government jobs, though this never applies to the top posts which, for reasons previously outlined, are kept in the hands of the Pakistani government. For most Mirpuri men a government job or marrying abroad are the two main routes to financial security. The recent development of a university in the state and a large number of government colleges has ensured a supply of graduates competing for the few government jobs. The primary effort made by these young men is to migrate, not necessarily to England, but to any part of the world where there are better economic opportunities. Many of these people are the sons of migrants left behind because of immigration laws or, at the very least, relatives of large kin groups settled abroad. Their educational opportunities have been largely funded by remittances and the standards that they aspire to are once again determined by a set of criteria established elsewhere (Ballard 1983). Therefore, for many of these young men employment in brick kilns or in the catering sector as waiters are routes that are no longer attractive given their levels of aspirations and the availability of cheap labour from Pakistan.

The service sector economy in Mirpur, as in Oldham, relies on migrant labour to the area. These come in two varieties - economic migrants and political refugees. Economic migrants come from poorer regions in the Punjab and NWFP whereas political refugees are from Afghanistan and from Indian-administered Jammu and Kashmir. Refugees from Indian administered Jammu and Kashmir are more likely to receive local and state support, especially in terms of housing. Many British Mirpuris have let their houses to these refugees and share accommodation with them when visiting the area. Present day Mirpur Town and the region as a whole employs a substantial amount of migrant labour. A local contemporary idiom sums up this migration: 'For these people Mirpur is like England'. The relatively high standard of living in the area, supported by remittances, ensures a source of income for those in the service sector. There is also the added incentive of a generally higher level of wages for services as returnee visitors tend to be out of touch with local rates.

Mirham and Oldpur

More than thirty years of migration has led to dramatic effects of the economy in the region. Ballard has typified the economy in terms of dependency reliant on emigrant remittances and effectively with no productive base. Now that Mirpuris have settled in Britain, remittances are not sustained at the same level, yet there seems to be no apparent slow-down in property speculation or growth in the retail sector. Two possible explanations for these continuities also point the way to future research in the region. If Mirpur/(Azad) Kashmir and Oldham/England are considered to be a single space in which certain social and economic relations are played out, then the question of remittances exhausting themselves does not arise. Money invested in Mirpur is as good an investment as a bank account or property in England. Similarly, certain monetary transactions take place which involve regular transfer of funds from England to Mirpur, for instance as pensions or as expenditure on funeral costs. Ballard (1990) has perceptively noted how burial in Mirpur ensures a sense of 'rootedness', as family will be inclined to visit the graves of their departed relatives. However, even this situation is changing with the development of Muslim graveyards in Britain.

This chapter traced a historical journey from the period of colonial rule to the present day, highlighting the reasons for and consequences of migration from Mirpur/ (Azad) Kashmir. Beginning with the colonial period, infra-structural and political factors led to Mirpur becoming a place of migration from the beginning of the twentieth century onwards. This initial bout of migration combined with continuing, post-partition, structural constraints, particularly the building of the Mangla dam, combine to produce mass migration from the area. The consequences of mass migration have been profound on the region and present both continuities with the past and new challenges for the future. Indeed, the recent political and social history of Mirpur is inextricably entwined with Britain and leads to the combination of Mirpur and Oldham which forms the subtitle of this chapter's concluding remarks. In the next chapter the migration story is taken up from the other end, with an analysis of the cotton textile industry of Oldham.

---

[1] For more detailed accounts of the political situation in the valley of Kashmir and its relationship to (Azad) Kashmir, see:. Noorani, A. (1971), *UN Mediation in Kashmir: A Study in Power Politics*, Gupta, S. (1964). *The Kashmir Dispute* Puri, B. (1993), *Kashmir; Towards Insurgency*.

[2] Subsistence follows Sachs (1992) definition.

[3] This was part of a general increase in political activity in the whole of the state, which ultimately led to the formation of the National Conference. The reasons for the uprising in Mirpur were, initially, more specific to the locality and relate to the tax assessment of the area.

[4] As with all British documents, especially the District Gazetteers, it is important to remember these documents were produced as a product of utilising knowledge of the natives in order to control them (Inden 1992). In that respect, they need to be treated with caution, especially when it came to relating histories of opposition and strife.

[5] Land acquisition in this early phase of migration is a significant continuity with the way in which remittances from Britain were spent.

[6] See Knight, E. (1895) *Where Three Empires Meet; A Narrative of Recent Travel in Kashmir*, and. Lawrence, W. (1895)*The Valley of Kashmir*, Vol 1.

[7] Figures from *(Azad) Kashmir at a Glance 1985* Planning and Development Department of the (Azad) Government of the state of Jammu and Kashmir.

[8] This information is from the India Office Records, Political Service Files, *Kashmir Affairs,* L/P+S/13/1260, November 1931-32. India Office Records, Political Service Files, *Kashmir Affairs*, L/P+S/13/1260, August 1932-December 1934.

[9] The main caste groups in Mirpur are land-owning. According to Salisbury (1932), the main land-owning *biraderis* were Jat, Sau, Bains, Gujar and Maliar.

[10] According to the *Glossary of the Tribes and Castes of Punjab and NWFP* the Khasbi are more commonly known as Juluha and are the most numerous of a floating class of artisans. Their traditional occupation is weaving. As this is the highest occupation open to scheduled castes, many of the other low caste groupings initially attached Juluha to there names. So you have Mochi Juluhas and Koli Juluhas. In time the lower caste association was dropped and only Juluha remained. It is quite obvious that this process has occurred in Mirpur, as there were very few other named caste groupings that people were particularly aware of. This also makes sense, given the post partition anti-Hindu sentiments in the country. This is further confirmed by the fact that 92% of Juluha's are given to be Muslem.

[11] Ballard (1985) estimates that eighty percent of the people in his fieldwork sample were land-owners.

[12] These are political boundaries and are therefore subject to continual change.

[13] For Mirpur and Dudiyal this has only been the case since the construction of the Mangla dam.

[14] Even though the Maharaja had his own private regiment, it is unlikely that recruits were taken from Mirpur district, given the preference for Dogras or Muslims of the valley.

[15] In fact there are seven regiments which refer to troops coming from the 'Mussalman of Kashmir' and which geographically could only be referring to Mirpur and associated districts.

[16] Rex and Moore (1979) note that 70% of there sample came to Birmingham between 1960 and 1964. Deakin (1970) records 3450 Pakistani men in Bradford, The actual presence of substantial numbers of men from Pakistan only occurred after 1960, whereas previous to this there had been a substantial influx from India. In addition the number of migrants increased from 3450 in Bradford to 7500 over this period.

[17] Many thanks to Yunis Treyabbi (Kashmir Workers Association, Birmingham) for this particular perspective on partition.

[18] The division of Pakistan into Pakistan and Bangladesh in 1972, illustrates the problems generated in Bengal. The Sikh insurgency movement in Punjab has part of its explanation in the logic of partition.

[19] This is further complicated by India referring to (Azad) Kashmir as Pakistani occupied Jammu and Kashmir. Neutral terminology tends to favour Indian administrated Jammu and Kashmir and Pakistani administered Azad Kashmir. In this text, as a comparison is not being offered, (Azad) Kashmir refers to Pakistani administered territory and Jammu and Kashmir to Indian administered territory.

[20] Islamabad is the capital city of Pakistan.

[21] The letter he received from the UK High Commission illustrates this point well and is dated 1960. This all changed with the building of the dam.

[22] This also included the Tarbela dam which was bigger.

[23] See Order No. 17/17/1358-1405/67 Dated 28/3/67 of the office of the Senior Secretary, (Azad) govt. of the State of Jammu and Kashmir, Muzzafrabad, giving jurisdiction for mutation of the land to Pakistan. This boundary change is obviously disputed by Kashmiri independence activists.

[24] See endnote 9.

[25] The Commonwealth and UK Citizens Act of 1962 placed a ceiling of 8500 migrants per year via the vouchers system. Other entrances were discretionary.

[26] Male migrants I interviewed, when questioned about the reasons for migration from the area, made reference to the dam as well as the voucher scheme.

[27] See "Iqbal, M and Ara, S and Van Riel, R. (1990) ' *Just for Five Years ? Reminiscences of Pakistani Senior Citizens in Sheffield'* and Malik, R and Gregory, S (1991), *Living with Two Cultures.*

[28] Block F10 in Islamabad is also known as the Mirpur enclave.

[29] Even though this rule can be overcome, with sufficient contacts and money, it still acts as a barrier.

[30] This is another bone of contention, put forward by the Kashmir Liberation movement, as a result of their neo-colonial status within Pakistan.

[31] This change can not be underestimated. During fieldwork in 1995, I made a journey from Mirpur to Akaalgarh/Islamgarh, by boat and foot, covering about four to five km. The equivalent journey by road was twenty five kilometres.

4 Textile Tours

Introduction

The previous chapter illustrated how the process of migration from Mirpur was intimately linked to extra-local, particularly colonial factors. By returning to the imperial motherland and specifically to the development of the textile industry in Lancashire, another piece of the migration puzzle is put in place. The growth of the British textile industry and the colonisation of the Indian sub-continent form part of the same historical frame in which migration from Mirpur took place. Cotton textiles link together various corners of the world in a complex web of economic and social relations. Much has been written describing and delineating the various sinews of the cotton textile story. In this chapter, I take up one strand which spins together the colonial relationships instigated by the cotton textile industry with the lives of the workers who toiled in the mills of Lancashire. This is, therefore, a dense and complicated narrative, which attempts to 'double' - spin together - areas of the world as disparate as Oldham, Gujerat, Poland, Ireland and Mirpur to produce a yarn of many weaves.

Lancashire and the cotton textile industry hold a special place in the imaginary of Britain's industrial past. Indeed this area is credited as the cradle and cot of the industrial revolution. Previous historical accounts have, however, largely ignored the significance of Empire in the development of the industry or presented a naturalised and passive view of the relationship between Britain and her colonies. Thus, the first theme in this chapter describes the development of the cotton textile industry in terms of its relationship to Empire and particularly to the Indian sub-continent. A historical frame that also serves to contextualise the treatment mete out to South Asian labour in the mills of Lancashire. The second major theme of the chapter concerns the labour force composition of the mills of Lancashire in general and Oldham in particular. Critically, the presence of South Asian mill workers in the 1960s is framed in terms of continuities with other workers in the particular industrial location of the mill. This is not only in terms of other migrants, as Miles (1982) has illustrated, but also in relation to other groups of marginal workers, which in the case of the mills were white women. These continuities and disjunctions in the representation of the various types of labour, used through the history of the industry, serve to contextualise and historicise the presence of South Asian workers.

Lancashire, the Indian Sub-continent and Cotton Textiles

Around the year 1600, the weaving of Fustians - cotton weft and a linen warp - had reached Lancashire from East Anglia [1] (McPhillips 1981). Alongside the ancient woollen industry of Yorkshire, a new cottage industry emerged, producing coarse cotton cloth. The textile producer was often a small land-holder who earned part of his income from farming and the rest from the sale of cloth. In the damp, dank, rolling hills of Lancashire, coarse cloth provided a meagre means of living (see Figure 4.3). Meanwhile, three and a half thousand miles away, the centre of the global cotton industry was the town of Ahmedabad, in the state of Gujerat, on the west coast of modern day India. From the fifteenth to the seventeenth centuries, the Sultans of Gujerat reaped the benefits of exporting cotton via seafaring merchants from Ahmedabad to East Africa, Arabia and even the Far East. Ahmedabad became a town of artisans and businessmen, attracting the finest weavers from all over the Mughal-ruled sub-continent (Kulkani 1979). While small producers were manufacturing basic cloth in Lancashire, the finest cloth and designs were emerging from India. This situation was to change with the arrival of the British into India.

The British East India Company began its activities on the West coast of the sub-continent by trading with the textile merchants of Gujerat. Up to the beginning of the eighteenth century Indian cloth and designs were in great demand in England and a relationship of mutual benefit to both trading communities was in place (Kulkani 1979). However, the increasing political and economic power of the East India Company in the sub-continent and pressure from England for protection of its fledgling cotton textile industry, led to the subsequent destruction of cotton fabric production in India. It is necessary to consider the rise of the industry in Lancashire to fully understand the impact upon India.

From a small cottage industry to the centre of the global textile industry, the history of Lancashire textiles is a narrative that can only be presented in condensed form here. The historical period of rapid growth of the cotton industry was between 1770 and 1840, with a continued, but slower, expansion up until 1920 (Aspin 1981). Lancashire's damp weather and the proximity of coal and soft water enabled the transformation of a back-water of the eighteenth century England to its industrial centre in the nineteenth. The rapid development of about three hundred mill towns in Lancashire, the landscape of factories and often-typified 'dark satanic mills,' as well as the migration of labour from village to town are all factors which are now taken as defining characteristics of industrialisation.

Figure 4.1 Textile Types of the North of England

Source: *The Textile Industry of Lancashire*, Bolton

Liverpool served as an ideal port and Manchester an optimum market place. The actual processes of producing finished cloth were subdivided to ensure the cheapest supply and maximum return. Raw cotton was imported from the United States, spinning mills turned it into yarn, weaving mills produced the cloth, which in turn was finished by independent dye and bleach works. The final product was then sold in Manchester to traders who exported it via Liverpool to the far-flung corners of the British Empire. The bulk of the cotton produced in Lancashire during this period was in fact exported. In 1843, India was Lancashire's largest customer; to such an extent that in the small mill town of Great Harwood, all twenty three mills worked solely on turbans and loincloth (Pagnamenta and Overy 1984).

Even though the cotton textile industry continued to grow in Britain up to the 1920s, the rate of expansion was slower and the industry was developing at a far greater pace in other parts of the world, particularly in Japan. Between 1920 and 1935, Japan doubled the number of looms it had in operation and doubled its export of cotton cloth (Singleton 1991). The growth of the industry in India during this period was, as would be expected, not as spectacular as it was in Japan. The colonial control of Britain over India ensured an economic imperialism, which stunted the growth of the Indian industry and ensured the Indian market remained open to British goods. Kulkani states, 'Lancashire was in fact determined to see that Indian enterprise was saddled with increasing costs so that its goods might be procured out by the imported ones even in the home market' (1982: 43). It was in this climate that the Indian nationalist movement took up the issues of boycotting British imports, with particular emphasis on cotton goods. Mahatma Gandhi was the inspiration behind the campaign. He encouraged villagers to buy from India's own mills and more significantly to revert to handmade, home-spun cloth (*khaddi*). The spinning wheel became the symbol of nationalist resistance and Gandhi imposed a full-scale boycott of British cloth. Gandhi's own image, wearing only a *khaddi dhoti* (cotton loin cloth) embodied the philosophy of *swadeshi* (home made goods) that he was promoting . In 1931, Gandhi was invited to Blackburn to see the effects that the Indian boycott was having on the mill towns of Lancashire. In the colloquial history of industrial England, Gandhi's visit is remembered by one mill owner:

> He [Gandhi] was to see how serious the situation was. In Blackburn alone there were seventy-four mills closed within about four years. 'Well, he [Gandhi] said: 'You come to the villages in India, we're a lot poorer than what you are', and there really wasn't much to say about that' (Pagnamenta and Overy 1984: 39).

Figure 4.2 Gandhi with Mill Workers in Blackburn
Source: *All Our Working Lives* (1984)

Gandhi, standing in his *dhoti* (loin cloth) with the mill girls of Lancashire, forms a poignant image, not only for the historical connection it evokes between the mills of Ahmedabad - Gandhi's home region - and Lancashire, but also for those other textile workers from the sub-continent; male Pakistanis who would not be able to work alongside the daughters of these women, let alone be photographed with them. [2] As a juncture in history, it portrays a crucial turning point in colonial relations between India and Britain. Indeed, Gandhi's campaigning activities and the lobbying by the various Indian mill associations of the British government, eventually led to the removal of the tariffs which had worked against the Indian industry since its inception. However, by this time the British were well into the process of withdrawing from India. The advent of the Second World War and the subsequent partition of the sub-continent into India and Pakistan put the issue of cotton textiles onto the back-burner.

Decline of the Textile Industry in England

After reaching its peak in the 1920s, the Lancashire cotton textile industry began a steady decline nominally due to lack of technical innovation and increased competition. However, the economic imperialism that had fuelled the expansion of the industry was an additional factor. It was no longer as powerful a force and therefore not as able to offer the protection to the industry that it had given in the past. Between 1926 and 1945, one-quarter of all the mills in Lancashire closed down with a reduction of the workforce by one-third (Farnie 1967). The post-war decline was more accelerated and is illustrated in Figures 4.3 and 4.4, which illustrate decreasing production of yarn, and a dramatic decrease in the size of the workforce up till 1970. In 1959 Britain, once again, became a net importer of cotton goods closing a chapter in the history of one of its oldest industries (Pagnamenta and Overy 1984). By 1970, more cotton goods were imported into Britain than produced there (Singleton 1991).

The reasons for this decline are multiple, detailed and complex, and are also the subject of much debate. However, of main concern to this book is the way that the issue of 'cheap foreign imports' flooding the British cotton market became the main rallying cry for the representatives of the cotton industry owners. The Cotton Board, which was essentially an

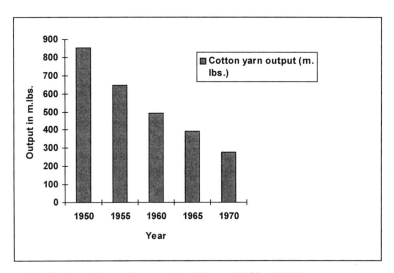

Figure 4.3 Cotton Yarn Output by Year: 1950 - 1970

Source: Cotton Board Quarterly Statistical Review; Annual Abstract of Statistics

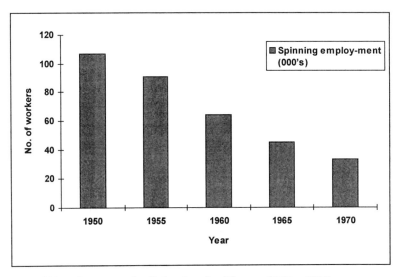

Figure 4.4 Employment in Spinning by Year : 1950 - 1970

Source: Cotton Board Quarterly Statistical Review; Annual Abstract of Statistics in Singleton (1991)

organisation of cotton textile owners, chose not to concentrate on the fact that the industry was antiquated in method and machinery but rather to,

> ...shamefacedly concentrate(d) on the single issue of restricting cheap Commonwealth imports. ....it warned that even a fully modernised Lancashire cotton industry could never compete with the products of cheap Commonwealth labour (Singleton 1991: 134).

Therefore, decline in the mills was attributed to the growing number of exports from the developing world. In fact, it was only in the post-war years that competition from countries such as India and Hong Kong was of any significance in the British market (Shepard 1983). The more substantial competition, which occurred in the 1970s, was from EEC countries who were not affected by trade tariffs. This fact did not stop the British government from imposing restrictive trading practices. To counter growing imports of cotton cloth, especially from Japan and Hong Kong, an agreement was reached in 1962, where import of cotton textiles to the UK was limited to a growth of five percent per year with 1961 as the base year (Renshaw 1981). This agreement lasted up until 1973, giving textile firms some breathing space. This was one of the factors that accounted for the upward swings in production that occurred sporadically though the 1960s. However, the protection offered by these agreements did not cover newly industrialised countries (NICs), nor the ever increasingly important man-made fibres market. In 1974, the Multi Fibre Agreement was negotiated which encompassed European Community Countries as well as NICs, and it is this regulatory framework which is still in place today, even though it has been re-negotiated, several times under the GATT and World Trade Organisation agreements (Renshaw 1981). The central premise of the Multi Fibre Agreements has been to 'protect' developed countries from the products of developing countries (Dicken 1992). Since 1974 this has resulted in massive penetration of the British market by American and European firms and vice versa, such that most of Britain's trade in textiles is with these two partners, rather than with NICs. Therefore, the notion that cheap imports from the Far East and from low-wage countries were mainly responsible for the decline in the textile industry does not hold up to close scrutiny. The rhetoric of the mill owners, the unions, and various government ministers during the 1960s, calling for a ban on the import of cotton goods, is similar in nature to the calls for bans on immigration. In both cases, the actual reasons for the decline in Britain's manufacturing capacity and subsequent unemployment lay elsewhere. [3]

In the meantime, following British withdrawal from the sub-continent in 1947, the textile industry in newly independent India and Pakistan continued to grow. India already had a large cotton industry in 1945, and this continued to grow despite periodic attempts by the government to protect handloom weavers by restricting the installation of modern automatic looms. The growth of cotton textile production occurred at a far more dramatic pace in Pakistan. Pakistan's cotton industry was established in 1947. Its development was assisted by public investment, the provision of subsidised credit, tax concessions for foreign investors, and state-financed export bonus schemes. In 1948, there was a fledgling cotton industry in Pakistan based around the port city of Karachi. At the time over ninety percent of the raw cotton produced in the country was exported for spinning and weaving elsewhere. The development of an indigenous mill sector took place in a very short period of time and by 1955 there were 1.4 million spindles in the country consuming about forty percent of the raw cotton produced. This growth continued up to the mid-seventies, when there was a slow-down in terms of production and development of new mills. This trend was reversed in the mid to late eighties, when there was a rapid growth in the industry under government sponsorship. However, the problem of under-usage of the current capacity is the issue of most concern for Pakistan's contemporary textile industry. [4]

A truly global history of the cotton textile industry remains to be written. However, this short review of the interlinkages between the Indian sub-continent and the development of the British industry should serve to illustrate the necessity of a wider perspective. Within this frame, the local histories of significant places in the spinning game also deserve attention. In this regard, the next section presents the history of Oldham, keeping in mind how it is produced by and productive of the transnational relations outlined in this section. [5]

King Cotton - Oldham

Oldham is distinctive in the history of the textile industry in terms of its central role as a producer of spun cotton and spinning machinery and also its relative obscurity in the narrative of industrialising Britain. Liverpool and Manchester are usually presented as pivotal in the growth of the North West and in particular to the projects of British colonialism and capitalist expansion throughout the world. Small towns such as Oldham do have significant roles to play in the global-local nexus and their development is deeply implicated in these wider processes. [6]

Figure 4.5 North and North West England
Source: OMBC Leisure Services

Towards the end of the nineteenth century, Oldham was one of the most important areas for the spinning of yarn, not only in Lancashire, but also the rest of the world. This comment from 1909 illustrates this fact:

> While the latter (*Manchester*) is the cotton centre of the world, the former (*Oldham*) is the cotton spinner....There is more cotton spun in Oldham alone than in Germany and France put together. (Daily Mail, 22 June 1909 in Gurr and Hunt 1989).

Over the last one hundred and fifty years, the town has been through a cycle of industrial development and decline. From a small hamlet in the eighteenth century it rose to become the premier spinning town of Lancashire. Unlike many of the other smaller mill towns in the region, Oldham was relatively undeveloped during the classic period of the industrial revolution from 1780-1850. A combination of factors contributed to the growth of the industry, the most significant of which was the American Civil War in 1861. While the rest of Lancashire, particularly Blackburn, relied on America to provide raw cotton, Oldham was the first town to use Indian cotton (Gurr and Hunt 1989). It therefore took full advantage of the low supplies of cotton during the American Civil War, taking over many of the markets that had once been controlled by other towns. The close proximity of Manchester, the greatest yarn market in the world, and of Liverpool, the largest port in the world, were also pivotal to the development of the textile industry in the town. The town reached the summit of its economic importance in 1890, when it was consuming one-quarter of all the raw cotton imports into Britain and was Liverpool's largest single client for export goods (Gurr and Hunt 1989). Figure 4.6 illustrates how the number of mills in the town expanded from 1794 to 1921. Oldham's mills developed in a series of waves with three major booms occurring in the 1860s, 1873-75 and 1904-8. Up until the mid-1920s, Oldham alone had, bar the United States, more spindles than any country in the world.

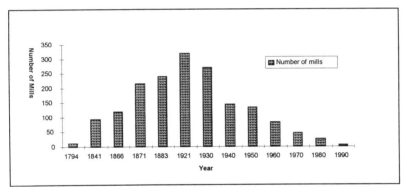

Figure 4.6 Number of Mills in Oldham: 1794 - 1990

Source: Gurr and Hunt (1989)

The benefits of the textile industry's evolution were widespread. The building of such a large number of mills ensured the construction trade a constant supply of work from the early 1860s up to the 1900s (Gurr and Hunt 1989). Another spin-off was the development of a textile machinery manufacture sector. The most famous machine producer to originate in Oldham were the Platt Brothers. This company's history bears witness to the rise and fall of cotton in Oldham. From humble beginnings in 1770, Platts went on to become the renowned name for textile machinery throughout the world. Many of Oldham's monuments and civic buildings owe their existence to the financial support of Platt Brothers. Even though the company invested much time and money in the development of the textile industry in Oldham and Britain as a whole, it is important to recognise that their machinery was also exported around the world. After

1843 the cotton textile equipment built in Oldham was exported to India and China, enabling them to compete for and eventually take over the markets that Oldham once solely provided for. In fact the first mill in Bombay was opened with the co-operation and support of Platts of Oldham (Kulkani 1982). The central role that Platts played in the cotton textile industry began to wane after World War II. Changes in the technology of spinning meant that new equipment was being brought into Britain from Europe. As with the rest of the British textile industry, competition from the French, Swiss, Germans and Japanese led to the ultimate closure of Platts in 1982.

Oldham's textile decline reflects the wider changes in the industry illustrated in the early part of this chapter. The last mill constructed in Oldham was the Elk, built in 1926, by the Shiloh group of companies. At this time over thirty percent of all the spindles in Lancashire were located in Oldham. This scenario was to rapidly change over the next thirty years. After reaching its peak in the 1920s the steady decrease in the number of mills in Oldham is illustrated in Figure 4.6. However, the most dramatic decline in the industry came about after World War II. The 1955-59 peaks reflects the effect of the Cotton Reorganisation Act of 1959. This was also the beginning of an almost steady decline in the industry which continued through the 1960s and 70s. By the late 1980s and early 1990s the small numbers of mills left (see Figure 4.6) meant that even a few closures had a dramatic effect on the overall rate. The patterns of decline in Oldham largely follows the trends in the whole of Lancashire, which were significantly influenced in the post-war years by government policy.

This Cotton Reorganisation Act of 1959 was one of the main measures taken by the government in terms of restructuring and rationalisation (Clairmonte 1981). This law made available grants for the scrapping of machinery and for upgrading of spinning technology. The government target for a reduction in half the spinning capacity was achieved over a period of two years. Though this was heralded as a success, it also resulted in thirty percent of the workforce being laid off. Despite this law, the industry was not able to reverse the downward trend. The last attempt at restructuring was the instigation of mergers; the premise being that if the processes of spinning, weaving, finishing and selling could take place within one firm then there was some hope for cost effectiveness. A similar scheme in the pre-war period had resulted in the setting up of the Lancashire Cotton Corporation, and it was these semi-nationalised mills that were sold off at a tremendous discount. Two firms,

Courtaulds and Viyella, effectively bought up most of the remnants of the cotton industry in the mid sixties (Clairmonte 1981). In 1964 Courtaulds began to buy mills in Oldham at what was, by then, a relatively cheap price.

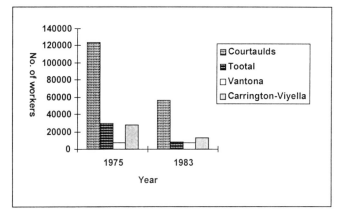

Figure 4.7 Workforce in Major Cotton Mill Companies: 1975 - 1983

Source: *Greater Manchester Industrial Profile* (1985)

By the end of the 1960s over one third of the mills in Oldham were owned by Courtaulds. This take-over by Courtaulds did not result in any dampening on either the absolute numbers of closures nor the rate of closure. The only possible positive effect of the Courtaulds buy-outs may have been to provide a period of stability in the early seventies, before the final end of the industry in the 1980s. However, to ensure a monopoly situation, Courtaulds in particular put many small family firms under tremendous pressure to sell. Courtaulds was not interested in any sort of 'Save Lancashire' campaign (Pagnamenta and Overy 1984). Their programme of modernising and closure of mills ignored any local interests and significantly served to protect their man made fibre business. [7] Figure 4.7 illustrates that in the space of eight years the work force in Courtaulds mills halved. From a beginning of twelve mills in 1794, it took one hundred and twenty-seven years for Oldham to reach its peak at three hundred and twenty mills. However in only seventy years the number of mills reduced back to twelve (Gurr and Hunt 1989).

In Oldham in 1995, there were six textile manufacturing firms, of which, only one undertook cotton spinning, while the others specialised in cotton mixes and man-made fibres. In the 1980s the last of the cotton mills in the town finally shut down. Between 1979 and 1983 the number of people employed in the industry in Oldham was halved (Oldham Chronicle 5/10/88). Between 1985 and 1988 there was something of a recovery which prompted a strike in 1988, the first in the mills for forty years, which resulted in short-term pay gains. But the fruits of this were short lived as the late 1980s and early 1990s saw the closure of most of the other remaining mills in the town.

The growth and decline of Oldham's textile industry illustrates how local processes are intimately tied in with national and international shifts and trends. The detailed history of the industry and as a corollary the town of Oldham also highlights and pinpoints the demand for labour at various stages. Changes in the industry both at the technological and economic level had profound effects on labour demand and particularly the types of labour employed. It is to these issues that we next turn.

Labour in Lancashire and Oldham

There has been considerable research on the textile industry of Oldham in terms of the number of mills and the amount of cotton produced therein (Gurr & Hunt 1989). However, little detailed investigation of the workforce composition in terms of gender, age or area of migration has been undertaken. This is surprising given the large numbers of people that the industry historically employed; though understandable, given the difficulty in obtaining evidence on composition of workforce in particular industries in post-war Britain. [8] In order to contextualise the arrival in the mid 1960s of South Asian workers in the cotton textile mills of Oldham, it is necessary to consider the changes in labour force composition from the beginning of the industry to the present day. There are two distinct, but overlapping, routes through which this analysis of the presence of South Asian labour in the mills of Lancashire can be traced. As migrants, they came last in a path trodden initially by Irish, and then European workers. As male workers, their presence in the mills, in such concentration, is a disjuncture in the labour history of the textile industry. After the 1880s, young girls and women began to be taken on in large numbers in the mills and eventually were present in a greater concentration than male workers. The presence of male South Asian workers is therefore an anomaly in terms of gender composition of the labour force but can be explained in terms of an overall general representation of labour in the mills, an issue which will be explored in some detail in this section.

In the late seventeenth and early eighteenth century, as the cotton industry began to first develop in Britain, cotton spinning was carried out in the home. A small farmer would gain additional income to farming by undertaking production of yarn (Aspin 1981) This was an activity for which all members of the family would provide labour. This situation changed with the introduction of small-scale factories in the mid-eighteenth century. The demand for labour in these small mills was fulfilled by migration to the area from surrounding villages. Signalling the onset of industrialisation, the process of rural to urban migration was taking place, at the time, throughout England. However, in the Oldham area, this did not lead to the development of a town with an associated working population. The average mill at the time only employed about ten to twelve people, therefore, the workers would usually live in close proximity to their place of work. The rolling hills around Oldham tended to favour the development of hamlets with three or four houses rather than clusters of mills and houses. It was the introduction of the factory system, in the early to mid-nineteenth century, that led to the development of the town and a working male population.

By 1866, nineteen thousand people worked in the cotton mills in Oldham, the majority of whom had moved to the town from other parts of Lancashire. McPhillips (1981) argues that there was a great fluctuation in the composition of the labour force in the cotton mills of the times. Boys and girls under the age of fourteen were employed alongside adult men and women. [9] Mill owners claimed that the smaller hands of children meant that they were better at controlling the spinning and weaving machines (MC Phillipps 1981). The employment of children was prevented by the introduction of factory legislation after the mid-nineteenth century. However, in practice it was not until the beginning of the twentieth century that child labour ceased in the mills. Another major shift in the composition of the workforce also occurred towards the end of the nineteenth century. With the introduction of the ring-spinning process in 1884 more women were enlisted for work in the mills than men (McPhillips 1981). Figure 4.8 illustrates that the trend towards using women workers had begun in the 1860s. However it was only after 1881 that a significant divergence between male and female employment occurred. The reason given by mill owners for the employment of women was their superior dexterity and precision in the handling of yarn, which the new ring-spinning mechanism required. This increase in the use of women's labour was not met by protest as might have been expected when male jobs were being taken. The reason for this acceptance was that the excess male labour was easily accommodated by the expanding construction and textile machinery-making industries. It is also worth noting that the employment of women for their 'dexterity and nimbleness of finger' is a similar reason given by mill owners twenty years earlier to justify the employment of children. In both cases, the fact that women and children were paid less than men, and this was sanctioned both by law and the unions, is the economic corollary to the reasons forwarded by the mill owners (Turner 1962). By 1914, seventy-eight percent of girl school leavers were entering the mills compared to only fifty-four percent of boys (Gurr & Hunt 1989).

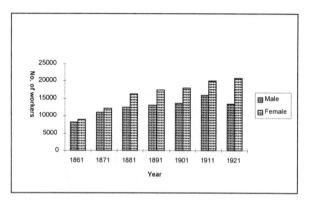

Figure 4.8 Employment by Gender in the Cotton Mills of Oldham: 1861 - 1921

Source: Oldham Census 1861 - 1921

Despite the large number of women in the mills, there were still areas of work which were the domain of men. 'Women were excluded from the mule room by the unions, they constituted a majority of weavers, while most all of the operatives in ring spinning were female' (Singleton 1991: 9). The jobs of foreman, overseer of the shifts and the skilled manual work were almost exclusively male domains. [10] It is during this period that the association of cotton mills with working women and the stereotype of the 'Lancashire cotton girl' comes into conceptualisation. Though it is not possible to fully explore the impact that this long history of working class women's paid employment has had on the region, it is possible to allude to some of the various economic and social effects: The introduction of 'fast food' in the form of 'fish and chips,' flexible working time and the ability to take more holidays are all a result of a changing role for certain women, fostered by industrial work and the availability of a double income (Penn et al 1990b). More specifically, the presence of large numbers of working class women in the mills served to create a particular type of working environment. This can best be described as one where a matriarchal hierarchy prevailed within the confines of a male-managed work space. Young girls who came into the mills were first placed with a more experienced spinner who decided when the new recruit was ready to handle a machine on her own. By the First World War, two and often three generations of women from the same family would be working in the same mill. Even though many younger women would leave the mills after a few years to have children, once they were of school-attending age they would go back to work, usually, to the same mill.

Lancashire reached its economic peak in 1920, at which time the mills of Oldham employed sixty percent of the workforce in the borough. A massive decline in the number of people employed in the industry occurred between 1920 and 1945 - from 600 000 to 200 000 (Singleton 1991). However, the two world wars and the development of new industries absorbed much of this labour. The development of new manufacturing industries in the aftermath of the Second World War meant that new sources of employment were now available to the 'Lancashire cotton girls'. These new factories producing white goods or packing/bottling offered a cleaner and safer environment, more pay, and better hours of work than traditional mill work. One positive aspect of this dwindling supply of labour was that mill owners attempted to make working life in the mills more attractive. Bus services to pick up their workers were introduced, and canteens and nurseries were opened in an effort to retain female labour. It was not the case that workers left jobs that they already occupied in the mills. Rather, female school leavers had more options for work, in other factories or in an office environment (Millet 1995). It is only in the final demise of the textile industry in the mid-1970s and 1980s that large numbers of women actually left or were made redundant.

The gender composition of the mill labour force is a unique aspect of a study of labour within industrial Britain. Indeed, their presence also provides an opportunity to compare their position as marginal workers, with migrant groups. However, it should not be assumed that the women in the mill were a homogenous group, as we shall illustrate in the next section, as migrant workers came into the mills, this also resulted in changes of the type of women workers.

Migrant Labour

The first migrants into Oldham, as with the rest of Lancashire, were the Irish. In a similar fashion to the capitalist penetration of India in the beginning of the nineteenth century, the British colonial control of the Irish market led to famine and subsequent migration (Davis 1991). The exodus of labour from Ireland was mainly to America, but large numbers also came to England. However, as this immigration was not legislated against, it is very difficult to assess the actual numbers of people involved. The census figures for those born in Ireland and other resources can give some sort of estimate of the population of Irish in Oldham. Heinrick (1990) puts the Irish population in Oldham as ten thousand in a general population of ninety-nine thousand in 1872. Even though this is an estimate, based on local knowledge and census figures, it nevertheless is probably the most accurate available. Beginning a pattern that other migrants were to follow, the Irish in Oldham worked primarily in the textile industry. Indeed it is safe to assume that one of the factors that caused their arrival in the town was demand for labour from the mills.

In the beginning of the nineteenth century, the Irish were to be found in the unskilled trades of the textile industry in the card and blow rooms, or doing labouring work. The skilled trades of weaving and spinning were in the hands of the English workers. Irish migrants were treated largely with indifference up to the middle of the nineteenth century. From the late 1840s onwards, however, there was a high level of hostility had developed towards the Irish in Lancashire. There were two broad excuses given for the emergence of anti-Irish agitation: firstly, the perception that the Irish were undercutting the pay of local workers and siding with employers in strike, and secondly the fact that most of the Irish were Roman Catholics, who were a popular target for hostility in any case (Walton 1990). In addition they were ascribed a number of negative cultural characteristics, for example drunkenness, violence and the spreading of disease.

Negative stereotypes about the Irish and specific hostility to the Catholic church continued well into the 1950s and 1960s.[11] In this sense, there are many continuities as between the treatment of South Asian workers and the Irish. Both were concentrated in semi-skilled and unskilled occupations in the mills and both groups faced hostility. However, at their time of migration, the Irish joined the textile industry at a period of historical expansion, whereas South Asians joined in a time of decline. [12] This distinction is significant in terms of subsequent post-mill work histories and also to explain that the hostility towards Asian workers was not directly as a result of a perception of 'undercutting' pay. In terms of comparison with South Asian workers migration, the European workers are perhaps a better group than the Irish, as far as the state of the textile industry and labour demand from it are concerned.

The presence of Irish men in the mills in large numbers lasted up until the end of the nineteenth century, by which time young women were numerically predominant amongst the workers. There must have been Irish women in this working population, but there are scant references to this presence in the literature and it is not possible to cross reference using the census data of the time (Pinchbeck 1969). The availability of female labour meant that the next batch of migrant workers into the industry came after the Second World War. Pre-war bouts of unemployment, underemployment, and short-time working in the cotton textile industry combined with post-war opportunities in other manufacturing industries meant that attracting labour to the mills between 1945 and 1951 was an almost impossible task (Singleton 1991). This demand was initially fulfilled from Europe, specifically war refugees and working migrants from Eastern Europe.

In the post-war redevelopment and restructuring of Britain, the government attempted to fulfil the demand for labour by encouraging the settlement of European labour. There were two main sources of European labour after the war. The first involved the resettlement of members of the Polish armed forces and their families. This group of people accounted for about ten thousand of the one hundred thousand Europeans who settled in Britain after the Second World War (Isaac 1954). However, the most significant source of new labour was from the European Volunteer Workers Scheme. This scheme was initiated and managed by the British government with two main aims. The first was to tackle the problem of labour demand in the restructuring of essential services and industries in post-war Britain. The second objective was to help to resolve the massive problem of displaced persons that had arisen as a result of the war. A large number of countries was represented in this group of people. The most significant were the Latvians, the Ukrainians, Yugoslavs, Polish and

Lithuanians (Isaac 1954). After 1950 the scheme was stopped for men as it was felt that there was sufficient labour to fulfil the demand. This was not the case with women, as there had been a disproportionate number of male recruits - about two to one - in the scheme. A majority of the men were employed in agriculture and coal mining, whereas, the women were mainly employed in domestic services of various kinds and, significantly, in cotton weaving and spinning. The demand from the cotton textile industry for more women workers led to the scheme being extended and to the active encouragement of women workers to come to the country. The European volunteer workers were required to spend three years in an essential industry - agriculture, coal mining, textiles - before they had rights to stay in Britain and therefore to take other work. Despite this ruling, a survey in the early 1950s revealed that about seventy five percent of the workers had actually moved on to jobs with better pay before the three year ruling. This was especially true for those employed in agricultural work, but applied to all of the industries in which the workers had been placed (Isaac 1954). The low number of women immigrants and the movement of labour offer a partial explanation of why there was a further labour shortage in the late 1950s and early 1960s in British industry but several other factors combined to attract South Asian labour.

The post-war boom in Britain's manufacturing industry is often cited as the reason for the employment of Black immigrant labour (Rex and Tomlinson 1979; Cross 1992). The argument follows the line that the new factories were in need of labour and it was these jobs that the immigrants took. This may have been the case in other parts of England, however, in the case of the Lancashire textile industry, the South Asian workers were coming into an industry which was diminishing. To appreciate the precise conditions which were faced by the South Asian workers when they arrived in Oldham, a much longer view is needed. This requires an understanding of the conditions of the industry at the time when the men were arriving and the kinds of opportunities that were open to them. In the next chapter the exact ways in which the men got to Oldham will be described; whereas here the focus is on those factors within the textile industry that resulted in it employing a large concentration of South Asian workers. This entails an appreciation of changes in technology, governmental and union intervention and an understanding of how the South Asian workers are located within the histories of migrant and women's labour.

As previously illustrated, the decline in the cotton textile industry in terms of absolute numbers of people employed and number of mills in operation, began around 1920. Subsequent to this, the industry went through a series of cycles of boom and recession, with an overall downward trend. During the growth periods sufficient labour was not available to fill demand for production, as was the case after the Second World War. However, the overall demand for labour was always contracting in the industry, due to technological change and increasing productivity, even in boom periods. In the post-war years, the expanding job market was actually in the light industrial and engineering sector and it was these jobs that white men and women were taking. In Oldham, for example, the aerospace industry, electrical engineering and specialist industrial engineering firms became the dominant force in the industrial sector. In parallel, the development of the warehousing and distribution sector provided part-time low-skilled employment that many women workers took in place of mill work. To argue, as many writers have done that South Asians were in 'competition' for jobs with white men is therefore a fallacy.[13] Rather, the jobs taken in the mills had not been desirable to Oldham's white men for a generation or so and in the post-war years were no longer attractive to white women. Perhaps the most significant element of this point is the differentials in pay that had opened up during the post-war years between textiles and other manufacturing. Between 1948 and 1965, the wages of cotton operatives fell by thirty percent relative to those of workers in other industries (Devons et al 1968) Though this point has been made before it is worth re-emphasising that the jobs taken, initially by European workers and subsequently by South Asians, were those that were unwanted by the indigenous white majority (Fevre 1984).[14]

Given the general decrease in employment in the textile industry, the specific demand for South Asian workers came from the introduction of a number of measures most prominent of which was the introduction of the night-shift. As noted in the first section, by the end of the 1950s, the cotton industry was in the process of restructuring. In addition to the steps taken by the government in the form of the Cotton Reorganisation Act and the introduction of import tariffs, further measures were deployed within the industry. For present purposes, the most relevant of these changes was the introduction of a twenty-four hour working day via a three-shift system. This system of production organisation had actually been in operation in Japan since the 1930s. However, it was only in the post-war years that it was introduced into Lancashire and even then at a slow rate. By 1954 there were only one hundred and sixty-three double shifts in receipt of formal union authorisation (Singleton 1991). This relatively late introduction of shift work follows from the fact that it was only with the 1959 Cotton Act that the investment in new equipment took place which, for economic viability, had to be operated twenty-four hours a day. Mill owners found it almost impossible to fulfil the demand for labour on the night-shift from white workers. Fevre (1984) has noted how many firms in the woollen industry in Yorkshire would have never considered operating a night-shift if it had not been for the availability of South Asian labour.

A similar situation existed over the Pennines in Lancashire. A generation before, young white working class women had been commonly available for working in the mills, but they were now gaining employment in factories with better pay and conditions. Two additional factors limited the recruitment of white women on to the night-shift. Firstly, it was illegal for women to work during the night and had been so since 1844. [15] Therefore, even those women, such as those from the European Workers Scheme and other migrants, were available to work, they were barred by legislation. Secondly, the twenty-four hour, three-shift system mitigated against the kind of flexibility that suited family life. Historically, shift work in the mills had been organised to take into account child care responsibilities. Women were allowed to work around school opening and closing times and to take time off, if a child was ill. This system worked well within the historical 'family firms' which dominated the industry (Penn et al 1990b). However, the take-over by multi-national corporations such as Courtaulds, and the introduction of twenty-four hour working, required a workforce that was flexible in terms of working longer hours, not fewer. In 1955, sixty-four percent of spinning operatives were female (Cotton Board 1958) which, given the changes in shift system, reflects the pressure mill owners were under to find male labour to employ on the night-shift.

With the competition from the indigenous workforce at almost nil, several other factors favoured the recruitment of South Asian workers into the mills of Oldham. The installation of new technology which required twenty-four hour running but was also relatively simple to operate. A new worker on a spinning machine could be trained in only six weeks and by someone who had learned only six weeks before that. In previous times this training might have taken from three to six months. The mill owners quickly realised that South Asian workers could attract others from their circle of family and friends to work in the mill. Therefore, the responsibility for recruitment and training passed on to the individual who had brought in the new workers. This was ideal for the management in a time of such acute labour shortage. All that was left for the white foreman and managers to do was to exert control to ensure unhindered production. The process of recruitment and training of South Asian workers has some resonance with the practices of white women, fifty years before. The sense of people employing their own relatives and therefore looking after and over them in the mill environment is one that is familiar to South Asian workers (Brooks and Singh 1973). However, the crucial difference in these experiences was that the South Asians were considered as 'foreign' or 'alien'. There was a great deal of antipathy and hostility towards them. This was obviously not the case in the relationship between the foremen and white women workers.

The position of South Asian workers in the mills of Lancashire, in terms of their relationships with management and workers can be seen in terms of a combination of their migrant status and as male labour in what was considered female work. As migrant labour they were treated similarly to the Irish in the 1850s, as unwanted foreign labour. However, the Irish came to the textile industry in a time of relative economic prosperity. More concrete continuities with the South Asian workers can be drawn with the post-war experiences of European workers. Singleton describes the situation:

> In other words the European Voluntary Workers, despite their formal membership of the trade unions, were treated as second-class citizens. The Poles, in particular, complained of segregation at work, and in hostels, and claimed to be the victims of Communist propaganda which portrayed them as fascists (Singleton 1991: 55).

In the next chapter, a similar picture is drawn in terms of the treatment of Mirpuri/Pakistani workers, by management and unions, in the mills of Oldham. Perhaps the most important connections between different types of labour in the mills was the ideological construction of their presence by mill owners and managers. In the pre-war context, mill work was considered to be women's work, a supplement to the income of the male, main breadwinner. This notion, in many ways, justified the poor pay and working conditions that women were subject to. One of the reasons given by textile mill owners for the employment of South Asian men centres on the idea of Asians being of nimble finger: 'You need nimble hands for spinning and weaving - women and Asians are good at it' (Fevre 1984: 111). As previously stated this is also one of the reasons for the increasing employment of women in the late nineteenth century. These representations are very local examples of the discourses described by Said (1978) in the seminal text *Orientalism*. The 'oriental' in these constructions is considered feminine and therefore sly and untrustworthy. [16] What is perhaps of most interest is the way in which this perception of the feminine oriental was enunciated and then contradicted in practice. The Adderton mill in Oldham illustrates the contradictory nature of this form of representation: South Asian women have been employed in the mill on the day shift since the 1960s. Similarly, mills in Ashton and Bolton have long taken on Asian women workers. However, it is only since the mid-eighties that the day shift in Adderton has seen the presence of many South Asian men. The employment of the South Asian women illustrates that there was a demand for labour on the day shift. However, the exclusion of South Asian men was a direct result of management perception that South Asian men on the day shift would be considered an affront to the white women working there. This view of South Asian men as somehow threatening to white women posits a sense of sexuality which is in opposition to the notion of the 'feminine' oriental which was deployed to justify their employment. These contradictions of representation and practice highlight how different stereotypes can be utilised in different contexts to justify social control and to legitimate exclusionary practices.

Migrants have formed an integral part of the labour composition of the textile mills in Lancashire. At different points in history, a particular configuration of labour demand and supply ensured a central place to migrant labour. South Asians came into the textile mills following a path followed by Irish and European migrants and there are continuities as well as differences in the migration stories of all of these groups. However, what is critical to recognise is the central role that these groups played in the growth and sustainability of the industry, a factor which is often missing in generic histories of cotton textiles.

Routing Mills

The mass presence of South Asian workers in the cotton mills of Oldham is ironic, given the long and entwining history of the cotton textile industries of Britain and South Asia. The slogan, 'We are here, because you were there' coined by the Institute of Race Relations (Sivanandan 1981) is perhaps the best summary of the issues the last two chapters have dealt with. Both Mirpur and Oldham are implicated in a history of colonialism and imperialism which brings together disparate parts of the world in a complex web of relations at the political, economic and in recent times social level.

Given the uneven and unpredictable nature of capitalist growth the links between Oldham and Mirpur are not direct up until the era of labour migration. However, this flow of people is prefigured by movement of capital and goods. Cotton cloth in the nineteenth century is sold to the subcontinent by Lancashire; at the same time raw cotton to fuel the British industry arrives from all parts of the world; and machinery made in Oldham forms part of the flow of technology to India as part of the development of the textile industry there. Evoking Appadurai's (1990) notion of techno- and finanscapes these flows mark particular paths and create particular worlds, but at the same time throw a wider net of influence, one which can take in peripheral areas such as Mirpur and propel them into the centre of a migration network.

At the level of historical analysis and over the time frame adopted in this chapter, it can be argued, that global flows and links are relatively easy to construct and create. However, the next three ethnographic chapters which focus on the narratives of South Asian migrant workers, over a much smaller time frame, equally well illustrates how the global and local become entwined.

---

[1] The weft refers to the horizontal strands. The warp refers to the vertical strands in the cloth.
[2] See below for details.
[3] In contradistinction, Dicken (1992) locates the descent of the industry in a much wider context, attributing it to a combination of technological changes, shifts in centres of production and inability to compete in a global market. For the cotton industry, the fact that the raw material is not grown in Britain, the historical legacy of old machinery and, thirdly, the cost of labour were additional but not primary factors. Dicken (1992) argues that employment change within a nation's industry is the result of the operation of several interrelated forces; the most important of which are: changes in domestic demand, in productivity - output per worker - and in exports and imports. Of these, the biggest source of employment loss in the textiles and clothing industries was productivity growth (Dicken 1992: 264). In simple terms, the fact that more could be produced with less labour inputs, due to technological advances, was the main reason for the loss of jobs. The shift from

cotton to man-made fibres, and the presence of cheap imports were contributory factors but not the most significant..

[4] See Editorial of *Pakistan and Gulf Economist* December 2-8 1995 Vol. XIV NO. 48.

[5] A comparison of Ahmedabad and Oldham would be a fruitful and consistent endeavour, however, given the limitations of this specific project this can only be flagged up as an area of future research.

[6] This is not to argue that Oldham itself is unique in this regard, but rather that theories that place cities such as New York and London at the centre of a global stage often ignore how these processes are much wider than the metropolises.

[7] Dicken (1992) argues that Courtaulds take-overs resulted in spectacular mismanagement and a ruthlessness in the closure of mills.

[8] The post-war census of industries amalgamated the categories of cotton and woollen workers to that of generic textile workers.

[9] Boys and girls in this case would be under fourteen years of age and adult was defined as over twenty-one in this period. There is, therefore, some discrepancy in the statistics.

[10] There are three types of skilled manual worker in textiles: general machine maintenance, crafts and electricians. In addition there were historically specialist production workers like mule spinners, tapesizers and beamers and specialist maintenance workers such as overlookers and strippers and grinders. Access to any of these jobs was via an apprenticeship or lengthy tenure of stay both of which barred women workers.

[11] See Millett (1996) pp.22-23 for examples.

[12] The targeting of the Irish as scapegoats, for a series of social and economic ills, is therefore more compatible with the historical period in question than with contemporary racism against South Asian workers. This is because the jobs the Irish occupied were open to competition from other sections of the newly developing working class. A close analysis of the position of South Asian workers reveals how there was no competition for the jobs that they were doing. These literally were the jobs no one wanted and therefore the reasons for racial discrimination are not the same for both groups - as Miles (1982) argues.

[13] See Saifullah Khan (1977) and Ballard (1987).

[14] This point is worth emphasising as the white perception that 'they' are taking 'our' jobs (Ballard 1987), was not the case for textiles where no one wanted these jobs.

[15] The night-shift in the textile mills was stopped after the introduction of labour law in 1844 which banned the working of women and children at nights (Gurr and Hunt 1989).

[16] A similar stereotype for South Asians of the time was that of 'childishness', which was also applied to the Irish.

5 Of Mills and Men

Introduction

The previous two chapters served as a historical background to the narratives of the working lives of the (Azad) Kashmiri men which will be presented in the next two chapters. The macro factors for migration from Mirpur and the demand for labour from the textile mills of the North West of England emerge in the stories and detail of the working lives outlined here. This chapter explores the role of the mills in structuring the lives of the *babas* during the historical period from the late 1960s. It is during this time, that the majority of *babas* arrived in Oldham and found work in the mills. Finding employment in the mills, living in all male households and relying on mutual support networks are the pivotal characteristics of this period. In exploring the lives of the *babas* working in the mills of Oldham, this chapter centres on the structuring role of mill work. Hopping from mill to mill, the individual narratives presented here attempt to evoke a sense of constraints that were put upon the *babas'* activities.

Previous studies of the working lives of South Asian migrants have been influenced by the work of Badr Dahya whose research in England in the late 1960s set the scene for subsequent analysis. Dahya (1970; 1974) outlines three factors which are central to the analysis of the socio-economic position of Pakistanis. Firstly, Dahya considers 'the actor's frame of reference' as a crucial starting point for the understanding of the Pakistanis' position in British society. He believes that the immigrants' perception of their situation in the context of their socio-economic background, their motives for migration and their ideology or 'myth of return' are essential for a meaningful comprehension of their behaviour. Secondly, in the context of a debate about housing, he goes as far to say that poor housing is 'related to their motives and orientations and is not an outcome of 'racial discrimination' (1974: 105), flying in the face of the earlier analysis produced by Rex and Moore (1967). Thirdly, and pre-dating the work of Modood (1992) by almost twenty years, Dahya argues that it is necessary to distinguish the housing needs of West Indian immigrants from those of South Asian immigrants: 'The two cannot be subsumed under the blanket category of 'coloured' immigrants' (Dahya

1974: 106). There is little in the work of Dahya about the specific conditions of employment that Pakistanis are in. This lack of concern is explained by reference to the supposition that the men are in Britain 'only to earn money and leave' (Dahya 1970: 95) and therefore the actual work situation is unimportant in terms of their aims and objectives. The interviews and views presented in this chapter often contradict and occasionally support the perspective forwarded by Dayha particularly in terms of the relationship forged in and with the work place.

Of more direct relevance to this present chapter is the study by Anwar (1979) of a Pakistani community in Rochdale. His main focus is on the textile mill workers in the area and, as such, there are many continuities between his findings and those presented here. In Anwar's 1979 book *The Myth of Return: Pakistanis in Britain* the explanation for the occupation and labour market position of migrants from Pakistan tends to rely on the centrality of kinship and the extended kin grouping: the *biraderi*. The *biraderi* plays a central role as an agent of social change and stability. In the search for employment, coping with redundancy, provision of labour and capital for small business enterprise and general welfare, the *biraderi* is noted as a system of organisation. Implicit in these roles assigned to the notion of *biraderi* has been a consensual and co-operative view of how kinship networks operate. In the following sections the role of the *biraderi* is examined in light of the work structures that were present in the mills of Oldham.

The ethnographic section of this chapter begins with an analysis of the process by which the *babas* came to Oldham. This provides a useful, though not often explored, example of a place to which migration occurred because of the agency of the (Azad) Kashmiris, rather than the result of chain migration extended to chain economic location (Anwar 1979; Werbner 1990). Therefore, the reasons for migration to Oldham illustrate the *babas'* understanding of the working of the labour market, rather than simply following others to working in the mills. Once in Oldham, the various routes by which the men obtained work in the mills and in other areas of work is explored. The core of this chapter focuses on the organisation of mill work and the role of kinship networks in its structuring. Drawing parallels with the effects of mill life on white women workers in the 1930s, the position of the (Azad) Kashmiri workers becomes better understood as a combination of their class position and racialised exclusion.

Routes to Oldham

The procedures of migration, from Mirpur to Britain, were briefly considered in Chapter Three. Obtaining a visa, collecting the money for a ticket, travelling to Karachi for the flight and finally landing in Britain involved an immense expenditure of labour and effort by the *babas* and their families. These aspects of the migration story have been covered in detail in other publications and are therefore not explored in any depth here. I take up the migrant's story upon their arrival in Britain. My central concern is to understand how and why the town of Oldham became a site of immigration and ultimately an area of settlement for the *babas*. In answering this question, the determinant role of 'chain migration' and structural push-pull factors in migrants' areas of destination are problematised. Rather, I demonstrate that the demand for labour from the mills coupled with the *babas'* understanding of the conditions of the labour market made Oldham an attractive destination.

Unlike cities such as Bradford, Birmingham and Manchester, Oldham was not the first port of call for the *babas* on their arrival in Britain. While the first South Asian in Oldham's post war history was likely to have arrived in the mid 1950s, the arrival of a mass population did not take place until the late 1960s and early 1970s.[1] Census figures from 1966 reveal small numbers of Pakistanis in Oldham relative to Bradford and Birmingham.[2] However, in the following thirty years the town's Pakistani population has risen from seven hundred and ten to eleven and a half thousand, a much greater percentage increase than in other cities.[3] Perhaps the most sophisticated analysis of the process of Pakistani settlement and the creation of urban population concentrations has been developed by Werbner (1990). Along with Anwar (1979) and Shaw (1988), Werbner deals with migrant choice of city primarily in terms of links made through 'chain migration'. As previously detailed, this involves the transfer of people through chains of relatives and friends, who help each other through the process of migration and settlement. While 'chain migration' is a useful description of the way in which the *babas* arrived in England, and even to cities such as Birmingham and Bradford, it is not a sufficient reason to explain the formation of secondary conurbations of Pakistani settlement, such as Oldham, Nelson, and Bury. In these cases other factors, which emphasise the role of the labour market, have played a crucial role. Indeed, an analysis of the way in which the *babas* migrated to Oldham highlights how their understanding of the working of the labour market and the types of employment available in the town were crucial in the decision to move there.

Almost all of the *babas* I interviewed during my field work had lived and worked in other cities before coming to Oldham. 'Chain migration' ensured that most new arrivals to England had an address of someone to stay with, but this did not mean that work was readily available in that area. Mohammed Khan's situation is typical of a widespread experience:

> I came to England in 1967 and stayed with my *chacha's* (uncle) son in Bedford. I looked for work there for four months, but I could not find anything. I went to the labour exchange and because I couldn't speak English they gave me nothing. Then I was told by my *chacha's* friend that there was work in Bradford. I went there and started working in a mill.

For the *babas,* the search for work opportunities in the 1960s was characterised by movement, within cities and throughout the country. Bradford, Birmingham, Maidenhead and Luton are just some of the main stop-overs in these job hunts. Areas such as Birmingham and Bradford claimed more stability as they commanded greater markets for the labouring work that the *babas* were looking for and being offered. Mohammed Ibrahim's case is illustrative, if a little extreme.

> I came to England in 1961 to Derby. I worked in an army depot in the battery slag unit. I was there for one and a half years and I then worked in Peterborough in 1963 for two months in a plastic factory. I then worked in Maidenhead in a Brillo pad factory for 5-6 years where there were quite a lot of our people. I went to Pakistan in 1966 and came back a year later in 1967. I then went to Bradford and worked in a textile mill for two years, then I worked in a mill in Huddersfield. I came to Oldham in 1974 and I have lived here ever since. Well, I've also been back to Pakistan.

A combination of several factors resulted in Oldham becoming an attractive stop and ultimately an area of long-term settlement on the *babas'* working tour of England. The demand for work on the night-shift in the textile mills is obviously one of the critical structural factors. However, this should not be seen as solely determinant. Chapter Four illustrated how, in the 1950s, the demand for labour from the introduction of the night-shift was met by European workers. The South Asian population only began to grow in Oldham in the mid to late 1960s and therefore the arrival of the *babas* was not a *direct* response to the needs of the night-shift. I would argue that the main reason for the move to towns like Oldham was the changing circumstances in which the *babas* found themselves in the mid 1960s combined with a specific type of local labour market. The crucial change in the *babas'* circumstances arose due to the arrival of young male dependants. This took place in a relatively short period of time due to the enacting of the Commonwealth Immigrants Act 1968. Prior to this date, vouchers were needed for Commonwealth immigrants to Britain, a restricted number of which was allocated to various categories of employment. After 1968, the voucher system was stopped and primary migration to Britain from Pakistan and other Commonwealth countries halted. After this point, only dependants of existing migrants were allowed into Britain. This resulted in an influx of young men, under the age of sixteen, who joined their fathers. Zaffar Ikram exemplifies the process by which the *kakas* came to Britain:

> I came to Oldham in 1969. My mother came with me and then left me with my father. He had arrived in Bradford in 1963, and then we moved to Oldham. He went to Oldham when I came because the money in the mills for a new worker at age 16 was the same for someone who had been older with more experience, even though it was the same job. I went to school for a year at Fitton Hill and started to work when I was 15, as a labourer in the ring room.

Zaffar's story illustrates the attractiveness of Oldham to newly formed father-son teams. In the Bradford woollen industry the newly arrived *kakas*, when they first joined work, were paid an apprenticeship rate at half of their father's pay. The arrival of dependants meant that the *babas* were looking for the best opportunities for both their sons and themselves. The cotton mills of Oldham and surrounding areas provided work which paid an equal wage for both. It was the availability of work, for both father and sons in the mills, which made Oldham an area of immigration. This did not, however, lead to the creation of a Mirpuri women and children population in Oldham. Rather, as in the case of Zaffar Ikram, families would arrive for a short amount of time to leave sons and then return to (Azad) Kashmir. In either case, by the early 1970s *babas* and *kakas* would be working together in the mills on the night-shift. This was a continuity in the labour history of the textile mills, as in previous time periods when two to three generations of white women would be working together in the same mill.

Figure 5.1 North and North West England
Source: OMBC Leisure Services

Several other factors also influenced the decisions to 'go to Oldham' made by the *babas*. The shift system in the Oldham cotton mills was more attractive compared to the woollen mills of Bradford. Mohammed Khan reflects a general opinion:

> I came to Oldham from Bradford in 1973. My relatives who lived there had told me at a *mattam* (funeral) that the shifts were better there. In Bradford we worked on twelve hour shifts; in Oldham it was only eight hours, six to two and two to ten. I first got my job in the card room, doffing at a mill in Chadderton.

Experience of working in the woollen mills of Bradford was an additional help in securing employment for the *babas* in Oldham. As a result of technological developments, the transfer between working with cotton and woollen textile machinery was relatively easy. Geographical proximity between Bradford and Oldham also facilitated this shift from wool to cotton. Bradford, Oldham and Manchester form a corridor across the North West of England which, with the development of the M62 motorway, are now within easy commuting distance - see Figure 5.1. This relatively short distance meant that it was possible to maintain obligations to friends and family in Bradford while working in Oldham. Migration to towns such as Oldham was therefore a result of the combination of several factors. Central to these was the labour market condition, the type of work available and the terms and conditions of that work. These elements have often been overlooked in the literature on minorities, migration and work. As outlined in the beginning of this chapter, Dahya (1974) and Anwar (1979) argue that the acceptance of poor conditions, by the *babas*, was a result of the 'myth of return'. Furthermore, the *babas'* status as migrants meant that they were unable to distinguish between various types of occupation and were largely unaware of the workings of the industrial system (Bonacich 1972). In contrast to these perspectives, the pattern of *babas'* migration to Oldham clearly illustrates a detailed understanding of industrial pay and conditions: Appreciating, firstly, that their sons could earn the same amount of money as themselves and secondly that the shift system in the cotton mills was not as strenuous. Similar detailed studies of other migrant male worker groups during the industrial period may also reveal a pattern of worker mobility which reflects a degree of agency, rather than an assumption of the exploited, unaware migrant worker.

Routes to a Job

While employment in the textile mills of Oldham forms the main focus of this study, it should not be assumed that this was the only source of employment for *babas* in the town. Work on the buses was an alternative for some and, for others, running shops providing groceries and provisions to their fellow countrymen was a source of income generation. However, these jobs were limited to those who had some knowledge of English and initially access to capital. The background of the majority of the *babas*, as explained in the previous chapter, was rural, and with little opportunity for formal education. Given this background, it should not be assumed, however, as Penn et al do: '[that] most of those [South Asians] who entered paid employment, would obtain work in non-skilled occupations .in Britain because of their previous occupations' (Penn et al 1990a: 22). It is disturbing, given Penn et al's (1990a) stated concerns about the lack of research on South Asian entry and movement in the local labour market, that they place the industrial and occupational location of South Asian workers in terms of their skills. In so doing they choose to ignore the significance of racially exclusionary practices operated by employers, which have been well documented elsewhere (Allen et al 1977; Fevre 1984). This viewpoint denies the fact that even those *babas* with qualifications also ended up working in the mills. Allen et al (1977) note: 'Many clerical workers, lower level accountants, policemen, secretaries, lawyers, clerks, shopkeepers and businessmen were to be found in Britain in manual work' (1977: 148). The cases of Anwar Khan and Firdauz Khan are illustrative of this point; both men were graduates in textile engineering from Pakistan. On approaching a mill for technical posts, they were told to: 'Go and work on the factory floor with the rest of the 'Pakis''. [4] The best jobs that qualified *babas* managed to get were on the buses, as conductors or drivers.

Notwithstanding the role of other occupations, mills were the employers of the overwhelming majority of South Asian and African-Caribbean men whom came to Oldham. At the time mills were not the major employers in the town. As stated in Chapter Four, the economic growth areas in the 1960s were in the new manufacturing and industrial service sector. The jobs the *babas* took in the mills were unwanted by most white males and peripheral to the overall economic growth of the town. In this context it was relatively easy to secure employment as there was little competition for mill jobs. Family relations, extended *biraderi* connections and friends from Mirpur/(Azad) Kashmir or other South Asians, were the sources of introductions to work in the mills. The response to the question, 'How did you get your job?' was from a standard stock of, 'My relative worked there' or 'My friend told me they were hiring' or 'I knew someone there from my village'. The presence of Pakistani foremen in two mills in Oldham in the mid-1970s also facilitated this process. They were often mentioned as contacts for getting work. Points of connection through the army and navy also proved invaluable in securing employment and gaining the trust of white employees. The presence of white foremen and managers who had served in the British Indian army and, therefore, had a smattering of Hindustani also aided in this employment process. Similarly, those men from Mirpur who had previous army experience usually had a little knowledge of English which they could put to good use. Ikram Khan explains how he gained employment:

> I was told there was work in the mill by my friend. So I went there in the morning. There were twenty to thirty men, mostly Pakistanis, but also some Indians. The white man came and he told us to line up and then he asked everybody: 'What can I do for you ?' No one could answer him. He stood in front of me and said: 'What job do you want ?' I said: 'This is the first time I've seen a mill'. He asked me: 'What had you done before this?' I said: 'I am in naval service now retired'. He then took me to his office and filled in the form for me.

Anwar (1985) explains the presence of large numbers of Pakistanis on the night-shift in the mills of Rochdale in terms of 'chain migration' and the obligation upon 'Pakistanis' to help each other. Those men, who migrated from the same village, would often find work for their kinsmen. Anwar's fieldwork showed a high concentration of men related to each other in each of the three mills he studied. This process was further helped by the presence of a kinsman in the position of a foreman or with long standing in a company. There is no contradiction between Anwar's findings and my own in the description of this issue. However, Anwar (1979) asserts that this process occurred because of a 'cultural' predisposition for Pakistanis to 'help' and 'obligate' each other. However, the pattern of gaining employment through family and contacts of existing workers has a long history in the textile mills. Previous to the employment of South Asian workers, the predominantly female workforce was also closely related through ties of kin and locality. Therefore, this pattern of employment was as much a facet of the organisation of labour recruitment in the mills as it was a reflection of the continuation of 'chain migration' and a 'cultural predisposition'.

In the previous chapter it was noted that approximately eighty mills were in operation in Oldham when South Asian labour arrived in 1960. Practically, all of these mills took on South Asian workers which reflects the mobility of the workers rather than large numbers of actual migrants.[5] In the same way that England was traversed in the search for work by the *babas* a similar mobility took place between mills. Movement from mill to mill was a result of a number of different factors, partially concerned with seeking better pay and conditions, but also to do with mill closures which took place through the 1960s and 1970s. However, the significant factor in this regard was the frequent breaks in employment that the *babas* took for visits to (Azad) Kashmir. These factors, in combination, meant that a *babas'* length of tenure in one mill was, often, only between one and five years.

Mobility in the labour market is often a sign of the individual seeking better pay and conditions from a new job. Even though it is clear that many of the *babas* left jobs when they felt they had been treated badly, there was little difference in terms of pay, conditions, and availability of overtime between mills. The close proximity of mills in Oldham, in some cases five to six on one road and after 1964, their ownership by Courtaulds, meant that each offered broadly similar pay and conditions. Baba Quyuum illustrates how frustration with an employer can result in movement:

> We worked in Adderton Mill and there was a foreman called Droof. He had been in the Indian Army. He treated our people really badly. He paid single time for overtime and was always swearing at us and calling us names. I knew English better than most and I wouldn't stand for it. I left that mill and got a job at Lilac Mill. It was easy to get a job in those days.

Quyuum's experiences also provide a balance to the view that some prior knowledge of India by the foreman was a help to the men. In his case it proved to have negative consequences. Ashfaq's experiences in the Aleck Mill, by contrast, illustrates how loyalty to a mill developed given the right conditions. Experiences of this kind were common only to the few family owned mills that were left by the time the *babas* arrived in Oldham.

> It was better working at the Aleck Mill - that was still like a family. In Courtaulds everything was business like. They did not care if you lived or died. (Ashfaq Razak)

However, despite greater commitment to the Aleck Mill, visits back to (Azad) Kashmir took priority for the *babas*. Holidays in the mills were normally only for two weeks in the year and often did not coincide with meaningful family and social events in (Azad) Kashmir. When a man left for longer than two weeks, his job would be filled by someone else and he was effectively given the sack. On his return from (Azad) Kashmir, it was unlikely that his vacancy would still be available, so he would find work wherever it was available. Mohammed Yaseen worked in six mills from 1969 to 1982 in and around Oldham. Prior to this he had worked in Birmingham and Luton. In between each job he would go home to (Azad) Kashmir sometimes for a rest, at other times to attend to family business. [6] This lack of flexibility on the part of management was supported by inaction on the part of the unions, an issue which will be returned to. The long-term consequences of this type of work pattern were serious. The next chapter provides a detailed illustration of how this fragmentation in employment tenure meant that few *babas* were able to claim unemployment benefits that arise from redundancy.

Length of stay in an individual mill increased with the *kakas*, who, after training at one place, usually stayed there for four to five years before moving on. This is especially true of those men who went on to become foremen or took an active role in union activities. *Babas* would attend to the responsibilities in (Azad) Kashmir while the *kakas* continued working in the mills. Thus, the *kakas* were less likely to have the opportunities to return, other than to be married. Dahya (1970) perceptively notes how this type of organisation of family labour resembles work patterns set in earlier economic migration. In the beginning of the twentieth century, leave from the British Indian Army and Royal Navy encouraged and developed a pattern of long visits home followed by longer periods of service. Unfortunately, the mills of Oldham did not allow for long periods of leave and it was for this reason that the men hopped from mill to mill.

Organising Mill Work

The typical spinning mill that the *babas* would have come to in the 1960s was an impressive building. Ashfaq describes the scene:

> When I first came to Oldham, the chimneys of the mills were as numerous as the trees in my village. I had never seen so many factories in such a small area of land.

Mills were often of five to six storeys in height, with each level organised according to a separate part of the spinning process. The basement was used for storage of both raw cotton and finished spun thread. The ground floor would usually house the card room and the blowing room, with the remaining floors used for spinning, roving and doubling. In the 1960s, mills were dusty places, often quite damp and extremely noisy. These conditions gradually improved throughout the 1970s and 1980s, such that on my visit to Elk Mill in 1995, there was full air-conditioning and very little dust, even though the uproar from the machines was still present. Razak Ahmed relates this incident:

> After I had been in England for two years, my father came to visit me. I was working in Lilac Mill on the night-shift. My job was as a labourer. I would bring the cotton up from the carding room. My father wanted to know what this work was that so many members of his family were involved in. The night-shift supervisor was a *gora* but he was good with us Pakistanis. So I said to him that my father would visit one night. I told *abbaji* (father) to come at 1 am when we would have a tea break. When he got to the mill, he went to the spinning room and looked for me. I saw him come in and went to talk to him, but he couldn't recognise me because my hair, clothes and face was covered with the dust of cotton ends. When I told him that it was me, his son, he was shocked and said: 'This country had made you into a ghost!'.

On the night-shift, the *babas* occupied almost all of the various jobs that were available, from labourer to doffer, and up to foreman. Historically, the job of doffer was the most skilled in the mill. However, by the 1960s, as a result of de-skilling caused by the introduction of new machinery, six to eight weeks training was sufficient to operate most of the new machinery. The worst working conditions in the mills were to be found in the carding and blowing rooms, and as would be expected, there was a concentration of Black/South Asian workers in these jobs. Labouring paid less than spinning, but, with overtime taken into consideration, this was a better job in financial terms than that of the foreman. The most significant distinctions amongst the *babas* were those based on management hierarchy. Shoaib was a spinner in the Lilac Mill:

> In the Lilac Mill there were sixty-eight frames. Each spinner would be in charge of six frames. A doffer would have control of a full ring. Two labourers would bring the bobbin from the card room to the ring room. The whole room was controlled by the General Manager of production. Each room would then have a foreman and depending on the size of each department, an assistant foreman. On the night-shift, there was only the foreman, no manager or general foreman, so that was good.

The foreman was the most important person in terms of everyday contact with the workers. In Oldham there were two foremen who actively encouraged the employment of Mirpuris/Pakistanis in their mills. Attique Ahmed, also a spinner in the Lilac Mill, explains why more *babas* did not become foremen:

> The foreman's job was worse than a dog. The ring jobber would get better pay than him. The foreman's pay was fixed at £96 per week, but we would get seventy-five pence a frame. I could deal with thirty frames in eight hours so you can see how much I could earn. I'd been working in the mills all my life, so I could keep them in control. The job of a foreman was easier than that of the worker. It was not as hard work and you did not feel so tired. But then there was the mental stress, timetable to be met and then dealing with the management. The worse parts was not having the option of getting overtime. The life of a foreman was worse than that of a dog.

The management and organisational hierarchy in the mills in Oldham reflects the more general status of (Azad) Kashmiris, particularly Mirpuris, in comparison with Pakistanis, specifically Punjabis. For example, the assistant manager of production in the Adderton Mill was a man from Lahore. A fellow Lahori was a visiting manager in a Courtaulds Mill in Oldham in the 1970s. The training manager for Courtaulds, with a specific brief for Asian workers, was the previously mentioned Anwar Khan, who was from Sialkot in the Punjab. Throughout the mill period, there was little sense of conflict across this regional divide. Most of the *babas* interchanged the use of the terms Pakistani, Mirpuri and occasionally Kashmiri in describing themselves to me. However, this hierarchical divide became significant as work shifted from the mills to the service sector. A point which will be elaborated in later chapters.

The Night-shift in a Mill

While workers in the mill were organised according to a management hierarchy, the most significant structuring element of mill work was the shift system. Working on the night-shift in the mills of Oldham ordered the organisation of the days and weeks for the *babas*. When overtime is taken into consideration, the working week could stretch over seven days. Each facet of the day, from getting to work, to organising food, to working on the night-shift generated a set of practices which reflected the mould of industrial working life. The organisation of workers into units of labour within the capitalist mode of production takes on specific meanings when associated with notions of scientific Taylorism (Braverman 1974). A central aspect of working life therefore becomes a concern with the control, management and utilisation of time. The resistance by workers to this appropriation of time by management has been well documented elsewhere (see Powell 1976; Grant 1983) and is taken up in the next chapter. The focus here is on the way in which the mill structured the *babas'* days, weeks and months.

Transport to the mills was organised either by utilising public transport or by catching a mill bus, and then later by the men's own vehicles. Early reliance on local buses led to some problems, especially when it came to getting back home after the night-shift in the early hours of the morning. Baba Quyuum relates a humorous story of this period:

> As you know, all the houses and streets look the same [in England]. There is no tree or pond to mark the way. We could never tell which bus stop to get off at. So someone said: 'Let us tie something around the bus stop so we can tell it is ours.' But what happened. Let me tell you. On the way home we spent all the time looking for the bus stop with the cloth tied

around it, but it never came. Some child or someone must have taken the ribbon off the stop. That day we got home later than usual.

After a few years, *babas* began to invest in cars and work groups formed with the men picking up each other on the way to the mill. Living in close geographic proximity to each other helped this process develop. This system has lasted to present day in Oldham with car-sharing being common amongst those few men still working in the mills.

Once the *babas* arrived at the mill, their general working practice would be the same, depending on occupation, across all of the mills. [7] However, individual experiences within the mill depended on a range of factors; who they were working with; who the foreman on the shift was and the length of their stay in the mill. If the shift was predominantly of *babas*, with a Pakistani or Mirpuri as a foreman, then the atmosphere would be relatively relaxed. In contrast, if the foreman was white and the shift also had some white workers on it, then the atmosphere was slightly more formal. On the night-shift, the *babas* would arrive at work at about ten pm, though this could be flexible depending on the foreman. In the Lilac Mill, where a *baba* was foreman, the men were not as worried about time as they were able to cover for each other. Whereas in the Maple Mill, the foreman was known to be 'anti-Pakistani' so there was more pressure to arrive on time. The night-shift would run until six am with a thirty minute break for food at about one am. As Anwar (1979) notes, in his study of workers in mills in Rochdale, very few of the men actually ate the food provided in the canteen.[8] Razak Ahmed describes his nightly routine:

> We would go to work on the buses all together, government buses. We stayed there from nine forty-five pm until six am. We would have a half hour food break at about one am. We would eat in the canteen, but would have our own *dal roti*. In any case, it [the canteen] was closed at night. We would keep the food on the machines to keep it warm and when it was time to eat, we would go into the canteen.

One small concession wrought by the *babas* and *kakas* was the employment of an Asian cook in the Lilac Mill in 1989. The canteen subsequently began to offer *dal*, *roti* and halal meat. Unfortunately, the mill closed down three months after the cook arrived. For many of the *babas*, life revolved solely around work. After leaving the mill at eight am, some would buy their provisions and then after breakfast go home to sleep. After seven to eight hours sleep, there would only be enough time to get ready for the next shift. Sunday became the only day on which letters could be written back to Mirpur, friends visited and family responsibilities fulfilled. [9] It was the *babas* routines which fitted into working life. In fact mill life remained remarkably resilient to any efforts by the *babas* to bring in change. Even on those issues, such as extended holiday leave, which would benefit all workers, change only occurred as the mills were finally closing in the mid-1980s.

In Chapter Four, the reasons for the night-shift being re-started in the 1960s were outlined. The concentration of South Asian workers on the night-shift was attributed to the blocking of opportunities in other jobs and to the deliberate organisation of time to minimise contact between South Asian men and white women workers. However, from the perspective of the (Azad) Kashmiri workers there were also some clear incentives for working on the night-shift. The shift system was organised in combination with overtime to ensure sufficient cover for the incoming and out-going shifts. Shifts would be extended to begin at eight pm and finish at six am or even from eight pm to eight am, which guaranteed maximum cover for the change-over periods. These comments reflect a general body of opinion:

> I get more money at night. There is no *gora* (white) management to bother you. We are all together so that is good also (Imtiaz Khan).

> There was no trouble on the nights. If you worked during the day, sometimes, the *gore* would give you a lot of trouble (Mohammed Khan).

> They didn't want us to work on the day shift because they were scared we would steal their women away. Once my family were not well and I asked to be transferred to the day shift for a few weeks. I knew the general manager, I had been working there for a few years. He told me that all I wanted to do was to look at the white women and that I should stay on the night-shift: 'with the rest of your lot' (Yunis Bhatti).

These comments reflect both the advantages to the *babas* of night-shift work and the recognition of their restriction to this type of work. A few more points need to be considered that reflect the agency and choices of the *babas*. The processes by which work came to be obtained, as described in the previous section, fostered men working on the same shift. The night-shift, therefore, offered a sense of security that was provided by working with people who spoke the same language, and who were fellow migrants and often kin relations. Perhaps most consequential in terms of economic choice, the night-shift paid more than the day shift and when combined with overtime could make a great impact on the weekly wage. A snapshot view of these arrangements could conclude that working on the night-shift was therefore advantageous to *both* the management and the *babas*. However, the benefit of hindsight and the fact that even in 1984, 44% of Pakistani males were still working on the night-shift across all industries (Jones 1993), allows us to realise that the *babas* were restricted in their long-term employment opportunities by extended working on the night-shift. [10]

Mills and Men

It is evident from the narratives presented in this chapter that the outline offered by Dayha in the introduction to this chapter is not sufficient to explain the experiences of the (Azad) Kashmiri workers in the mills of Oldham. This is not due to differences with field sample, in that Dayha was ostensibly not distinguishing between Pakistanis and (Azad) Kashmiris in his work, though this is a point of relevance in other contexts. [11] Rather, it is an overt concern with placing the migrant workers out of the context and relationship with the work place. Rather than attempting to work out how the mills placed constraints and therefore created new forms of social organisation, Dahya's perspective leads to an unproblematic set of continuities with a particular migrant outlook. This chapter addresses these questions and recognises the central role that kin groups and male working groups made in organising and coping with a new environment and industrial working. But, this role is set in the context of working patterns set by previous bodies of labour.

It would be naïve to simply state that Black migrant workers simply slotted into the working cultures of the white working class. Chapter Four indicated the profound gender aspect of the organisation of labour in the mills. The presence of previous generations of migrant labour is also an important element. Indeed, the fact that the labour market is and always has been ordered in relation to factors such as ethnicity, community, gender and household (Joyce 1987) is central to my concerns. However, as Aronowitz notes: ' For mature capitalist states of the 19th century and the first half of the 20th century, social and cultural identities were forged by the categories of class and strata: everyday life, aesthetic expressions, and cognitive mappings articulated with production relations' (1992: 23). In the shift from the countryside to the town which marked the industrial revolution in Britain, social relations were reformed which intersected with ties of kin and locality and emerged in terms of class. If this discursive perspective on class formation is taken, then it is clear that the (Azad) Kashmiri workers were involved in a process that had taken place with previous groups of workers.

Amongst the *babas* and other racialised male workers, class formation was taking place that intersected and crossed ties of kin and locality. During my interviews, there was the constant sense of the *babas* sharing a common camaraderie with other South Asian and black workers. This was re-enforced by living in the same inner areas of Oldham, in the same kind of housing and having a similar status as migrant workers. In particular the presence of Indian Gujeratis and some Bangladeshis provided a broad South Asian cross section, while mill workers from the Caribbean shared residential and public spaces. The development of Mosques/Mandirs/Churches, pubs, and clubs separate from the bulk of white male mill workers did not mean that these sites, however culturally marked, did not share the same function as those for the white working class. What is clear, though is that class did not provide the basis for unity. Even though, as we will see in the next chapter, the participation by Black workers in the union was substantial their incorporation into the broader union movement was not.

The mills played a central role in restructuring and organising the lives of the *babas*. In this chapter the focus has been on the way in which they responded to the demands of industrial time and the rhythm of working life. Despite this their role as active agents was reflected by the means and reasons that drew them to Oldham. Indeed, it is this role, of the *babas* and *kakas* wresting some form of control from the imposing mill structures that is taken up in the next chapter.

---

[1] Kahil Mir states he was the first arrival in 1954 in a personal interview and in Millett, F. (1995) *Oldham and Its People*.
[2] 1966 Special Census Figures for cities in England show the population of Pakistani born people as: Birmingham 10280 Bradford: 7030, Manchester: 1730, Oldham: 710. There is a need to be careful about the Pakistani figures, in that up to 1972 they also include Bangladeshis, formerly East Pakistanis.
[3] See Appendix I for a full breakdown of Oldham's Pakistani population.
[4] In personal conversation with Anwar Khan.
[5] All of the mills in operation in the 1960s and 1970s were mentioned to me by my respondents.
[6] Mohammed Yaseen's work history by town and year.

Town	Place of work	Year
Birmingham	Factory	1960
Walsall	Foundry	1963

Luton	Factory	1967
Oldham	Maple Mill	1969
Oldham	Belgrave Mills	1970
Shaw	Lilac Mill	1974
Stalybridge	Ray Mill	1976
Pakistan		1977
Ashton	Cedar Mill	1978
Shaw	Lilac Mill	1980
Redundant		1982

[7] Those mills still in operation would have invested in the same type of machinery and therefore occupational profiles across a range of mills would be similar.

[8] This only applied to those cases where there was a canteen in the mill.

[9] Anwar (1979) offers a detailed breakdown of the impact of the night-shift on family and social life.

[10] In the next chapter the deleterious effects of working on the night-shifts for the post-mill employment prospects of the *babas* are considered in detail.

[11] See Methodology chapter for a theoretical argument and Chapters eight and nine for evidence about distinguishing between Pakistani and (Azad) Kashmiri.

6 Of Men and Mills

Mill work played a major role in structuring the day to day life of the *babas*. Their presence did little to alter the relations of work that had been set in previous generations and indeed the previous chapter illustrates how there were many continuities and minor adjustments with the previous employment of young white women. In an attempt to reflect the agency of the *babas*, it is necessary to shift the perspective from 'Mills and Men' to 'Men and Mills'. By considering the issues of visits to Pakistan and holidays for Eid, it is possible to see the specific ways in which the *babas* took control of their time, and in some senses subverted aspects of management control. The issue of control is central in the struggles over Eid and extended holidays for visits to (Azad) Kashmir/Pakistan. These two issues formed the central points of resistance for the *babas* and the *kakas*. Support from the unions was minimal in these struggles despite the fact of mass enrolment by South Asian workers.

Despite some success in gaining rights for holidays on Eid and for extended visits home, the state of the textile industry was such that these concessions were wrought in mills that were often due for closure. Mill work left the *babas* with little by way of transferable skills and given the geographical nature of industrial decline in Britain, few opportunities in areas like Oldham. From entry into the mills up to the period of decline the *babas* situation remained that of marginal workers. Nonetheless, this chapter illustrates that the *babas* and *kakas* did not constitute the passive workforce, that previous literature has alluded to (see Chapter One).

Eid and Trips to (Azad) Kashmir/Pakistan

A central aspect of working life is concerned with the control, management and utilisation of time. The resistance by workers to this appropriation of time by management has been well documented elsewhere (see Powell 1976; Grant 1983). If the night shift illustrates capitulation to the workings of mill life, the issues of Eid and trips to (Azad) Kashmir best represent resistance to time control by the migrant workers. Anwar (1979) persuasively argues that the majority of problems that Pakistani workers faced in the mills of Rochdale were the same as those that affected the workforce as a whole. These were the issues of pay, working conditions, and health and safety standards. In so doing, Anwar (1979) makes light of disputes over issues such as a holiday for Eid, a space for prayer and problems concerning extended leave for visits to (Azad) Kashmir/Pakistan. However, if union records and the work of Fevre (1984) are consulted, they reveal that there were many points of conflict in the mills, which concerned the month of fasting and a holiday for Eid. A contemporary focus on these issues resonates with the hostile marking of Muslims in the last fifteen years in British society. [1] This is particularly inscribed by the festival of Eid which is a celebratory and public acknowledgment of the presence of Muslims. [2] However, it is necessary to be careful when consulting union documents on the issues of Eid and visits to Pakistan as this is the only time that differences such as Asian, Muslim and immigrant are highlighted. [3] For other matters, such as pay and conditions, it is not possible to separate workers out in this way. Therefore, it should not be assumed that these were the only concerns over which Muslim workers engaged in protest.

Protests over the Eid holiday are of great consequence, if viewed from the perspective that Fevre (1984) puts forward. He writes that Eid was meaningful, not just as a religious festival, but also as a site of resistance for Asian workers in the Bradford woollen mills. During Eid in 1994, when I was present in Oldham, all of the (Azad) Kashmiri, and other Muslim, men still working in the mills took the day off. Greater flexibility was adopted by the management throughout the month of fasting. This was made possible by negotiations, prior to *Ramadan*, between workers and management. [4] Cordial relations of this type were not always the case, as Issaq relates:

> During *Ramzan* in the summer months, when there was eighteen to nineteen hours for *roza* (fasting), when we broke the fast we would have to have food in the mill. So we would always take it with us. We used to take a holiday for Eid, but the management always complained. They didn't know about Eid; this was 15-20 years ago. They didn't give us any time for *namaz* (prayer), but we found our own time. I was the first person to start *namaz* at the mill I was at. I was doing my *namaz* and a manager came and saw me and asked me: 'What are you doing ?'. I told him I was doing my prayer. He told me: 'You can't do it in the machines'. He said that 'If you want to do *namaz* there is a free room'. After me, they all started praying.

A series of agreements were negotiated throughout the late 1970s and early 1980s by unions and workers allowing for a holiday on Eid. As Fevre (1984) has noted for the woolen textiles industry, Eid posed a problem for management for two reasons. Firstly, the date of the festival was not fixed - varying according to the lunar calendar- and secondly almost every Muslim worker would take the day off irrespective of management compliance.

Contention over a holiday for Eid reflects the wider issue of the control of time that was a major struggle for the Mirpuri/Pakistani workers. Frequent trips back to (Azad) Kashmir meant that tenure of employment in one mill was never for more than a few years. This often resulted in short periods of unemployment or a necessity to take a worse job on returning from a visit. To increase their length of tenure and accommodate trips home the *babas* sought those mills that offered a multi-shift system. In this work scheme, large amounts of time off could be accrued, and therefore the necessity to give up a job to go to (Azad) Kashmir was avoided. Faizal Karim explains:

> The mills and jobs most favoured by us were those that ran the multi-shift system: This was a three days on two days off, two days on three days off type of rotation. The advantage of this system was that if you arranged with friends and relatives to do part of their shift you could amass a large amount of time off. In many cases you could make up to eight weeks off and then go back to Pakistan. The Kent Mill ran this type of system but it was only in certain departments, so everyone wanted these jobs so we could go home and come back to a job. This system of working changed in 1980. In fact it was stopped.

Once the contraction of the industry began, the *babas* became increasingly aware of the importance of remaining in one job and keeping it secure. Therefore, extended holidays and leave for Eid were issues that became sites of formal struggle with management. The *kakas* were at the forefront of these conflicts, as they were more likely to be in one place for more than five years. In turn, their relationships would be better developed, and they would therefore have more secure employment rights. Ashfaq Ahmed, a *kaka* who is widely respected in Oldham and still working in a mill, describes the situation in the Adderton in the mid-1980s.

> The main thing we fought over was to get Eid recognised as a holiday and we told them that we would want to take a day off and they agreed, but as long as we gave them some warning of when it would be. The other thing

> was about visits home to Pakistan. Normal holidays in the mills were only four weeks during the year. After spending so much money [for the ticket], we would want to go for longer periods. After all, when seeing family after such a long time, it was important to spend more time. We negotiated with the management that after five years, you could take eight weeks holiday, but if anybody took more than that then they would not be given their job back.

The Adderton case is not unique as many such local agreements were forged. However, what is apparent from the narratives of these micro-struggles with management undertaken by the *babas* and the *kakas,* is the minimal role played by the unions. More often than not, it was the *kakas* in the mill who would, by themselves, organise to demand concessions. Inactivity on the part of the textile unions on this issue was symptomatic of a more general hostility towards Black workers.

Union Membership and Participation

Experiences of unions stretch far into the migratory history of men from Mirpur/(Azad) Kashmir. This quote highlights how their forefathers working on the steamboats from Bombay contributed to union coffers:

> Perhaps the most notorious is the £30 per head that was paid by the ship owners to the National Union of Seamen for every Asian seafarer they employed. Until last year, that 'blood money' which was paid straight into the union's central fund helped to prevent any official union objection to complaints that Asian seafarers were receiving one quarter the pay of 'British' seafarers. It was formalised in 1911 to pay for settlement of the seamen's' strike of that year' (Short 1984: 14-15).

There has been mass union membership amongst South Asian men through entry into the cotton textile industry up to the present day. However, the relationship between the various textile unions and their South Asian members has not reflected this level of support. Anwar (1979) points out the irony of a situation where the Pakistani men who joined the textile unions in the 1960s in Rochdale did not know the name of the organisation they joined. The following quote, from the year book of the Rochdale and Oldham branch of the ATWU - Allied and Textile Workers Union- illustrates the meaning of good 'race relations' at that time.

> In Rossendale they had had an outstanding example of co-operation with coloured workers. When a question of large-scale redundancy arose it involved about 300 people, many of them immigrants. At the meeting to decide policy on redundancy it was found that some of the immigrants had longer service than some of the local women, but representatives of the Pakistani workers said that because local women had roots in the area, and the immigrants were mobile, they felt they should be made redundant and that the local women should keep their jobs (ATWU 1972: 52).

This response by the union demonstrates how the South Asian workers were viewed as alien, foreign and temporary, and significantly not part of the general working class. As Short (1984) notes, support for the Pakistani workers on the issue of extended holidays would have benefited all workers, yet the union was not supportive of the demand. This is lamented in the report *Lancashire United ? Black Workers and the Trade Union Movement in Lancashire*:

> If you were absent for more than four weeks, it was assumed that you had resigned. Sometimes, you were re-employed in the same position by the same firm, but were deemed to have broken services. But in virtually all the cases where agreements were signed, the black workers were pushing and the white workers were hostile. And how many white workers would ever have dreamed of getting time off before retirement to have a holiday with their family in Australia? Or have pushed the union into fighting for that as a right? The demands initiated by the black workers would have benefited all (Short 1984: 18).

Beyond the specific issues of Eid and holidays, union activity and involvement was far greater amongst the *kakas* than the *babas*. As illustrated by the concessions over Eid and holidays, it was the younger men who fought at the front-line. However, when it came to becoming shop stewards or to take any active role in the union, their response was similar to that of their white counterparts: apathy. The present textile branch secretary of the GMB in Oldham is Mohammed Dawood who relates these difficulties:[5]

> The remarkably few numbers of Asians active in the shop stewards and general union affairs reflects the general state of affairs. It is very difficult to get *anybody* to become a shop steward.

Where the role of the unions was to protect individual workers rights, the response to the *babas'* needs was also not always positive. [6] Despite this some of the *kakas* did make an active use of the union, as Peter Bashir explains:

> I've been a member of the union since I came to work in the mills. I hurt my hand in the machines once and my thumb was cut off. The union took a case out against the company so I could get compensation, but I lost the appeal. There were always little conflicts going on all the time with the foreman or the mechanic who were white and sometimes with the management. If something happened we would threaten to close down the machines.

Despite Bashir's comments, it was made apparent through my interviews that Shoaib's feelings reflected a more widely held opinion:

> I have had very little contact with the union. The only time that they had become relevant was during a strike for short working day in 1988. I was in Dee Mill at the time. I never knew the name of the union until they amalgamated with the GMB. My own experiences of the union have been very negative. When I was in a disciplinary hearing for taking off too many days sick, my union representative was useless.

The 1988 strike Shoaib refers to was the first national strike for forty years of textile workers for better pay and conditions. Throughout this period, union documentation illustrates that the Asian workers supported the strike action and were actually worse affected by subsequent redundancies and mill closures. [7] It is clear from Union records that the union played a role in various negotiations between the (Azad) Kashmiri workers and the management and by the 1980s showed a willingness to tackle issues such as racism in the workplace. However, this was near the end of the textile industry, and by this time the unions power base and therefore ability to assure effective change had diminished.

Another significant role that unions play in the work place is in terms of health and safety. Work in textile mills has long been known to have deleterious effects on health. This quote from the BBC documentary book, *All Our Working Lives* discusses the effect on a woman mill worker from the 1930s:

> She grew up with 'bad legs' from many years of standing besides a loom, with diminished hearing from the weaving shed clatter, and with breathing

difficulties from inhaling cotton fluff or irritant dust from the size used for wraps - size that contained zinc chloride (Pagnamenta and Overy 1982: 19).

General ill health from working in the textile mills was also present amongst the Black/South Asian workers. Abdul Ghaffoor relates his troubles:

> I worked until 1987 when my knees went bad and I had to go off sick. I'm still on the sick note since 1989. They [Mill management] still want me to go back but I'm not well enough. I worked for 25 years without going off sick and now look at me.

Mills in the 1960s and 1970s, however, were not as dusty or damp as they had been in previous eras. The main health problems that affected the Mirpuri workers resulted from working on the night-shift. Master Razak:

> Working on the night-shift has meant that my eyes have got a little bad, but the rest of my health is okay. But at night my vision is bad. I have had an operation in my eyes as well. I worked all my life in the card room. Sometimes in other rooms as well.

Perhaps most tragic of these cases is that of Rashid, previously foreman on the night-shift at the Aleck Mill. He was in his late forties when made redundant due to long-term sickness.

> I did not want to leave the job. But after working on the night-shift for so many years I could not sleep at night. The doctor gave me sleeping pills, which worked at first and I thought I could go back to work, but they stopped working after a while. Then I went to Mirpur and even though I could sleep there, the rest of my health suffered. While I was there, I went to a *desi hakim*, (doctor) who gave me some *apna* (local) medicine with which I was getting better. But it's not the same level of health care. Now, I can only sleep by taking pills and they make me feel sleepy all the time.

Industrial accidents, bone complaints and breathing problems are just a few examples of the effects that prolonged working on the night-shifts on the mills of Oldham have had on the health of South Asian workers. Ill health was and is one of the central reasons for the high level of unemployment to be found amongst *babas*. Years of working on the night-shift took their toll and resulted in weakened bodies not able to even undertake light labouring work. Indeed, the decline of the mills coincided with an increasing toll on the health of the *babas*.

The struggles over welfare and social needs that constructed the working class and union movements in Britain excluded Pakistanis and other Black workers. Thompson (1978) brilliantly illustrates how the unity of the white male working class was forged, not only by working together but through working mens' clubs, meetings in pubs and other social institutions. These spaces were effectively off limits to the *babas* and therefore their social participation was not with white members of the union. In fact, working on the night shift and the struggle over Eid illustrate the alternative public sphere in which the *babas* socialised and forged unity. This racialised division was further reflected in workplace relationships.

Interaction and Relationship at Work

With the notable exception of Duffield (1988), few studies of strikes, union activity and general political activity have emerged in the academic study of Britain's visible minorities. [8] Indeed, certain studies have contrasted these positions maintaining a consensual view of industrial relations. Brooks and Singh present the foreman as someone who is 'helping the natives help themselves' (1979: 102) and not as a person in a position of management and control. The only conflict noted is that amongst the ethnic groups themselves. Comments such as: 'Whites were far less likely to complain about the presence of another white ' (Brooks and Singh 1979: 102) litter the text. Similar themes emerge in Dahya's (1974) study, where criticism of the 'host' society does not feature as an issue for the Pakistanis. In a similar fashion to that of Wallman (1979), the power relations in each situation are levelled out. Therefore, antagonisms between workers are equated with those between workers and management which side-step issues of unequal power distribution within the workplace. My fieldwork illustrates the fact that tensions within the workplace hierarchy could be managed within the *biraderi* setup, but ultimately the mills management structures matched and mirrored existing divisions, rather than expediting them.

Relationships at work can be divided into two broad categories: those amongst workers, and those between management and workers. These lines, in some cases become enforced, and in others, blurred when divisions along racialised and gendered lines are taken into account. In terms of the overall management hierarchy, the division between the South Asian workers and white management succinctly highlights how racialised boundaries intersect with class creating a hierarchical and exploitative set of relations. At the same time, worker solidarity was enforced by the close knit relationships of the *babas* and *kakas* outside of the mill context. This strict divide is crossed when considering the role of a Mirpuri/Pakistani foreman whose alliances shift between being one of the 'workers' and being part of management.[9]

Practically all of the mills in Oldham employed some South Asian labour: men at night and women on the day shift. The night-shifts on Aleck Mill and the Adderton Mill provide useful cases studies of how relationships at work were determined by who the *babas* were working with, and who was overseeing their night-shift. Both the Aleck and Adderton Mills are still in the spinning trade in Oldham and therefore bridge the working period between the *babas* and the *kakas*. However, the Aleck is a local family owned company, whereas the Adderton is owned by Courtaulds. In the mid 1970s, a man called Rashid, a *kaka*, became the foreman on the night-shift at the Aleck Mill. Due to his activities, the mill in popular speech amongst the *kakas* and *babas* was called 'Shida's Mill'. This name reflected the influence he exerted over recruitment and his general high standing amongst Mirpuris/Pakistanis. Rashid joined his father in Oldham in the late 1960s, attended school for a brief spell and subsequently worked in the Aleck. Due to his hard work and consistency he was promoted to the job of foreman. In this post, over a period of time, Rashid ensured that all the men who worked on his shift were '*apne*'(ours). This term was broad enough to include all South Asian workers, but could also narrow to only include men from his small hamlet, in Mirpur. All of the men who worked the night-shift during Rashid's period as foreman remarked on how supportive and communal the experience was. A selection of responses are presented below:

> We never had anything to do with the white people. In the Aleck Mill we all worked as a team and helped each other out. If someone had family problems we would cover for him. If someone wasn't well he wouldn't have to work as hard. There was such a good atmosphere in the mill. It was not like that in the Lilac. Even though we were all Kashmiri, the foreman was still white (Kaimer Shoaib).

> Rashida was our relative and he was a really good foreman. We could go to the smoke-room every hour and have a chat. There was no problem if

> you got in late. If you needed to go to Mirpur in a hurry, he would make sure to keep your job. The management liked him because he made sure everything ran smoothly (Mazzer Rehman).

> At 9.45pm my friends would come with their car to take me to work. We would clock in at Adderton at exactly 10pm. At Aleck it was not so important because Abdul Rashid was the foreman, so he didn't mind if you were a little late (Mohammed Anwar).

These examples of male camaraderie, within an industrial working environment, are not unique to the *babas* and *kakas*. They are found repeatedly in studies of white working class and other Black groups. However, it is apparent from the narratives about the Aleck Mill that the presence of a *kaka* as foreman allowed the space of the mill to be, albeit temporarily, subverted from the control of white management. Aleck Mill, in 1995, still provides employment to *kakas* in Oldham on both the day and night-shift. There are, relative to Rashid's time, more Mirpuri/Pakistani foremen in the various departments of the mill. However, the rest of the management hierarchy remains, as it always has, predominantly white male. The presence of all Mirpuri/Pakistani night shifts nurtured and sustained ties of kin and friendship that were present historically amongst the *babas* and the *kakas*. However, despite this there was little-long-term impact on the actual hierarchy and structure of the mill.

Adderton Mill provides a contrast, both in terms of worker relationships and impact on management hierarchy, which is further complicated by the fact that there was a Pakistani - though not (Azad) Kashmiri- foreman employed in the mill. Faizal Hussain came to Oldham in the early 1960s and, though trained in textile engineering, found himself working on the shop floor. In the 1980s he became the assistant manager of production at a mill in Oldham. While he actively promoted and encouraged other Pakistanis to work in the mills, his interests appeared to be with the management and to promote his own position. [10] This quote from a *baba* who worked with Faizal is illustrative:

> I went to Adderton Mill and the foreman was Faizal. He told me to go and see which job I wanted to do. He recommended that I go to the filter room where there isn't too much work. I went to see and there was so much dirt and stuff. Uncle Jeevan also worked there. Faizal asked me if I wanted that ? I said: 'No'. He said: 'Tell me what you want ?' I said: 'Give me the winding job. If I can do it then its fine.' He said: 'Winding isn't under me

that is under another foreman, a guy from Lahore, Aziz.' He phoned him but he would not take me. These men were useless (Baba Razak).

The workforce in the Adderton Mill was also more diverse than the Aleck. This was not only in the sense of employment of Ukrainians and Italians, but also in terms of other South Asian groups. [11] Baba Nazir illustrates the point, when he joined Adderton in 1964:

> I started work at 6.30am and worked through to 9pm. This woman from Sri Lanka would make the slips and I had to put those slips on to the bales. There were many people from India there also. Once we had three young Sikh men come and work, but they did not like the mill and so they left.

Ashfaq describes the situation thirty years later, in 1994:

> When I arrived I began working in Adderton Mill. There was a vacancy for a dubbler and I took it. I worked there for the last eleven years. There were about one hundred Asians working there. There were quite a few Gujerati Indian women on the day shift. With me there are Jamaicans, Bangladeshis, Indians, Pakistanis, some *gore*, but mainly Kashmiris. All *kale* and *gore* mixed up.

This quote from Ashfaq illustrates that relationships fostered in the workplace could cross boundaries that may at other times be more strongly enforced. [12] It is only possible to speculate if it was the presence of a Pakistani man at a senior level in the management hierarchy that ensured the mill was kept relatively ethnically mixed. In this way, his position could ensure that the workforce would therefore be acquiescent or at least not as unified in their demands.

Relationships amongst workers were found to be racialised, in the sense that white and Black/South Asian workers minimally interacted. As Anwar (1979) notes working on the night-shift in predominantly Pakistani work forces did not allow for a great deal of interaction with anybody, let alone the wider general public. However, many of the *babas* had a certain romantic attitude towards their early days in England. On reflection they reasoned that things were much worse now - 1994 - in terms of race relations, and conflict with white people in general, which partially explains the view of the past that Baba Ashfaq presents in this quote:

> We were treated very well in those days. When we got off at the railway station people would tell us where to go. Our neighbours lent us *bartan*

(pots and pans) and in winter when it was cold they gave us brandy to keep us warm. I could not speak English so I had a letter with an address, to where I wanted to go. People told me where to get the taxi from. There were not many of us in those days. Now you know there are so many of us.

These rosy reminiscences did not extend to working in the mills. Interactions with the foreman at the Adderton provide a clear contrast. Baba Ashfaq in the same interview:

> The manager was Jones. He was trying to place me in a job. Firstly, he made me do labouring work. He phoned packing and they needed someone so he sent me down there. The packing foreman was a white guy, when he saw me he said : 'No pakis'. Then Jones came, he was a tough guy. He said to me, 'What do you want? What do you want?'. I said, 'What do you mean ?' He said, ' I am boss. I am foreman'.

Contact with other white workers took place even less often than those with the foreman. However, in the early 1960s there were some notable incidents that illustrate a begrudging camaraderie amongst workers across the racial divide. Baba Razak relates his first day at the Maple Mill.

> An old white man was sent to train me. He asked me if I wanted to smoke a cigarette. I said yes and he sent me to the toilet to have a smoke. Every hour he would do the same thing. I was supposed to learn by watching him and the machine. He had just given me the tool when he told me to go and have cigarettes. So, I got home and after twelve hours work, sitting down is hard. In the morning my back was hurting, and I thought working is hard. But I had to do it. I got to work and the old *gora* said to me: 'You saw what I was doing yesterday, now you do it and if you can't do it I'm here and you can ask me'. Anyway I carried on doing it and he helped me on the third day he said to the manager he can manage it. After he said to me, 'I'm still here so I can help you. If you got an extra machine you can get over time, another £2.50-3.00 a week'.

This situation of a white worker training a South Asian did not occur too often, because workers such as Baba Razak would themselves train other Pakistani/South Asian men. In this way, contact with other white workers was progressively limited.

The lack of contact with white workers in the mills was also increasingly matched by the phenomenon of 'white flight', where inner areas of Oldham were becoming increasingly populated by visible minorities. Family reunions and the increasing need for housing for mothers and daughters, joining fathers and sons, meant that areas of Oldham were becoming more and more densely populated with (Azad) Kashmiri families. Interactions with white people were therefore lessened in both the workplace as well as in the general public sphere. It is ironic that just as all-male households were being replaced by settled family units, the income that was needed to sustain these new migrants was drying up. For the majority of the *babas,* the night shift in the mills with occasional visits to (Azad) Kashmir became a pattern of working life that lasted for twenty years or more. Few of these men could have predicted how their lives were about to change with the onset of recession and decline of heavy industry. A shift almost as profound as that from the rural setting of Mirpur to the urban industrial landscape of Oldham.

Decline of Mills

The decline in Britain's industrial manufacturing base during the late 1970s and early 1980s had a widespread and devastating impact on working class communities throughout its industrial heartlands. Steel workers and miners seem to have attracted the most attention, of what is a scant academic literature, on the implications of this industrial decline. [13] For Black workers, the de-industrialisation of Britain had no less severe implications in terms of employment and poverty. However, in general there has been little academic concern for the consequences of de-industrialisation on this group of workers. [14] The cotton textile industry had been in a state of contraction since the 1930s. Throughout the 1960s and early 1970s the decline in the mill sector was steady and reflected wider changes within the British economy. South Asian workers occupied a niche - working on the night-shift- that was created in a final attempt by mill owners to maintain the industry. Therefore, the impact of the industrial decline was particularly marked on this group of workers.

During the recession of the early 1980s, certain jobs became susceptible to massive redundancy. These were in manual and semi-skilled occupations, and it was these very jobs that were the main sources of employment of (Azad) Kashmiri men. Burnett (1994) argues that occupational status was the single most important factor in determining which groups of people were most likely to become unemployed. The statistic that manual workers constituted eighty-four percent of unemployed men in 1983 is a stark illustration of the vulnerability of this section of labour (Burnett 1994). As noted in the previous chapter, the majority of South Asian mill workers in Oldham were concentrated in the least skilled areas and on the night-shift, in those jobs that were, by that time, conceived of as semi-skilled and manual labour.[15] A double jeopardy comes into play here, firstly concentration in an industry in decline and secondly in those occupations which were increasingly becoming redundant across a range of industries.

In previous chapters, the fact that labour in the mills was racialised and gendered was demonstrated. White women workers numerically dominated the day-shift, with the occasional South Asian male, while the night-shift was predominantly manned by South Asian workers. During the late 1970s, the day-shift became increasingly mixed as fewer women entered the mills. The closure of mills also had an effect on white women workers. However, they were not as severely affected by the changes that were taking place in the structure of the labour force. New work in the expanding service sector targeted women, offering part-time and flexible working hours. White women workers were, therefore, able to take up the part-time service sector oriented work which was becoming more readily and increasingly available.[16] Penn et al (1990b) note how this process began in the mid 1970s when mill work became less flexible and fewer young women entered the industry. Ironically, it was the flexibility of mill work that attracted women to working in the mills a generation previously. While the contraction of the textile industry therefore caused redundancy amongst all members of the labour force, the severity of the impact was greatest on Black workers.

Factors for Redundancy

The economic recession of the early 1980s in Britain was so widespread that its effects were relatively indiscriminate in terms of who was rendered unemployed (Burnett 1994). Despite this fact, three trends can be isolated which when combined increased the likelihood of unemployment. These were regional location, occupational sensitivity, and age discrimination. A middle aged mill worker in Oldham would be likely to fulfil all three criteria, irrespective of being South Asian or not. In addition, there were certain factors specific to the *babas* of which their status as 'international commuters' and discrimination against racialised minorities are the most significant.

In the early 1980s, working in Oldham or other towns of the North West was a significant factor in terms of loss of employment. The North

West was one of England's worse effected areas in terms of industrial decline (Martin and Rowthorn 1986). These areas of old industrial concentration were not those that became centres for new employment, despite government schemes, such as enterprise zones. Development of new manufacturing sites tended to be closer to areas where skilled and white collar labour was available. Large retailing centres, a growth area in terms of employment in the 1980s, were also located outside of city centres. These general shifts were reflected in changes in Oldham's economy where rapid closure of mills and employee redundancies led to marked shifts in the distribution of labour. In 1971, in Oldham, there were 18234 employed in textile manufacture. By 1981 this had fallen to 13324 and by 1991 there were only 3254. The most recent survey in 1995 revealed that only 1827 people were employed in textiles. [17] Even though this decline was not as severe in terms of number of mill closures as it had been after the Second World War, the difference here was that it was not compensated by employment growth in other manufacturing sectors. The main areas of economic growth in Oldham, during this period, were in warehousing and distribution. [18]

If the decline had been restricted to textiles only, then the resulting effect on the South Asian workers might have not been so damaging. Shaw (1988) has shown how a mini economic recession in the late 1960s resulted in Pakistani men moving from Birmingham to Oxford in search of work. However, in the 1980s the decline in industrial jobs was widespread and significantly affected semi-skilled and unskilled occupations, closing many of the labour market options that had previously been open to South Asian workers. The processes of de-industrialisation effectively blocked off any job opportunities in the traditional manufacturing sector. This was also the sector where there was a concentration of South Asian male workers. Mohammed Yaseen's story is typical:

> I arrived in England in 1960 and worked in a factory in Birmingham for a few months. Then, I shifted to Walsall where I worked in a foundry for two years, then on to a bolt making factory in Luton for a year. I came to Oldham in 1969 where a friend was living and told me there was lots of work. I began work in the card room and worked in six different mills over a period of thirteen years. I had a variety of jobs from labourer to doffer. In 1982 I was made redundant. My age was about fifty-three. I have not worked in full time employment since then. I tried to get work in other factories in Oldham, but they told me I was too old, or not experienced.

The fact that many of the *babas* were in their late forties and early fifties when they were made redundant was an enormous disadvantage. Azar Khan relates his experiences:

> I spent all my time in England working, one factory to another, then in the mills. All my life working hard to make money. Then, in 1983 I went to a funeral in Mirpur and when I came back the mill had closed down. I looked for work in many other mills, but they told me: 'You too old, no work for you'. When they wanted us then they treated us well. Now there are no jobs. The white people treat our young boys so badly.

Research in Rochdale found that in 1982 over sixty per cent of the over fifty age group of Pakistani men were unemployed in the area (Penn et al 1990a). This is a statistic which starkly illustrates the effect of age on redundancy. During the 1980s, as more and more *babas* increasingly entered the world of long-term unemployment, age and health in combination became the main reasons for restricted access and entry to the labour market. The *kakas* were also becoming unemployed at the same time, and for much the same reasons as the *babas*. However, those few jobs that were still available in the mills were preferentially offered to them. For many of the *babas* who considered themselves fit and able to work, the retort 'too old' was a bitter one. Ishtiaq Khan comments on the situation:

> Why is there so much illness ? Why so much depression ? We spent all our lives working hard for our money. Now, we are like women, we sit around in the house all day.

Age, regional location and occupational sensitivity affected all working class communities in one way or another during the process of de-industrialisation. In addition there were certain factors specific to the *babas*, primary of which was their status as 'international commuters'. As previously explained, the *babas* would leave a job every two or three years to return to (Azad) Kashmir. In the late 1960s and early 1970s, when jobs were plentiful and readily available, this lifestyle was sustainable. Given the demand for labour in the mills, the *babas* were almost guaranteed to find work on their return from an extended stay in (Azad) Kashmir. Even in those cases where the actual mill they had left did not have vacancies, another nearby mill would usually have some openings. The *babas'* transitory existence served the management of the mills. For instance, workers' benefits, in terms of redundancy and sick leave payments, accrued with length of tenure with the company. Any break in employment meant that the employee's tenure began again from scratch, with no previous service being taken into account, even if the worker returned to the same company to do the same job. Abdul Rashid's story is a marked illustration of the effect of this rule:

> Every two to three years I would go back to *vatan* (home), for between six months and a year. You know there was always someone's wedding or funeral to attend to. But I knew when I got back to England I would always get my old job back. The general foreman in Asia mill knew I was a good worker and always told me to come back to him when I needed a job. In all I worked there for sixteen years. Then in 1981, I went back to Mirpur in a hurry for some family emergency. I only went for three months, not as long as other times. When I got back to England, I went to the Asia mill but was told there were no vacancies. Another friend of mine, from the same village, had told me that I should get redundancy pay after working there for so long. When I asked the general supervisor about my redundancy money. He told me that I had not worked there for long enough. *Bhen choud* (sister fucker), is all my youth not long enough ?'

Rashid's case is typical, as few South Asian/black workers actually managed to claim redundancy payments when mills closed. [19] Whatever benefits accrued from redundancy packages were not applicable to these workers, as even by the late 1970s and early 1980s many of the men had kept up their status as 'international commuters' and not gained the required length of tenure. In this way they were ideal workers for management, as they did not incur extra costs to the company. The *babas* I questioned on the issue of redundancy blamed a lack of awareness of the system and unsympathetic responses from union officials as the main reason for not being able to claim redundancy payments. However, the low availability of redundancy payments and the low take up was not unique to Mirpuri/Pakistani workers. Burnett (1994) states that the total number of workers who received redundancy payments in 1987 was only twenty-one per cent. Overall, more than forty per cent of workers received no payment at all on being laid off or being made redundant. Once again the *babas* were more likely to suffer from this loss of benefits as the *kakas* would usually not go back to (Azad) Kashmir as often, and were therefore more likely to accrue a longer tenure in one mill. [20]

During the mill period, work forged the *babas'* patterns of mobility, the daily routine and the long-term organisation of months and years. They managed to accommodate and in small ways subvert the system in a pattern, which while culturally specific, resonates with organisation by sections of the white working class. The last two chapters have crucially illustrated that the role of the *babas* in the industrial setting cannot be simply viewed in terms of cultural factors and the workings of the 'myth of return' or chain migration. In addition the separation of the *babas* from the 'out of work' institutions of the white working class males also indicates the culturally specific forms of social action. This ethnography clearly illustrates the enmeshed nature of culture and structure, without a romanticisation of the *babas* agency.

Despite the evidence of micro level struggles and the considerable concessions wrought over holidays for Eid and visits to (Azad) Kashmir, the inexorable processes of global economic change, shifts within the textile industry and the local conditions of Oldham led to the decline of the industry. In this sense, the structured position of male South Asian/black workers in the textile industry ultimately led to their long-term unemployment. Indeed, the contrast between the mass redundancies of the 1980s and the concession wrought from management at a micro level are largely incomparable in terms of scale and effect. However, the next chapter focuses on the ways in which the *babas* reconstructed their lives after mill work disappeared.

---

[1] See, Runnymede Commission (1997) *Islamophobia: Its Features and Dangers*, for a full discussion of the concept.

[2] It is not by accident that Amer Rafique was blinded in one eye by racist police in Manchester on Eid in 1995 (Eastern Eye 11/3/1995).

[3] From immigrant, to Asian, to Muslim reflects the shifts in the naming process in the union records from the Oldham and Rochdale branches from 1969-1973.

[4] Ramadan and Ramzan are both words denoting the Muslim month of fasting.

[5] The main textile union, when the *babas* arrived in England, would have been the Allied and Textile Workers Union. By 1986, its membership was so small that it had to merge with the GMB.

[6] Racism in the unions is well documented; see Phizacklea, A. and Miles, R. (1992) 'The British Trade Union Movement and Racism'.

[7] See Oldham Chronicle 28th July 1988 for details of the strike.

[8] In fact there has been a considerable amount of work on these issues from Sivanandan (1982) and the Race and Class Collective.

[9] Tensions of this type will be more fully explored in Chapter Nine, where owners of taxi ranks and take-aways work alongside kinsmen, who are workers.

[10] This is not to imply that this attitude was a function of his migration from Pakistan rather than (Azad)Kashmir. It is more a reflection of his general class disposition when compared to the majority of the workers and the fact that he left

Adderton Mill to set up a small spinning plant with other members of the management team.

[11] The mobility of all South Asian labour meant that a stream of men passed through Oldham in the 1960s and to a lesser extent in the 1970s looking for work. They would stay in Oldham, for a few months to a year, and then move on.

[12] See Westwood (1984) for similar findings with Indian Gujerati women in a garment factory in Leicester.

[13] For example, Warwick, D. (1992) *Coal, Capital and culture: A Sociological Analysis of Mining Communities in West Yorkshire* and Docherty, C. (1983) *Steel and Steelworkers : The Sons of Vulcan*, London: Heinemann Educational.

[14] The main exception being the work of Cross (1992) on the economic decline in the West Midlands foundries.

[15] Pre-Second World War, the job of a spinner would be considered skilled. Increasing mechanisation meant that by the time of the 1980s all jobs on the mill shopfloor, were effectively semi-skilled or manual.

[16] While part-time work offered greater flexibility to women, their employment rights and working conditions were usually severely eroded when compared with working in the mills.

[17] Greater Manchester Research: *Employment Trends: Bulletin* 1990-1995.

[18] Warehousing developed in Oldham as a result of the empty mill properties, which provided cheap and large storage facilities. However, even these industries were subject to a great deal of fluctuation. See Appendix I for breakdown of Oldham's economic base.

[19] These findings are similar to those found by Penn et al (1990a) in their study of Asian mill workers in Rochdale in the late 1980s.

[20] Smith (1981) found that 36%, in a survey sample, of Asian men left their job to visit 'country of origin'.

7 Redundant not Despondent

Introduction

From the mid 1960s to the early 1980s the textile mills of Oldham and surrounding areas were the loci for the activities of the *babas* and *kakas*. Working on the night-shift in the mills organised their days and nights into a routine punctuated by Sundays and occasional visits to (Azad) Kashmir. Few of these men could have predicted how dramatically their situation was to change as a result of the economic recession of the late 1970s and early 1980s. As the mills began to close down, men who had known nothing but hard work and labour were suddenly faced with the prospect of not working in formal employment again. An appraisal of the *babas'* and *kakas'* responses to long term unemployment reveals the remarkable way in which many of the *babas* managed to cope with the loss of formal employment. This was mainly achieved through an increased and active involvement in religious, community and family life. However, despite this ability to maintain an active life, the problems of financial constraint and its effect on coming generations meant that the *babas* were still unhappy about being in England, and in this sense shared the despondency of white long term unemployed men.

Even though the collapse in the textile industry affected both the *babas* and their sons, the primary concern here is with the *babas*. The *kakas'* story is taken up in subsequent chapters. An exploration of the post-formal working lives of the *babas* reveals how a renewed commitment to religion and an increased regard for life-cycle rituals has served to off-set many of the more negative consequences of unemployment, at least in the social and psychological arena. The *babas'* ability to cope with unemployment, throws a different light on the structuralist 'deprivationist' perspective, illustrating their active agency. At the same time, this chapter also problematises the notion that renewed commitment to family and religion are simply a 'natural' phenomenon, a result of migration into an 'alien' culture. As argued in Chapter One, both the 'myth of return' and the 'fear of the west' as organising principles for migrant life can also be related to particular socio-economic factors. In this chapter, it is the effects of unemployment and subsequent free time, that plays a crucial role in the development and maintenance of religious and social institutions amongst (Azad) Kashmiris/Pakistanis in Oldham.

Initial Responses to Unemployment

As previously stated, economic growth in Oldham in the mid 1980s was concentrated in the service sector predominantly in retailing and distribution.[1] This sector of the economy mainly offered part-time and temporary work. Developing a small business, working for clothing manufacturers or driving a taxi were some of the possibilities open to the *babas* in England. Another option that was unusually open to the *babas* and not to their white peers, was to fulfil the 'myth of return' and to set up a business in (Azad) Kashmir. It is at this point that the story of the *kakas* and the *babas* diverges. The next chapter takes up the issues of working in taxi ranks and take-aways and the cruical role of these businesses in securing employment for the *kakas*. Here the central issues of concern are the initial responses by the *babas* to unemployment. Before proceeding, it is important to recognise that unemployment was not a discrete moment, and many of the men spent periods of time pursuing opportunities in both England and (Azad) Kashmir.[2]

Working in warehouses in Manchester - usually owned by other South Asians and with informal employment status - was and still is one of the main alternatives to unemployment in Oldham.[3] The geographical proximity of Manchester and the availability of work in manufacturing of garments was a source of labour for both men and women. The low-skilled, low paid work that the Manchester clothing manufacturers offered provided short term employment for many of the *babas*. The unexplored history of this labour forms the flip-side to Werbner's (1990) analysis of Pakistani elite and business families in Manchester. The large Pakistani clothing manufacturers with warehouses in the Ancoats area of Manchester, employ a workforce of men from the surrounding mill towns of Oldham, Rochdale and as far as Nelson.

During this period, the *kakas,* in contrast, were working as taxi drivers, on market stalls and in other small business. No such options were open for the *babas*. A lack of capital, no previous experience of business and a concern for the fact that there were so many other people running shops and other small businesses already were some of the reasons that the *babas* gave for their lack of involvement in setting up a business. Many took labouring jobs in factories and warehouses often at worse pay than they were receiving in the mills. Many others, with failing health stopped working altogether. In the late 1970s and early 1980s taxi driving was an attractive opening for the *kakas*. But for men in their early fifties, gaining a license, first for driving a car and then for driving the taxi were not simple tasks. For the *babas*, going to Mirpur with the possibility of setting up a business was probably seen as a more manageable route.

Babas returning to (Azad) Kashmir in search of business opportunities fulfil Cross's formulation literally: 'ethnic minorities have unwittingly become involved in a massive transformation of the British economy which has turned the story of migration on its head' (Cross 1992: 56). Cross is referring to shifts in the economy from labour demand to labour excess, but his comments are equally appropriate to the return migration that many of the *babas* embarked upon. Loss of work in the mills was viewed by some of them as an opportunity to fulfil the desire of returning to their homeland, with their savings, to settle. This reverse flow was not organised in the corporate terms that the migration to Britain had been. There was no reverse chain migration with its concomitant support structures. Often the decision to return was a complex of various factors, reflecting degree of settlement in Britain, amount of family left in Mirpur and sense of alienation from Britain. Each of these was in turn influenced by individual experiences of migration and labour.

Whatever the mix of motives for return, there were few possibilities for economic security to be found in (Azad) Kashmir. The politically indeterminate status of (Azad) Kashmir has led to a skewed economy - as was outlined in Chapter Three. The economy has an almost total reliance on emigrant remittances. The initial flow of capital from Britain went primarily into the construction industry resulting in a great deal of land speculation and property construction. It was to these two areas of economic activity and other service-providing retail businesses that the returnees turned when looking to re-establish themselves. This took the form of shop construction, often in the most remote of locations and sometimes attached to their own property.

During my fieldwork trip to Mirpur in 1995, I met several *babas* who had successfully transferred from England. The majority of them had set up businesses in Mirpur town itself, in the hotel, retailing or transport business. In terms of actual presence of other returnees there were many transient visitors who were investing in property and building family houses, but very few actual re-settlers were identified. The local state in (Azad) Kashmir actively encourages business connections and for overseas

Kashmiris to invest in (Azad) Kashmir. Mohammed Buta relates his experiences:

> Two friends of mine went back to try and set up a business but were unable to because of family disputes and other such problems. One time the *Wazir* (Prime Minister) of (Azad) Kashmir came to talk to us, we people with businesses in the area. He wanted us to come and set up in Mirpur. I said to him: 'First you stop the corruption and the bureaucracy.' He said nothing.

Despite the few success stories, a more general pattern for the *babas* was to spend a few years attempting to set up a business, but failing and then returning to Britain. Master Sadak is a good example of this process:

> In 1986 I took redundancy from Asia mill. I went to Mirpur for two years to try and settle there. My family have quite a big tailoring business there so I went back and didn't have any trouble with money. After working on the night-shift for so many years I could not sleep at night. Even though I could sleep in Mirpur, my health was not good. I came back to England for a while but did not like it. So I went back to Mirpur. Then I had to come back because my health was so bad. My family joined me here only two years ago [1992].

Very few of the *babas* managed to establish themselves in Mirpur after losing work in the mills of Oldham. This is not surprising in light of the poor infrastructure, the elaborate and often intransigent bureaucracy and the limited opportunities for long term investment to be found in Mirpur. Even though the Azad Jammu and Kashmir government encourages returnees to invest, the problems of organising a business proved to be too much for many of the men who had dreams of re-settlement in Mirpur.

Despite the multiple strategies adopted by the *babas* in finding employment, there were many factors that mitigated against them. Age, regional location and work experience were all factors which resulted in redundancy and were also significant hindrances to gaining employment. There are general issues that faced all the workforce. In addition there were factors which were specific to South Asian groups. A central reason identified by the *babas* was the issue of language. Anwar (1979) notes how working on the night-shift meant that South Asian mill workers had little to no contact with the world outside of their mill and their place of residence. The *babas* would have relationships and interaction mainly with fellow Mirpuris/Pakistanis or other migrant workers in the mill. The closest continual contact with a white person would be with the foreman or the

General Manager of production in a mill. One of the main consequences of this situation was that the only English the *babas* learnt were those words and broken sentences needed to function in the mill. In this way the *babas* developed a limited vocabulary, in some ways quite technical and specific, but nevertheless not applicable to other types of work. This lack of spoken English was a distinct disadvantage when looking for jobs in comparison to their white co-workers. Karim and Abdul's stories are common:

> I went for a job at the big Mirror factory in Oldham. My friend had told me they were taking people on. When I got there, they wanted me to take a written test. I just looked at the paper and left (Karim Shah).

> While we were in the factories, there was no help with speaking English. But we stuck together, so someone could always help you out. Now we have to run around to these *parre likhe* (people who can read and write) to get any money. So many forms to fill out (Abdul Quyuum).

However, this lack of English language skills should not be taken as an indicator that racialised discrimination was not a major factor. The next chapter illustrates how *kakas*, with an equivalent level of spoken and written English to their white working class peers, were also unable to get jobs. The *babas* themselves had a clear understanding of their position as unwanted labour:

> When we first came here they treated us so well, but then they needed our labour- hard work. Now look at the young men running around with nothing to do. Now the *gore* spit on us (Baba Afzal).

> All the factories have closed down. Just like in Bosnia, they will throw all Muslims out of England. They don't need us now to do their dirty work (Master Bashir).

Racism works through practices of exclusion, and for the *babas* this became most significant when they faced long term unemployment and a lack of new jobs that they could take. There was a sense from the *babas* that they had worked hard, all of their lives, only to be repaid with no future prospects. It can be argued that the specific impact of industrial change on the *babas* was the predictable result of their initial racialised position within the labour market. Their concentration in semi-skilled jobs, on the night-shift of a declining industry and in the wrong region of the country all add up to inevitable unemployment. However, while these are significant factors, there are wider issues which also need to be accounted for. Critically, it is necessary to recognise the multiple levels on which exclusion operates, and how these practices impact on the individual. For the *babas*, as the quote above from Master Bashir illustrates, redundancy and the closure of the industry was perceived as a direct attack on Asians in general and Muslims in particular (Lancashire Industrial Language Training Unit 1987).

Language difference and racial discrimination are hindrances to employment specific to South Asian/black workers. It is useful to distinguish these elements from the more general issues that affected all workers such as the lack of transferable skills between jobs, and the lack of experience in finding work. The 1987 report, *In Search of Employment and Training, Experiences and Perceptions of Redundant Asian Textile Workers,* outlines the reasons for the low level of re-employment amongst South Asian workers in the North West. It forwards four issues of primary concern: poor English language; lack of skills as those gained in the mills were not transferable; discrimination; and lack of job seeking skills. While poor English and racial discrimination are issues specific to South Asian workers, it is important to recognise that white workers would also suffer from the issues relating to skill shortage. [4] The fact that discrimination in entry to retraining for new work may be an issue for the *babas* and the *kakas* should not be used to confuse the fact that all the workers who were made redundant from the mills had few skills to offer other industries. The textile industry did not develop transferable skills in any of the workers other than the willingness to work hard, for relatively low wages. This story is not unique to textile mill workers, but applies to all manual and semi-skilled workers. Finally, the issue of lack of skills in finding work implies that the method of utilising contacts of kin and friends which had sustained the presence of so many (Azad) Kashmiri men in the mills was no longer effective. However, as Daniel's (1981) findings show, semi-skilled and unskilled white workers also used friends, relatives and former work-mates as sources of information about new jobs. This was the most successful route to gaining work as opposed to job centres and advertisements in the press. This simple set of comparisons emphasise how critical it is to distinguish between those factors which are specific to the unemployed *babas* in the context of widespread redundancy for all semi-skilled and manual workers.

Despite various strategies for finding work, the obstacles that the *babas* faced were by and large, insurmountable and a new phase of long term unemployment began. Ibrahim relates his story:

> I went to the employment exchange. They told me to sign somewhere and I would get money. I was shocked. All my life I had worked hard to get money and here they were giving it to me for doing nothing ! ....The woman asked me what work I could do ? All I had known was work in mills, from Bradford to Oldham (Ibrahim Mohammed).

> The biggest problem I see for myself is the unemployment of my children. They should pension everyone off at sixty. Then there would be enough jobs to go around. We never had enough time to get in to the sort of trouble that the younger generation are now in because we were always too tired [from working so hard] (Ishaq Khan).

Once it became clear that work in the mills and other factory work was not available, welfare benefits became one of the primary sources of income for many Mirpuri/South Asian families in Oldham. For some *babas*, their sons might still be working in the mills or in other jobs, though this was not always the case. The change in actual income from working in a mill to claiming benefits was not as dramatic as would be expected. This was for two reasons. Firstly, by the early 1980s pay in the mills was, relatively, so low that the difference in weekly income was negligible. Secondly, the welfare benefits system favours those with large families which was the case for the *babas'*. However, state support was not the most significant initial source of income. An important element to financial survival was the communal support system that existed amongst the *babas*. In the same way that they had relied on each other when they first came to Britain, family members and friends in work provided a short term financial fall back.

The system whereby men would pool money in *komittees* - rolling credit associations- provided a source of funds for the unemployed *babas* in case of emergencies. [5] In Oldham these *komittees* would vary in purpose and size, from large *biraderi* based organisations whose function was to provide finances for funerals, to small local rolling credit associations amongst groups of related families and occasionally friends. These smaller associations were of most importance to the support of financial hardship. Each *komittee* operated its own mechanism for collection and distribution of money. This process varied enormously ranging from fixed handouts to members at a given month of year; to an assessment of need of the family concerned; to others where a lottery type drawing of lots take place to see who should receive the money. In any case, and most significantly, this system provided an alternative source of cash for the *babas*.

This ability to pool resources and to live in a frugal manner is critical to an understanding of the way in which the most severe financial implications of long-term unemployment were offset by the *babas* and their families. The financial consequences of redundancy were faced by all members of the family and, to a large extent, it was in the domestic setting that the effects of limited income were most felt. The ability to survive with few resources was not something new to women raised in rural Mirpur. Even when the effects of emigrant remittances are taken into account, the running of the household in Mirpur depended on women's ability to manage on very little (Ballard 1985). This ability to live on little cash is also reflected in the reminiscence of white working class people of the depression of the 1930s. As Seabrook notes: 'Working-class people used to be proud of how much they could do with very little money; now people feel ashamed of how little they can do without a lot of it' (1982: 3). Similar sentiments were forwarded by many of the *babas* when questioned about the financial problems of being unemployed. For example, Master Sadak:

> What do we need ? People have become so greedy. We have food and clothing. The rest *Allah Tallah* will see to.

This ability to cope with poverty does not imply that the process of survival was easy or without negative consequences. A shortage of money was an essential component to the way that many of the *babas'* lives were organised. However, very few men were willing to relate this as a problem that they faced personally. Rather, it was something that had happened to their friends or it revealed itself in terms of a curb on their activities, particularly trips to (Azad) Kashmir for themselves and for their grandchildren. Concern for the future of their children in Britain also inevitably turned to the issue of money and the difficulties of living off 'the dole'. Indeed, the *babas* were less concerned with their personal material well being, and more interested in the future of their children. For many of them, the changes in their life organisation, outlined in the next section, meant that their time was filled and to some extent fulfilled, such that the issue of earning an income became a secondary activity.

Changes in Life Organisation

Look *sardarji*, our story is a simple one. When we worked in the mills we were in the pubs and drank beer and ate kebabs. Now we are out of work we spend our times in mosques saying: 'Allah Allah'. (Haaji Mehrban)

Mehrban's somewhat tongue in cheek statement encapsulates the fact of the shift that the *babas* made from labouring twelve to sixteen hours a day, to spending most of their time at home. This involved a radical change in their lifestyles in terms of arranging the day, general time usage, and their relationships both with friends and families. This section illustrates how religion, extended family and, for some, involvement in community and political associations, became sources of 'work' for the *babas*. In contrast to studies which account for the formation of social, religious and community associations as a 'natural' phenomenon of migrant communities, my central assertion is that unemployment is one of the factors that has led to an increased activity in these areas. Therefore, the formation of Islamic and Pakistani/Kashmiri organisations are not only expressions of 'community' self confidence and development, as Ballard (1994) asserts, but also particular manifestations of the social and economic conditions in which the *babas* found themselves. Werbner (1991) has explored this relationship, in terms of the role of 'community' association in business development. However, her work takes a perspective in which the economic activity is subsumed by or requires certain cultural forms to function. My fieldwork illustrates a process in which cultural agency is continually framed by economic limitations, but nonetheless the crucial issue of agency is not subsumed by economic determinism. Rather, as this section will illustrate, by comparing and contrasting the *babas* situations in the period of full employment with the period post-redundancy, what emerges is an engagement and renewed commitment to a set of activities which act to fill the space once occupied by employment.

The loss of a formal structuring to the day, boredom, a lack of physical activity, and being confined to the home were all mentioned by the *babas* as problems they faced after they found themselves unemployed for a long length of time. Days spent watching South Asian language films and dramas on television, and therefore staying in the house for extended periods of time, were the worse elements of joblessness. These long spells of physical inactivity often resulted in a deterioration of both physical and mental health. At the same time, there were many *babas* who led an active life involved in family and community affairs and for many these activities relieved the boredom of their everyday life. A deep sense of religious commitment meant that the mosque was a regular place for them to go and also a source of socialising. Burnett states: 'Unemployed people may be able to find the satisfactions of work in active leisure, in self provisioning, in voluntary service or political activities, or by engaging in the informal (black) economy' (1994: 296). Burnett's eurocentric perspective misses out the areas of greater involvement in family activities and religious affairs which became the backbone of the *babas'* coping mechanisms.

In the book *Coal, Capital and Culture*, Griffin (1992) notes that certain institutions and networks; churches, pubs, clubs and co-ops, were at the forefront of supporting the newly unemployed miners after the 1984 strike. Comparatively, for the *babas*, the mosque, relatives' and friends' houses and to some extent Kashmiri/Pakistani community associations, were the spaces and networks from which they drew support. Life cycle rituals, such as weddings and funerals, provided long term structure while kin and *biraderi* commitments took up day to day activity. The *babas'* concern with the politics of (Azad) Kashmir, with their land, and extended *biraderi* gave them an extra-local focus, which was outside of the problems of their day to day life in Britain. [6] Perhaps most significantly a renewed commitment to Islam provided a practical structuring of the day, week and year. Furthermore, Islam provided a moral framework for the *babas* with which to understand their predicament as unemployed men in a 'foreign' land.

As previously illustrated, Eid and the issue of praying during work was a point of mobilisation for the Muslim workers in the mills. Once the *babas* became unemployed, the tension between Western industrial and Islamic time was no longer found to be a problem. Islam provided a structuring to time that working in the mills once did. This entailed a division of the day into five zones for prayer times, the week into Friday as a day of rest, prayer and contemplation - which added specific meaning for Thursday evening - and the year revolving around the month of fasting and subsequent celebration of Eid. Whether the *babas*, after they became unemployed, actually prayed five times a day or kept all of their fasts is not actually important. The main point is that they could prescribe to an organisation of their lives which had equal if not greater meaning to the ordering offered by formal employment. During my fieldwork, Ramadan (the Muslim month of fasting) fell during the months of March and April. I was surprised by the difficulty I experienced in finding *babas* to interview during this period. On many occasions, I was told that it was difficult for them to talk to me because they were simply too busy. This was despite being unemployed and therefore supposedly with ample free time. A crucial aspect of Ramadan was the sense of purpose that filled many of the *babas* during the fasting month which was not present during the rest of the year. On a spiritual and practical level, the month generated a great deal of activity, revolving around prayer times and the beginning and end of the fast. During this period the mosque also became a central focus for prayer and meeting.

In terms of social space, the mosque has replaced the mill as a centre of activity. Since the late 1970s and early 1980s there has been a distinct increase of the number of mosques in Oldham, as well as an embellishment of existing mosques. The following account broadly illustrates the point:

Case Study A

> The first mosque in Oldham was set up in the late 1960s in Greengate St in Glodwick. This was followed by other mosques in the early 1970s. Significantly, these were, as in so many other parts of Britain's inner cities, terraced, two up, two down, houses. The expansion and development of mosques in Oldham began in the early 1980s. For example, in 1985, the Nagina mosque committee purchased a disused Co-operative grocery building and converted it into a mosque. The central figures on this committee were retired and semi-retired mill workers and bus drivers. Three months after the Nagina mosque was completed a second mosque, a converted warehouse building, fifty yards from the Nagina mosque was built. Subsequently throughout the 1980s and 1990s purpose built mosques have been built in Oldham's inner city. The most ornate of these being completed in 1995 and located in Glodwick.

A number of differing perspectives have developed to explain the growth and impact of mosques in Britain's cities. Shaw (1988) and Werbner (1991) link these developments to the re-creation of moral spaces by Muslims now that permanent settlement in Britain has become a reality. The development of mosques therefore reflects the maturity of the 'community'. Other accounts have remained more descriptive, focusing on the varied and factional nature of mosque organisation (see Lewis 1994). The themes of Islamic factionalism as a means of producing more mosques has also found wide currency in the anthropological literature (see Shaw 1988; Anwar and Werbner 1991). In contrast, more recent research has attempted to consider the symbolic meaning of mosques in terms of the uses to which they have been put (McLoughlin and Kalra 1994). For many of the *babas* the development of mosques was also driven by a, often rhetorical, need to reproduce and transmit religious and social norms.

Although, in practical terms these institutions find it difficult to fulfil this role. A critique of this inability of mosques to attract the young is found in accounts such as this one from the *Islamic Times*:

> What is the benefit that the Muslim community has gained from so many mosques? ...The thousands from the younger generation are becoming secular. It's discos and not the mosques that are attracting them. ....mosques have become a dead institution in Britain...It is understandable that the first generation of Muslims had very little time at their disposal and could not supervise the mosque administration (The Islamic Times (Stockport) June 1994: 4).

Given the wide academic and public concern with mosques, as illustrated in the above quote it is surprising that few studies have focused on the more mundane, non-religious or non-political aspects of running a mosque. Following from Shams (1993), mosques can serve to replace many of the functions that work once fulfilled, in terms of the organisation of their management and day to day running. Attique Rehman comments on the present situation:

> It would be right to state that if it wasn't for the presence of a large amount of excess *baba* labour there wouldn't be so many mosques.

The functional and humorous nature of this statement belies much of the complexity of the processes involved, but points to the way that mosques have become important sites for *babas'* activity.[7] Despite the protestations of organisations such as the *Islamic Times,* there is need to re-emphasise how poor facilities for the unemployed in Britain actually are. This is also the case for white groups, let alone for racialised and aged groups.[8] If the mosque provides this source of activity for the *babas* then it is to be welcomed rather than criticised.

The management and organisation of mosques, especially at festival times such as Eid, provides ample work for those involved in their day to day running. From the payment of electricity bills to overseeing the activities of the *maulvi* (religious instructor), to organising evening Koran reading and Urdu language classes, the mosque provides the sort of activities which are both 'busy' in the sense of time-consuming and more significantly status conveying. For instance, the piety which can be evoked by doing voluntary service for the mosque is second only to going on *hajj* (pilgrimage).

A mosque can also be viewed as one of a number of voluntary activities that the *babas* became increasingly involved in throughout the 1980s. [9] This period also witnessed a blooming of voluntary organisations once again reflecting the availability of recently redundant mill workers. Adalat Ali has written about the development of the Pakistani community centre in Oldham:

> In the case of the Pakistanis there were twenty voluntary organisations which were vouching for representational control, reflecting the large size and diverse nature of the population (majority Mirpuri- Azad Kashmiri, but also sizeable Pathan and Punjabi populations). These organisations were run by emigrant Pakistanis, usually unemployed mill workers and were quite involved in politics in Pakistan, some were also primarily associated with the promotion of *Pirs* (spiritual leaders) (Ali 1993:20).

The development of large centres such as the Pakistani Community Centre should not imply that there were no welfare organisations in Oldham during the early 1970s. An exhibition in Oldham libraries in 1994 focused on one such organisation, the Pakistani Welfare Association, and illustrated how it had been active since the 1970s. [10] However, greater participation in and the proliferation of voluntary groups was related to the availability of people with time to be actively involved in them and this took place during the 1980s.

Increased involvement in mosques and in other voluntary activities certainly occupied the *babas,* perhaps more importantly it also allowed them to be involved in an alternative world from work, which had its own rules of status and time structure. In a similar manner active involvement in voluntary organisations and local party politics was a source of influence over the direction of their local *biraderi* and their welfare. Active involvement of this sort tended to be restricted to a group of *babas* who would appear and reappear in a variety of different contexts. [11] For instance a mosque committee would only have fifteen to twenty members whereas its congregation would run into the hundreds. Attendance and organisation therefore need to be distinguished in this context. In terms of *babas'* main time commitments, it is to the family and the *biraderi* which is more pervasive.

Family Commitments

In towns like Oldham, large kinship groups of (Azad) Kashmiris living in close proximity to each other mean that there is an almost endless source of activity related to family in the everyday sense and in terms of life cycle rituals. For the *babas* active involvement with their own family could involve mundane and routine tasks such as grocery shopping, picking up grandchildren from school, and paying bills. For example, between three-thirty and four p.m. was another time in which it was difficult to find a *baba* to interview. This was the time that grandchildren would be picked up from school, perhaps dropped off at mosque school, from where they would be picked up later on in the evening. Everyday responsibilities to immediate family were interspersed with births, deaths and funerals in the extended family. Funerals, in particular, illustrate how an institution has developed and changed from the period of full employment to long term unemployment. In a similar manner, other life cycle rituals have become more significant both in terms of attendance and organisation.

In terms of funerals, a note on their general structure is needed in order to fully appreciate the changes that have taken place from mills to mosques. Once a person has been declared dead, the family house is prepared for mourning. The *mattam* (mourning) period can last from between three to five days. Men and women mourn in separate spaces. Family and friends visit the mourning house to offer prayers and condolences. After the mourning period, the body, accompanied by family members, is usually sent back to (Azad) Kashmir for burial.[12] During the mill period, funerals and mourning did take place, but their occurrence and structure fit around working times in the mills. Sunday, was the primary day for fulfilling these obligations with only close family members attending funerals on other days and subsequently to go to (Azad) Kashmir with the body. Two prominent areas of change have occurred in the period of unemployment, both of which involved greater time involvement and commitment in the funeral process. The first is illustrated by this complaint made to me by a young man at a *mattam* I attended:

> The old men just use the *mattam* as an excuse to have a gossip. They should be more respectful, go in, do their prayer, sit for fifteen minutes and then be on their way. Otherwise they will obviously get bored and want to gossip (Nadeem Khan).

The *mattam* is an ideal place to sit and meet with relatives and friends in the locality as well as to wile away a day. *Babas* from other parts of the country, often themselves unemployed, would attend as well, so the funeral provides an opportunity to meet relatives and friends. A second trend in

Oldham was the practice of holding a *mattam* for a relative who had died in (Azad) Kashmir. In the mill period, the effect of a death in Mirpur would involve close family members leaving Oldham to attend the funeral in (Azad) Kashmir. The death would not result in four or five days of official mourning in Britain, though people would obviously visit the family to give condolence. This is a sharp contrast to the present, where a death in Mirpur can result in elaborate mourning in Britain. The practice of mourning in Britain for a person who died in (Azad) Kashmir is a subtle reflection of the way in which a renewed commitment to a 'cultural' institution is closely related to the availability of people and time. Attendance at funerals, in contemporary Oldham, has become an obligation for the *babas*. In a similar manner to Eid, there were many times when I had arranged to interview someone and on arrival at their house, a family member would tell me that the interviewee had to leave in a hurry because a relative had died in Bradford or Derby.

Funeral attendance is only one aspect of an enhanced commitment and responsibility by the *babas* shown towards their families. Two other areas of concern were also reflected through the family. The first was the perceived lack of respect from young people towards them and the second was their own personal predicament. Moral panic about the young will be considered in the next section. The *babas* concern with their own predicament revolved around the issue of belonging, specifically where the *babas* felt most at home. In practical terms, their problem was simply that their families were 'divided', that is with some members in Mirpur and some in England. Indeed, one of the central reasons for the sending of bodies back to (Azad) Kashmir for burial was to enable the deceased to be buried in the family graveyard. The notion of divided families was a considerable source of tension for many of the *babas*. It complicated a simple desire to return to Mirpur and ultimately to die and be buried there. As one *baba* put it to me:

> *Sardarji*, when I die, where should my grave be ? Half of my family is here, half in Mirpur. If my grave is there, then my family here will be sad, if it is here then I will be buried in a foreign land. Allah ! What shall I do? (Nawaz Karim).

In the 1990s, those *babas* who returned to Mirpur were going as pensioners. Even though pensioners were not faced with the problems of setting up a business, as outlined in a previous section, very few actually managed to stay in Mirpur on a permanent basis. As Ballard (1985) notes, issues of health care and the fact that children and grandchildren were permanently settled in Britain were serious considerations for the *babas*. This was particularly the case in Oldham where whole *biraderis*, sometimes up to five hundred families in size, were now living in towns throughout England. Baba Quyuum's statement is telling:

> Home is where your family is. Most of my family are here, why do I want to go and live there? Yes of course I miss my land, but then what are we to do?

A feeling of being trapped, in some way unable to feel settled in Mirpur or England haunted and troubled many of the *babas* I talked to. They were not really happy in England, but they were also aware that, in the light of their age and health, Mirpur was a difficult place to live. Dawood Khan's response to a question about leaving Mirpur is telling:

> I haven't left my country [Mirpur]. I have a house there. I have land there. I would like to go back and live there, but this is up-to the *maalik* (God). I would like to go and die there, but this is also up to God. There are so many men who only go back in the coffin. There is a desire to go, but with my family here, what can I do. I go every few years and even the children went, but they were very ill. The little girl said that I don't want to go. She was so ill.

The possibility of spending time in both Mirpur and Britain seems the obvious solution to the tension that so many of the *babas* expressed in their lives in Britain. However, this route relies on the ability to afford airfares and the general costs of travel which, in the light of the general economic status of Pakistanis in Oldham restricts the possibility. For a minority of *babas*, the option of shifting base to Mirpur, effectively reversing the international commuter status of their early years in Britain, meant visiting Britain for family events as they once visited Mirpur. This could vary from a few months to years in Mirpur followed by a few months in England. An additional incentive to this process is that pension payments can be made overseas. However, these do not increase with the rate of inflation and the only way to update the pension is to regularly re-register in Britain for it. This was therefore another reason, alongside marriages and family visits to visit England. Baba Khan's case is illustrative of this process:

> I came to this country thirty-one years ago. Having spent six to seven years

in the army before partition, I served all over India and Iraq. I have five boys and five girls; two girls (married) and three boys here, with two boys and three girls in Kashmir with my wife. I've just spent nine months there and have come back to sort my pension out. I've not got it yet, but I should be due it from this year. Habib Bank send the money direct to Kashmir. None of my children are working in this country. I have a younger son in Germany. He has his own shop there, my elder son buys from Britain and they then sell it in Germany. I've been sick for the last fifteen years and last year I had a heart attack.

The narratives presented throughout this chapter illustrate how the *babas* have managed to offset the more negative consequences of unemployment runs by an engagement in religious and family affairs. The statistical picture of high unemployment and spatial concentration in infrastructurally 'deprived' areas distorts the means and ways in which collective actions can offset the more long term financial, social and psychological impacts of long term unemployment.[13] However, in making this argument it is also necessary to recognise, that in explaining their world, the *babas* expressed a profound sense of depression. The main source of this was a perception of a breakdown in society and general moral decay, especially amongst young people.

Moral Change - Ways of Explaining the World

In my interviews with the *babas*, our conversations would begin with their experiences of work, move through the period of redundancy and then come to rest on their contemporary lives. These conversations would often take convoluted paths, but would almost always end up with an explanation of their views of the contemporary world. These focused on the decline that they perceived had taken place over the last twenty years in the moral fibre of British society in general, and of Muslim youth in particular. These discourses were framed by reference to an Islamic moral framework and a general sense of persecution towards Muslims in the modern world. Their analysis of the lack of discipline and respect amongst Muslim youth was closely related to this group's lack of employment opportunities and feelings of being unwanted. Sentiments of moral decay and youth alienation are also present in the narratives of white working class men who have suffered from long-term unemployment. The congruence of white working class men and *babas* in terms of their concerns with moral decay, breakdown of community and the future of the young, diverges in terms of explanation of these circumstances. For the *babas,* Islam offered a means of understanding their predicament, whereas for many secular, white working class men, a similar framework was not present.

The theme of moral decline was illustrated by the *babas* in terms of the decline in the quality of their relationships with family and friends. Razak explains the predicament:

> You see, *sardarji, pyar kat giya* (the love between people has lessened). When we first came here, we lived and worked together. We had time for each other. Now even your brother is too busy to see you. We have lost our sense of duty to each other. *Allah-tallah* has said that these are the signs of a coming *quiyaamat* (judgement day), when family relationships break up and people live in barbarism. Look at Bosnia and Kashmir.......We came here to work and then to go back, but look at us now. We are stuck not of here nor of there. When I first came here I thought I would make 18-20000 Rs and go back home and now I think I'll make 30-35 lakhs and go home. The gap between what you've got and what you want always remains the same no matter what you have achieved. It is basically greed which is keeping us all here.

Similar issues emerged in interviews carried out by Seabrook with white unemployed people:

> Among these losses, apart from the damaged sense of function [as workers], have been some of the humanising responses to that older poverty, the solidarity and working people of values - dignity, frugality, stoicism - which offered an alternative to the brutalising destructive values of capitalism (Seabrook 1982: 221).

A crucial difference in these two sets of narratives is the way in which the world is explained. Many of the *babas*, when asked why they felt a sense of moral decline and injustice at their position in England, inevitably referred to the coming of *quiyaamat* and to the fact that as Muslims they were being oppressed everywhere. The issues of Kashmir, Bosnia and, in more recent times, Chechnya were paramount concerns in many of the conversations I had with the *babas*. There is no doubting that there was a sense of connection to these places, helped along by daily television news broadcasts and reports in the *Daily Jang*.[14] Razak was clear in his opinions when asked why he thought the world was in such a bad state:

> It is the coming of the *quiyaamat*. In our Koran, that which Allah has sent

to us. When you read it and look around you, you see that these are the things that are written. It says that there will be fighting all around, people will not relate to each other, especially amongst close relatives. These are the signs of *quiyaamat*. These signs are everywhere. That there will be fighting in mosques and this is happening. That the houses and the mosques will be *pacca* (permanent), but there will be no-one to read *namaz*. You see this in our village as well as here.

For the white men interviewed by Seabrook, the ability to understand and rationalise their position was met by a sense of despair rather than a renewed commitment to any cause or faith.

The increase in violence, disturbance and destructiveness among the young, which puzzles so many people, seems to have more to do with the obliterated function [as workers] of which they are the inheritors than with an insufficiency of money to buy all the things that are supposed to constitute the 'full' life (Seabrook 1982: 9).

The only possible analysis of this situation is despondency, Seabrook continues:

And yet, in all working-class communities, so many of them ravaged now by the extinction of their original industrial function, people have been talking ever since I can remember about their sense of loss (Seabrook 1982: 32).

Seabrook (1982), in this study, also interviews unemployed Pakistani workers in Balsall Heath - Birmingham. He finds that strength of religious belief gave the Pakistani workers a sense of purpose which he found was missing amongst the white workers.

Despite the ability to rationalise their position, the *babas'* greatest sense of loss is related to young people, and especially young men. Iqbal Rehman sums up widespread feelings amongst the *babas*.

The children *vigre ge* (are spoilt). Here in Glodwick all they do is sell drugs and thieve, even though it is true that 'if one person in a village is a thief then the whole village gets to be known as the village of thieves'. Another big problem here is single parents, there are too many of them. We have uneducated parents marrying their daughters and sons to people from Mirpur and then they get divorced. It is the fault of parents that these boys are in such a bad state. They have no sense of responsibility, they won't go to weddings or to *mattams* unless forced.

Worry about the future of young people in the light of high levels of youth unemployment, a growing drug youth sub-culture and alienation from society preoccupied the *babas*. For the majority, one of their primary motivations for migration was to provide a 'better' life for their families. The inability to deliver this therefore affected the *babas* in both emotional and physical terms.

Work to Non-Work

The impact on the *babas* of the shift from fields to textile mills to the 'dole office' in the space of one generation is difficult to gauge. It would be relatively easy to carry out research with a group of *babas* and not take into account these historic changes. Given their daily involvement with the Mosque and with their family, it would also be a simple task to assign this to a continuity with cultural norms and practices from 'back home'. This would be missing out a critical aspect of the reconstruction of practice and renewal of commitments. The radical changes in environment that the *babas* experienced are sufficient cause to note that contemporary commitments to religion and family are not only a defensive posturing to a hostile host society but the result of an active engagement with their conditions. Obviously, unemployment is not the only significant factor - other authors have pointed to family reunion and the need for recreating moral orders (Ballard 1994). But there is a need to forward recognition that the *babas'* economic status is a consequential element in the process of reinvention of tradition.[15]

Upto this point, the focus has been on the *babas*, and in many senses, the material covering mill work has been a reconstructed history from their memories and what few records are available. In ending this chapter with the contemporary situation of the *babas,* the focus has moved from a work place to other spaces which to some extent have become work-like. The *babas* may have become redundant from the formal labour market, but this has led to other activities rather than outright despondency. This contemporary focus continues in the next two chapters, but my concerns return to the workplace and to the working lives of the *kakas*. Redundancy from mill work and the issues covered in these last two chapters relating to difficulties in finding formal employment are pertinent to the *kakas'* experiences. However, the next two chapters are more concerned with the types of employment and the comparison with working life in the mills.

---

[1] See Appendix I.

[2] Ballard (1987) characterises this movement as a search for economic security in either England or (Azad) Kashmir and in fact not being able to find it in either place.

[3] *The Oldham Social Survey 1995*, travel to work data reveals that 23% of Pakistanis from Oldham work in Manchester. The full breakdown is available in Appendix II.

[4] It can be argued that literacy amongst white people in these kinds of jobs would also be low. English language skills should therefore refer more specifically to the spoken word.

[5] Werbner (1990) and Shaw (1988) also refer to *komittees* in their work. But these are run by women for the purposes of gift-giving. In contrast, the largest funeral *komittee* in Oldham had 734 members, across England. Though this was unusual in terms of its size.

[6] This overcomes one of the main psychological impacts of long term unemployment, where the man loses regard for the outside world (see Jahoda 1979).

[7] It is crucial to recognise the significance of events such as the Rushdie Affair, the War in the Gulf and the continuing situation in Kashmir to a renewed sense of commitment to Islam.

[8] See Mc Laughlin, W. (ed.) (1992) *Understanding Unemployment: New Perspectives On Active Labour Market Policies.*

[9] In contrast to Werbner (1991) who argues for a distinction between mosques, Community Centres and Local Authority arenas, the crucial point is that those men who are active in one sphere tend to be in the others as well. There is therefore an implicit overlap between the various fields of activity.

[10] This exhibition stands as an alternative public history of Oldham. From the first Pakistan Day celebrations in the city in 1976, a series of events are portrayed illustrating the work of the organisation. It is available from the Leisure Services Department of Oldham Metropolitan Borough Council.

[11] Indeed, the three areas of mosque, community association, and local politics outlined by Werbner (1994) in terms of Pakistani associations tend to involve an overlap of the same people.

[12] Oldham does have a Muslim burial ground, but in 1994 its primary use remained for the burial of children and on those occasions where the deceased had made a specific request to be buried in Oldham.

[13] In this sense the culturalist perspective outlined in Chapter One allows us to recognise the way in which the *babas* coped with structural hindrances.

[14] a) These conversations would be passionate on days that the BBC or ITV actually reported something on the events in these parts of the world.

b) The Daily Jang is an Urdu/English newspaper. It has the widest daily circulation of any South Asian publication in Britain.

[15] This is especially so with the increased commitment to Islam which has arisen from a much wider and complex set of reasons.

8 Take-Away Lives

Introduction

In the previous three chapters a historical map of the working lives of the *babas* and *kakas* was traced from working full time in the mills of Oldham to long-term unemployment. The *babas'* experiences of migration and of finding work in Britain provided the basis for their sons to come and work in England. Following their fathers' footsteps into the mills, the *kakas* retraced a route, previously taken by white daughters joining their mothers and grandmothers in the mills of the North West. When work in the mills began to decline the *kakas* faced similar problems to the *babas* when it came to finding work. However, the option of retirement was not there and the need to take on the responsibility of income generation became paramount. Hampered by poor training and lack of transferable skills, the *kakas* faced many of the same problems that the *babas* did. However, their better knowledge of English and in some cases access to their fathers' savings meant they had greater opportunities for finding work or setting up in business. The next two chapters illustrate the *kakas* working patterns which revolved around attempts at business activity followed by periods of employment and then further attempts at self-employment.

Entry into self-employment and the general working cycles of the kakas illustrates two theoretical themes that have come of recent academic interest. Firstly the literature on small business development amongst South Asian groups that builds on the broader theme of ethnic entrepreneurship. This notion is examined here with a case study of the establishment of a take-away businesses. Even though aspects of the business development argument are also present in the next chapter, the main theoretical concern there is to assess the extent to which the shift in working patterns from secure employment with little flexibility to high risk employment with a lot of flexibility is illustrative of Beck's (1992) notion of a risk society. Once again elements of the 'risk society' thesis are also present in the outline of business development presented in this chapter but the main focus is on business development.

South Asian Entrepreneurship

The Employment Gazette of March 1991 claims that only five million of Britain's workforce were employed in manufacturing with nearly sixteen million in the service sector. Approximately four and a half million of the group employed in the service sector were in distribution, hotels, catering and repairs, almost as many as in the whole of manufacturing. [1] This miscellaneous services sector also has the greatest concentration of self-employed people. Oldham has mirrored these national changes, but retained a considerable manufacturing sector. The Oldham Economic Development Unit's *Fact File For 1991* states the changes:

> Manufacturing activities, public administration, education and health and distribution, hotels and restaurants sectors amount for a large proportion of total employment in the borough. Oldham employs proportionally more people in manufacturing and within distribution, hotels and restaurants sector than both the national and regional averages (Oldham EDU 1991: 18-19). [2]

The general shift in the British economy towards the service sector sets the context for the particular growth in self-employment amongst South Asian groups.

Contemporary academic studies of economic activity and South Asians in Britain have concentrated on self-employment and entrepreneurial business development. [3] As Cater and Jones point out: 'Over the past decade or so, Asians have acquired an unshakeable reputation as entrepreneurs, a group whose future is that of the new Jews' (1988: 182). This concern has led to the development of a centre for the study of Asian businesses at the Roehampton Institute and a range of studies on South Asian business development. Despite this broad concern, studies of the phenomenon have paid an overt attention to retailing, while restaurants, take-aways, taxi-drivers and other areas of business activity have been somewhat neglected. Large surveys of Asian shopkeepers in various towns throughout Britain have constructed a somewhat limited model of the Asian entrepreneur (see Aldrich et al 1981; Jenkins and Ward 1984). The central concern of these studies has been to explain Asian entry into self-employment either in terms of an active choice to enhance mobility or as a result of limited opportunities in other parts of the labour market. In separate studies of Oxford and Coventry, Srinivasan (1995) and Basu (1995), respectively, both maintain that entry into business for South

Asians is the result of a conscious decision to 'improve' themselves. A similar account is given about Asian businesses in Leicester:

> The overall growth of ethnic minority business in Leicestershire can be attributed not to a transfer of business experience from East Africa nor the lack of job opportunities but to the positive desire of owners to be independent and to make money (Soni et al ix:: 1987).

In contrast the findings of *The Ethnic Business and Community Needs* report based on a study in Bradford carried out in the mid eighties found that the reasons for business entry for most Asians in the city was a result of negative push factors :

> A combination of deindustrialisation and racial discrimination in the job market has created unacceptably high rates of unemployment and underemployment for ethnic minorities, making self-employment an attractive option (1989: 1).

There is, evidently, no consistent set of reasons for South Asian entry into business which can be applied across a range of geographical locations or ethnicised groups. For instance, Pakistanis in Manchester form a group of successful businessmen in Werbner's (1990) accounts, whereas, Rafiq (1992) relates previous business experience as the most significant factor accounting for business entry in Bradford. Other studies view South Asian entry into self-employment as a result of the need to avoid racial discrimination and a confinement to low status jobs in the labour market (Aldrich et al 1982; Ram 1992). Experiences of racism in the wider labour market are, therefore, an additional factor in pushing some members of ethnic minorities into self-employment. Hence, their entry into self-employment is seen as a 'damage limitation' exercise to avoid unemployment (Aldrich et al 1984). Further evidence to support this view is provided by Ward and Jenkins (1984). In their survey of Asian businesses they argue that self-employment is an 'economic dead-end' with long hours of work and generally low returns.

Another area of interest concerns the use of labour in South Asian owned businesses. One of the repeated themes in the literature is the availability of extended family labour, which offsets the cost of production by acting as a source of free or cheap labour (Ward and Aldrich 1981). Indeed, this is seen as the main 'ethnic resource' and the central competitive advantage that these businesses have over others. However, Phizacklea

(1988) notes that this labour is often female and not made transparent in assessment of labour costs.[4] It can be argued that:

> The success of the male ethnic entrepreneur is at the expense of the health and well being of the women in the household and does not result in a general improvement in the life experiences of women workers (Afshar 1989: 224).

At the same time family labour with marginal status, whether female, or young men or *mangeters*, may feel they are contributing to the overall well being of their extended kin network, even thought this may be at their individual cost (Werbner 1990; Westwood 1984).

In a useful review of this literature Modood et al (1996) forward the need for an approach which takes into account factors of 'cultural' resources as well as the wider labour market. Developing Waldinger et al (1990) the suggestion is that to understand minority business requires looking at both opportunity structures in the labour market as well as group characteristics. This perspective still falls into the problems of the priorities associated to different factors, and Modood et al's (1996) work tends to rely on simplistic ethnic categorisations. Perhaps more fundamentally, there is still the empirical problem of the focus on retailing in much of literature on Asian businesses. These studies do not consider the self-employed status of taxi drivers nor the business ownership of taxi ranks and take-aways, both of which have long been entries into business ownership for immigrants and providers of low level service sector work for waiters and receptionists. Indeed, the patterns of working that this kind of business activity generates has also not been satisfactorily explored. By describing the setting up of a take-away, in some detail this chapter pushes the self-employment debate into some new directions.

After the Mills

An economic profile of the Pakistani male population in the early 1990s in Oldham reveals rates of unemployment in excess of thirty percent, a rate which is almost three times higher than the borough average. Fewer men are in full time employment than the borough average, with a larger percentage registered as self-employed. This higher rate of self-employment is one of the main areas of concern for this chapter.[5] It is very difficult to ascertain occupational breakdown for a small population in one area of the country from Census analysis. However, by considering broad social class categorisations, it is found that Pakistanis are most concentrated in the areas of, 'manual workers, skilled foremen, supervisors and self-employed' and 'personal service and semi-skilled manual workers'. These broad classifications include taxi drivers, take-away owners, as well as textile workers and would, therefore, confirm the significance of these areas of income generation. This section is concerned with the process by which a group of industrial workers found themselves unemployed and therefore in need of a means of income generation. Clearly, this was not an overnight or short term phenomenon. It took place over a period of a few years.

Decline in the textile mills occurred at the same time as massive unemployment throughout the manufacturing industry. A large number of white men were therefore available for working in the remaining factories. Discrimination against racialised minorities, lack of work for which they were qualified and a general shortage of jobs were all factors towards the *kakas* high levels of unemployment. Nawaz is eloquent in describing this time:

> My father was working in the Lilac Mill and I worked with him for two years. My younger brother was in school for a year after we got here and then he started working in the mills as well. Then I saw that the factories were closing down. This is around 1979-80, when things in the economy were really bad. Factories were closing down everywhere. Some of my friends were out of work. I realised that I was not going to make it in the mills. I also saw that having a market stall was not going to be very easy either. I knew some people in Manchester who had market stalls, that was too tough. Most people at that time were thinking of getting into shop keeping, of buying a shop. Trying to get some security.

As the 1980s progressed and more men became redundant and experienced difficulty in finding employment, a general perception formed amongst the *kakas* that formal employment was not going to be available. In light of this, the choices were simple and limited: employment in jobs with low pay, welfare benefits or self-employment. Attique Rehman describes his situation:

> I was working in the mills until 1982, then I was made redundant. I went to the job centre and then worked in a warehouse, packing. But the *gore* treated me badly. I was the only Pakistani in the place. So I left and then worked for Udin Textiles in Oldham. But it was dog's work and the money was no good. Now I have my own taxi.

The main source of factory employment for the *kakas* was to work in the clothing sector either in Manchester or Ashton. These manufacturing units were generally owned by Pakistanis or other South Asians. The conditions of work in these places were often so bad that many of the men actively sought other work, were saving money for a taxi or left at the first opportunity they were given. Tariq Khan's story is illustrative:

> I left Aleck Mill in 1987 and went to work in Manchester. The owner was an Indian and the work was ironing the clothes after the women had sewn them. They had video cameras on the floor to watch the workers. They treated us like dogs for shit money. If you stopped for one minute for a cigarette, the owner's wife would come and shout at you. I tried to get people to complain, but they were all *mangeters*, both the men and women. The owner threatened them with deportation if they said anything or made a noise. I only stayed there for two months.

Tariq's experience in the Manchester 'rag trade' is more common amongst male *mangeters* and other groups with little possibilities of alternative employment who, for a variety of reasons, are tied in with the employer. [6]

Racism from white manufacturing companies and poor conditions in Asian owned factories meant that the *kakas* often used these jobs as an opportunity to save enough money to gain entry into the world of self-employment, more specifically into retailing, taxi driving or the restaurant/take-away business. Studies of Asian self-employment have tended to focus on retailing. [7] The necessity of shops catering to the specific dietary and clothing needs of the Asian population has created a niche market which Asians have occupied since the mid-sixties. In towns such as Oldham these material needs were met, initially, by shops in Manchester and Bradford. The first Asian grocery shop was established in Oldham some time in the early 1960s by a Gujerati Indian, who is no longer resident in the town. The first shop opened by a *baba* was in the late 1960s, a grocery shop with the crucial element of the provision of halal meat. Long established shops in inner city Oldham tended to be owned by families who had some experience of shop keeping in (Azad) Kashmir and as such the majority of business were owned by Punjabi/Pakistanis. [8] During my fieldwork, I carried out a survey of twenty-five retail outlets in the Werneth and Coppice area and about twenty-five market stalls in Tommyfield market. [9] My intention was to gauge how many of the owners were ex-mill workers and the extent to which the hierarchical divide between Mirpuris and Punjabis, that had manifested in the mills in terms of the foreman - worker relationship, had reappeared in terms of shop ownership. Only seven of the twenty-five retail outlets were owned by (Azad) Kashmiris of which three were owned by ex-mill workers. The other shops in inner city Oldham were owned either by Punjabi/Pakistanis or by other South Asian groups. [10] Of the market stalls only two were being run by (Azad) Kashmiris while the rest were run by Punjabi/Pakistanis who were, by and large, not resident in Oldham and also attended several other markets in the region. In addition to confirming the hierarchy between owners and workers, which is also present in the manufacturing sector in Manchester, this survey also highlights the problem of focusing on retailing when considering a survey of the Mirpuri/(Azad) Kashmiri self-employed.

Ownership, of the clothing factories that the *kakas* went to work for in Manchester and of most retail outlets and other businesses in the region, is dominated by Indians and Punjabi/Pakistanis. This division highlights the point made in the Methodology chapter and the general thrust of this book, specifying Mirpuris/(Azad) Kashmiris in certain contexts as a separate group from Pakistani. The hierarchical line between owners and workers in the new self-employed business sector generally falls between Punjabi/Pakistanis and Mirpuri/(Azad) Kashmiris This is illustrated, even in the case of taxi ranks which tend to be owned by Punjabis with cars driven by Mirpuris, a point which will be taken up in the next chapter. Here, the case study of a take-away business helps to highlight the multiple problems associated with entry into the catering business and brings to the forefront issues relating to interactions with customers. Implicit in the narratives about take-aways is a comparison with life in the textile mills, specifically, whether life has changed for the better or worse varied according to individual experience, but general shifts in the organisation of time has affected all the men.

Take-aways

Take-aways, serving a variety of food from chips to chicken *korma* and rice, have become a feature of the urban landscape in Britain's cities, towns and rural high streets. They serve a varied clientele of pubbers and clubbers hungry for post-alcohol food, taxi drivers eating their midnight snacks, and the dial-a- curry brigade, preferring to have their chicken *biryani* and *naan* delivered to their homes rather than travel to a restaurant.

Poor cousins to the 'Indian' restaurant, the take-away has slowly come to replace the fish and chip shop as a source of convenient, cheap and filling food. This comparison is poignant given the historical claim by Lancashire to be the home of fish and chips. [11] In households where women worked in the textile mills, fish and chips on Friday night provided a welcome rest for women, who would be expected to fulfil domestic duties as well as a shift in the mill. One hundred years on, Wilmslow Road in Manchester can boast to be the home of the take-away kebab, while even Oldham has approximately twenty establishments. [12]

In contrast to cities such as Bradford, Manchester and Birmingham, Oldham's take-aways did not develop from a need to provide food for South Asian workers, hungry after their shifts in the mills. [13] The first take-away in Oldham opened in 1981 and was managed by a man from Lahore, Pakistan who already owned two take-aways in Manchester. It was located on Union Street, next door to two taxi stands. Other take-aways sprung up throughout the eighties primarily as the demand for 'Asian' food increased from the white clientele, and it became apparent to ex-mill workers that this was a business opportunity. Take-aways in Oldham offer fish and chips, American fried chicken, 'Genuine' Italian pizzas, hamburgers, curries and, of course, kebabs. In fact, there is now an almost generic range of take-away food, with few speciality fish and chip shops left. The majority of the take-aways earn their income from the predominantly white clientele, though for some, South Asian taxi-drivers are also an important source of revenue, despite the fact that for the owners' friends, food tends to be subsidised.

From working in taxis to being a waiter in a take-away to selling goods on a market stall to unemployment and back again is a pattern of occupational transfer that is commonplace with the *kakas* and to some extent the lads of Oldham. The take-away is an important way for a *kaka*, with a little capital, to set up in business. Similarly, those men working in the take-away after gaining experience could set up their own take-away, as an alternative route to self-employment. The intense competition in a relatively fixed market and a misplaced sense that hard work is all that is needed to make a business succeed meant that these establishments would often close down after six to nine months. [14] Many of these men would end up working back on the taxi ranks or in other people's take-aways. Simplistic accounts of minority business trajectories fail to account for the non-linear pattern of working and cycles of set-up and failure that are common in places like Oldham. Indeed, the central question of business entry so prominent in the literature on South Asian business development is relatively insignificant when considered as part of a cycle of unemployment, part-time employment, self-employment, unemployment, part-time employment etc.. It is the flux and fragmentation of the working career which is of more significance rather than the fact that self-employment features as a factor. Cheema's story is a pertinent example:

> I came from Bhimber in 1976 and worked in a mill. I got married and came here as a *mangeter*. I was made redundant in 1982. Some of my friends from the mill, they had a taxi. So while I was working in the mill I would sometimes take their taxi. It was an okay job and the money was cash in hand, so when I was made redundant I used my friends taxi until I had enough money to get my own. I drove for about two years. Then a relative of mine, who owned a take-away in Shaw had to go to Mirpur on urgent business. He asked me if I wanted to run it. I jumped at the chance. Then he told me if I gave him a bit of money I could have the place. I ran the place for nine months, then there was a family of *gore* in the area, they gave us trouble before, but one day there was a big fight with them. We thought: 'fuck this' and closed the place down. I'm working at Rose of Kashmir take-away now and thinking about driving taxis again.

The quick turnover of owners over short periods of time characterises the take-away business in Oldham.

Take-aways tend to be located close to taxi ranks, reflecting the importance of that clientele in the late hours of the night and their city centre/high street locations. In Oldham there are two main areas of concentration of both take-aways and taxi ranks, Union Street and Yorkshire Street, both of which are located in the central shopping area. Take-aways in other parts of the town tend to be on main roads alongside other shops or next to out of city centre taxi ranks. Taxi driving and take-away work have become as ubiquitous amongst Pakistani/(Azad) Kashmiri males as mill work once was. Both jobs have low entry levels in terms of skill and capital with little need for re-training or interaction with white owned business. On the other hand, low pay, long hours, and considerable interaction with, often hostile, white customers are also common characteristics to both jobs. On the latter point, these interactions can often be marked by conflict and violence, and each job comes with a certain level of personal risk. But it is also necessary to note that these jobs offer flexibility in working time, cash in hand, and the ability -for taxi drivers at least- to see themselves as self-employed. Factors, which for some of the drivers, balanced the negative aspects of the job.

Before considering a detailed case study of the rise and fall of a take-away it is useful to distinguish between the owners of take-aways and the people who work in them. In a take-away this is a relatively simple task, as there is usually one owner with a group of workers. The chef is the best paid of the staff with young lads serving at the bottom of the hierarchy (Yiannis 1988). However, the simple distinction of owner and worker is blurred by the fact that all the men work together and are related to each other by a multiple number of relationships. Brother, cousins and *biraderi* members are only the most obvious of these relationships. Less apparent but equally salient are former mill working mates, business partners, villagers or long standing friends. The fluid and changing nature of these relationships amongst owners and staff was reflected in the rapid turnover of staff and ownership in these businesses.

The Maharaba

In this section I illustrate some general points about take-aways in Oldham by reference to one case study. The 'Maharaba' take-away came into existence in December 1993 and closed down in December 1994. This period spans my fieldwork and therefore the case of the Maharaba gives an insight into the setting up, running and ultimate demise of a take-away. It also sheds an ethnographic light on the questions addressed in much of the South Asian self-employment literature about reasons for business entry, the type of businesses set up and the factors for lack of business success.

Location plays a crucial part in the success or failure of a take-away. If the premises are near a pub or night-club in the city centre or by a taxi rank, the business has a better chance of success, and this is reflected in the price paid for premises. During my fieldwork ready-fitted take-aways changed hands more often than conversions from other premises, though even in these cases, the owner could procure ovens, shop counters and other equipment in a thriving second hand market. Capital commitment to start a take-away can then vary from as little as a few thousand pounds, for goodwill and rent of premises, to over twenty thousand pounds for a full refurbishment.

Case Study

The 'Maharaba' is a kebab and fish and chip outlet near a large night club in Oldham which was taken over by Tariq Khan in December 1993. Tariq is from Mirpur. He came to England in 1972, as a twelve year old, and went to a local comprehensive school until he was fifteen. He left school with no qualifications and worked in the mills until he was made redundant in 1985. He tried his hand at taxis, but didn't like the hours or the risks and then worked as a waiter in a few take-aways. The Maharaba was his first venture in owning and running a take-away. His relatives are the owners of Silver Star take-away which is reputedly the most profitable take-away in the city. Tariq paid £2000 in goodwill for the premises and equipment and pays £500 month for the lease of the premises. His experience of running a business is minimal, though he has gained knowledge of the take-away business from working in other take-aways.

In the context of Oldham take-aways, the Maharaba in terms of decor, clientele and turnover fell somewhere in the middle range. It never became as successful as the Silver Star take-away which was acknowledged by most of the other owners as the most profitable take-away in the town. [15] At the same time, it was not at the kind of basic level that, for instance, the 'Rose of Kashmir' fell into. This establishment was located next to a taxi rank and a private nite-club, a little distance out of the city centre. The premises were distinctly basic and this was reflected in the prices and the quality of the food on offer. In terms of location and general facilities, the Maharaba was therefore well suited to develop into a stable business. The next stage in its setting up was the employment of staff.

Owners of take-away businesses in Oldham tended to be *kakas*, with moral and financial support from *babas* and physical help from close relatives, usually other *kakas*. The lowest paid members of staff would often be young men between sixteen and twenty-five, the lads, who would earn cash in hand and often be signing on or attending college at the same time. These lads were often themselves related to the owner, but were nevertheless usually treated poorly and were the most mobile in terms of taking and leaving jobs. In competition with these young men, *mangeters* would also work in the same conditions as the lads. [16] Indeed they formed a major source of competition to the lads for this kind of work. Often with young families, male *mangeters* were deemed to be more reliable than the young lads who were not usually in dire need of money.

Central to the whole operation was the chef who, by and large, would be Sylheti/Bangladeshi and commanded the best salary. Some of the older more experienced (Azad) Kashmiri take-away owners had learnt the trade and prepared the 'curries' themselves, saving the business a considerable amount in salaries. However, the predominant pattern was to employ a Sylheti/Bangladeshi chef. He would also be the most knowledgeable member of staff in terms of availability of work and comparative salaries on a local and national scale. [17]

Workers in the take-away, who were not closely related to the owner, were highly mobile, not so much in the hunt for wages, though this was significant, but for a multitude of other reasons. These ranged from not liking the boss, to boredom and occasionally conflict with other workers. Experience of working in a take-away was the essential commodity in this world. Good workers were often poached by new take-aways. Assistants to the chef were generally *kakas,* who would have good experience of working in a take-away and could therefore command a better salary than any of the lads. All of the owners I talked to complained of the difficulty of finding reliable, hardworking, staff. Once found it was subsequently difficult to keep someone who was good. Tariq:

> All the lads want to do is to try and get off with any woman who comes into the take-away. These youngsters have so much *jurat* (bad attitude). They are spoilt. Then if you take on someone mature like Imran, after they've learnt the trade they go and set up their own fucking business.

In the light of these staffing conditions, the role of the owner, his assistant and the chef were critical to the running of the business. It was these men who spent the most time in the take-away setting up before opening and clearing away after closing time.

Working in the cotton textile mills did not develop any transferable skills in the *kakas* to help gain employment in other manufacturing or the new service sector. However, the experience of staying awake on the night shift at least helped when working through the night in taxis and take-aways. On average a taxi driver could increase his earnings the longer he worked, whereas, for the take-away owner any longer hours meant paying more people for the time. Nevertheless, the pressure to increase cash flow meant that the Maharaba increased its opening hours.

Case Study:

> When the Maharaba first opened, its daily openings were 5pm to

1am Sunday to Wednesday and then 5pm to 3am, Thursday to Saturday. These times only reflect when the public were allowed access. At least an hour on either end is added for the staff. By the time they reached home on the weekends, it would be 4am. After six months with the business not going as well as it could have been, Tariq paid for one of the younger lads to open at lunch time from 12 till 2pm. This lunch time opening only offered chips, burgers and doner kebabs, an attempt to cash in on the lunch time market. For Tariq, who also had to buy supplies and ensure the payment of warehouses and other bills, the take-away was a twenty-four hour, seven day a week commitment.

For the workers, the hours demanded by take-away work were not much longer than those worked by the *babas* in the mills. However, unlike mill work, the take-away involved long periods of boredom with only a few customers, followed by spurts of intense activity. For example from nine-thirty pm to pub and club closing times would be a quiet period followed by the busiest time of the day. This was also a feature of taxi driving. Tariq expresses how this was probably the worse feature of the business:

> In the mill you knew how much work you were going to do. You knew how much pay you're gonna get. Here you don't know what the fuck's gonna happen. Somedays you make a lot of money and it's busy, other days nothing. Thursday, Friday and Saturday night you know you're gonna make money but other times...One hour one person, the next hour you don't have time to think, you get so busy.

The certainty of routine and repetitive work on the mill floor was replaced with uncertainty and risk, both of which are hallmarks of small business venture, and the take-away is no different. Daily income depends on a range of factors, such as the weather and simply whether their customers have the money to afford their services.

The fate of the Maharaba is common of many small businesses in Britain.

Case Study:

> In January 1995, after the Christmas rush, the Maharaba closed down. The Butterfly night club near the take-away had been under

renovation and re-opened in December 1994. Tariq had hoped that the fortunes of the take-away would change with the opening of the night club. But even though the Christmas period was 'good', previous debts had mounted to suppliers and to the leaseholder. After the closure, Tariq went back to driving taxis.

For Tariq this event was just another segment of a vicious circle of activities that he engaged in to make money. Tariq had few options after the Maharaba closed down to return to taxi driving, other take-aways or welfare benefits. Beck (1992) notes that the increased flexibility of employee working patterns means that they absorb a 'portion of the entrepreneurial risk' which is associated with business establishment. In the Asian take-away business, it is the lads and *mangeters,* those workers who are the most marginal, that bear the brunt of the closure. The chef is likely to find work while he other *kakas* can enter into the cycles of taxi driving and other activities. These distinctions amongst type of worker are evident throughout the relationships in the take-away.

Relationships at Work

Working relationships in the mills were one dimensional in that the main area of concern for the workers was with their immediate boss and the management of the mill. For the *babas* the presence of a fellow kinsman as foreman could even work to disrupt the hierarchical relationships present. The shift from working with machines as part of a manufacturing process to one where a service is being provided via the production and sale of food is marked by changing relationships. While the inter-relationship between workers is present, the role of the boss is immediate and one which is present on the shopfloor. Given the small numbers of people involved in an individual take-away, another aspect of relationships at work is present, that of competition between take-aways. This operates at the level of general business rivalry as well as the movement of staff. However, the most profound shift in terms of relationships forged at work from the mill period is the new set of interactions that come into play as a result of working in the catering sector, that between customer and provider. This adds a new and hierarchical dimension to interactions and relationships at work.

The distinction between the owner and the workers in the take-away was only present at times of stress and when it came to handling money and getting supplies. Working alongside the staff, the owner would only show his authority when the take-away was very busy and only to the lads. Depending on the turnover of the establishment, there could be between three to six full time staff which would increase on the busy nights of the week; Thursday, Friday and Saturday. Unlike work in the mills, where the close working on the night shift engendered a sense of camaraderie, this small number of men in close proximity for long hours generated both solidarity and tension, often played out in language. Urdu was the lingua franca of the take-away and Putohari/Punjabi/Bangla the informal languages of insult. However, these tensions were less to do with any essential differences between the Bangladeshi chef and the (Azad) Kashmiri owner/workers and more a result of the type of work; boredom and lack of activity followed by intense periods of activity, which required a general level of alertness not possible to sustain from five pm to three am. [18] In simple terms, when the men worked well together, there was a sense of purpose and camaraderie in the take-away. At those times when orders were getting late and people were queuing for food, there was tension.

    Work in the restaurant is divided into the front and back areas. The front is where maximum interaction takes place with non-friendly customers, those people who do not have ties of friendship or kin with the workers or owner. Those people who are friends, who tend to be either Mirpuri or Pakistani taxi drivers and family, break down the barrier between customer and worker represented by the front 'counter' (Parker 1995). They would come into the back space, to complain about or supervise the preparation of food they had ordered. Serving at the front is generally paid less than for the back work. Even though the front-line workers control chips and burgers, the backroom workers are considered more important. This divide is played out with lads at the front and *kakas* at the back, though on weekends everybody apart from the chef works in the back and front. Take-aways with delivery services extend the front area to encompass the inner city of Oldham, providing take-away meals and encroaching on the business of the 'Indian Restaurant'.

    On Friday and Saturday nights, from 10.30pm onwards take-away work is tense, not only in terms of the activity level, but also the unpredictability of the customers. Asif described his nightly life to me:

> Well I just take the piss, when they come in I go: 'Oh yeah, all right mate,

whadja want then. Right chips yeah...'. They're fucking always pissed. They can't walk straight. They're always shouting and then they eat their food like pigs, dropping chips and throwing their wrappers on the floor and being stupid.

Words are inadequate to describe the lowering of intelligence and sensibility that Asif had to undergo to describe his nightly life. Mostly young, white men and women, descend from pubs into the take-aways and form the large part of the clientele. Incidents of verbal racial abuse were common, but violence was not something that seemed endemic as in the case of the taxis. There were a number of reasons for this. In the Maharaba, for instance, the lad who worked in the front area knew a lot of the white customers from school and college In the small satellite towns around Oldham, like Middleton and Droylsden, the staff developed a rapport with their white customers, as many would become regulars. Another significant contributing factor to the low levels of violence in the take-away was the fact that these were predominantly male spaces. On a Friday or Saturday night five to six men would be working and often their friends would be there to visit or to eat.

Relationships between take-aways were naturally marked by intense competition.

Case Study:

> One evening at about nine pm, when the Maharaba take-away was not very busy, Tariq picked up the phone, dialled a number and began to talk: 'Fucking, who is it ? What, you know, what ? You fucking stupid. I want curry, You curry face. You go, and get me fucking curry. You do what.....' This conversation, if it can be called that, went on for about five minutes. When he got off the phone, he was chuckling and told me that he had just given a take-away order to his nearest rival, Silver Star take-away.

The owner of Silver Star, Quyuum, is one of Tariq's extended family members, and in some ways his success and earnings inspired others to go into the business. Tariq's prank telephone call revealed the frustration he was feeling at his lack of success in the business. This was compounded by one of the best workers, Imran, leaving to set up his own take-away. During his period working at the Maharaba, Imran was quite open about amongst take-aways and among former mill workers was one of the most significant aspects of the business.

Single case studies can often over-emphasise certain facets of a business and downplay others. Nevertheless the short life of the Maharaba take-away highlights many of the features that interviews with other owners/workers of take-aways in Oldham experienced. Setup with minimum business experience, these establishments rely on good will from family labour and often delayed payment of essential staff. [19] This kind of business/self-employment amongst (Azad) Kashmiris in Oldham and the region is commonplace but difficult to assess in terms of overall significance due to the transient nature of the establishments and the staff that work in them. However, it is necessary to consider whether ownership and employment of these businesses is anything more than a shift in working from the older and decaying parts of the manufacturing sector to the traditional low skilled and poorer paid parts of the service sector.

Self - employment or Survival ?

Two aspects of the South Asian self-employment debate have come under some scrutiny in this chapter. Firstly, the reasons for entry into self-employment have been shown not to simply be an either or in terms of personal preference (Soni et al, 1987) or due to negative push factors (Ward and Jenkins 1984). Rather it is necessary to take into account time of entry into business and type of entry. In the case of the take-away business in Oldham those who entered early were often showing a preference and a history of involvement in small business, while those who entered later were doing so out of an ability to follow a path to income generation. Indeed for this latter group the question of entry into self-employment is largely irrelevant, and the more important considerations are the employment patterns that these men engage in. Take-aways, taxi ranks and other forms of marginal work form part of a cyclical career pattern, usually associated with young people in the transition to full time employment (McDonald 1992). When viewed in this way, the question of self-employment loses its centrality and the question of entry into self-employment becomes less a matter of motivations and aspirations and more of a pragmatic decision. The competition amongst the *kakas* illustrated in this chapter does not illustrate an overwhelming desire to be self-employed but rather the ability and confidence, achieved through working in a take-away, to set up an independent establishment. This knowledge of the business and the methods to set it up, to design a menu and to attract customers is a crucial aspect of the ability to set up in business. [20]

The second area of the self-employment debate raised in this chapter has been that of the role of family labour. Once again the simple dichotomy between exploited, unaccounted for family labour needs to be sophisticated by differentiating between groups and type of worker. Those members of a family who have a direct investment in the success of the business and will (other than in terms of wage labour) share in the benefits of business success cannot be considered as absolutely exploited. Whereas, those workers who gain little benefit (other than wage labour) from the business are in a position of exploitation. In both cases the worker may be related to the owner and it is the depth of the relationship which is of concern. In the context of working in take-aways, the labour at work is not female, yet it occupies, in the sense of being marginal labour, a structurally similar position to women homeworkers,. Given the wages and length of hours worked, these take-aways would not be able to recruit in the open market. It is the ability to blur the lines between friends, relatives and employee which means that workers find themselves tied to the person providing the work in a knot of multiple relationships. This is particularly the case with male *mangeters*, whose precarious legal position in the first year of their residence makes them particularly open to exploitation. [21]

Entry into self-employment and the use of family labour are themes that are of concern in the next chapter, but which do not sit comfortably with the development of the taxi driving business amongst (Azad) Kashmiris/Pakistanis. This area of business development could have been included in this chapter under the general rubric of the ethnic entrepreneur debate. However, taxi-drivers and taxi ranks occupy a liminal position with regards to business establishment. Even though all taxi drivers are self-employed they are not considered 'business men' in the sense of a take-away owner. Indeed, it is more useful to look at the establishment of South Asian taxi ranks in light of the wider debates about the shift from industrial to service sector work and the associated notion of the coming of a risk society.

---

[1] Figures from *Employment Gazette* March 1991: Table 1.2: p.198.
[2] See Appendix I for full breakdown of Oldham's contemporary industrial make-up.
[3] See Modood et al (1996) for a useful review
[4] Phizacklea (1988) makes the crucial point that you can be self-employed and not an entrepreneur, as is the case with many women homeworkers.

[5] Figures from 1991 Census. A full breakdown is available in Appendix I.
[6] A corollary to these bad conditions of work is found in the rates of pay given to women as homeworkers.
[7] For example Aldrich et al (1981) and Ward and Jenkins (1984). The notable exception is Werbner (1990), who looks at clothing manufacturing.
[8] Allen et al (1977) found that many of the owners of businesses in Bradford were previously in business in Pakistan.
[9] Tommyfield market is the main open air market in Oldham.
[10] Either Indian Gujaratis or Sikhs or Bangladeshis.
[11] This quote from a book about popular culture in the North West illustrates the point: 'And however cosmopolitan the species has become- Pizza in Preston and rogan josh in Runcorn - there is still enough life left in tripe....' Jobes et al (1992: 52).
[12] This figure is based on my fieldwork in 1994 and is based on Oldham as a borough, not just the town centre. The number is always changing as take-aways close and open frequently.
[13] These take-aways feature in a Bradford Heritage unit meeting: 'And basically they used to be what you called cafe social bars, mainly for the Asian men. It's like the conception of the Pakistani take-away, that's how that derived basically'. Bradford Heritage Recording Unit (1994: 53).
[14] This is not to denigrate the hard work that these men put into their business, but to note that because the owner is locked into the business day and night, he often has no time to do the preliminary work, such as accounting and stock management, needed to make the business a success.
[15] The owners of the Silver Star are established caterers in the town, with a restaurant and catering business. During my field work period they also opened a second take-away, euphemistically called Silver Star II.
[16] Indeed, during my fieldwork in Mirpur, locals complained that *mangeters* would come back from England and act like DCs (District Commissioners), whereas DC really stood for dish cleaner.
[17] A good chef can earn up to £250 a week.
[18] Any tensions across ethnicised boundaries were often overcome by evoking a shared Islamic heritage or South Asian British experience.
[19] Several of the chefs I interviewed complained about lack of payment from various take-aways in the region.
[20] This is a similar conclusion to that drawn by Rafiq (1992) in his work in Bradford, though he looks at previous business experience, rather than the ability to gain knowledge of business through work.
[21] The socio-economic position of *mangeters* is precarious for a combination of reasons, of which the most significant is the operation of immigration rules. If the marriage through which the person came to Britain is annulled in the first year, the *mangeter* can be deported. Strict application of these rules and widely publicised cases have meant that *mangeters* can be subject to exploitation by members of the *biraderi* into which they have come.

9 From Textile Mills to Taxi Ranks

Introduction

Taxi ranks and take-aways are rather less imposing, less impressive and less significant sites than the mills once were on the post-industrial landscape of the former mill towns of the North West. Oldham's forest of chimney stacks overlooking red, rectangular, brick monuments to industrial capital are now reduced to a few warehouses, often with the tallest chimneys removed. The substantive buildings of the inner areas of the town, now shine with a different hue and pay homage to a different God. It is the presence of domed mosques, some of impressive size, that have replaced the dominance of the mills not only in the architectural sense, but also in their influence and significance for the *babas* and *kakas*

Take-aways as a source of employment and self-employment for *kakas* were highlighted in the previous chapter. Here the interest is in another self-employed activity that has become one of the main methods of income generation for South Asians in the North and North West of England: taxi driving. This section of the service sector along with catering has largely been ignored by many contemporary analysts of the rise of the 'service sector' economy in the UK. These sectors have been seen as part of the traditional service sector and have been long associated with migrant workers, given the conditions of low entry and low pay. However, in the case of the *kakas*, entry into the service industry was not a direct result of migration. Indeed, in a similar manner to the development of employment in take-aways, a combination of factors resulted in taxi ranks becoming sources of income.

As well as contributing to the self-employment debate begun in the previous chapter, one of the central concerns here is to explore how the shift into service sector employment from industrial working has effected the relationships amongst and between *kakas* and *babas* Beck's (1992) notion of the 'Risk Society' presents some useful insights to help illuminate the ethnography. Two strands of Beck's work are of central concern.

Firstly the processes of individualisation which are crucial to the development of a risk society. Changing work patterns have led to greater individuality and competition which has brought about the second aspect of Beck's vision, the need to manage risk. What was once managed by institutions, by work organisations or by the state, now has to be increasingly organised by the individual, who has to weigh up and assess risks before taking action. Beck's work is not really concerned with the traditional service sector or with manual labour which he argues always had associated risks. In fact, the main thrust of his thesis is on environmental issues. However, risk is a useful tool with which to explore the shift from textile mills to taxi ranks and the change in status from worker to self-employed.

In the next section, I present a general history of entry into the taxi driving market by Mirpuris and Pakistanis in Oldham which illustrates the endemic racism within the industry and the way in which this was circumvented by the Mirpuri and Pakistani drivers. The entry of the *kakas* into the industry was only possible by the take-over of taxi rank ownership, a process which mirrors the 'taking over' of certain shifts on the night shift in the mills. Everyday life as a taxi driver is marked by insecurity in terms of personal safety as well as income generation. In a similar manner, in the case study of the Maharaba take-away, the issue of risk is central to my description. Implicit in these narratives about taxi ranks is a comparison with life in the textile mills. An assessment of whether life has changed for the better or worse varied according to individual experience, but general shifts in the organisation of time has affected all the men. The final section considers how the increased time flexibility offered by taxi driving, has allowed the *kakas* to maintain their commitments to family and religion. In so doing, the *kakas* retain a point of connection with the lives of the redundant *babas*, thus blurring the boundaries of the lifestyles between those in and out of work.

Taxi Drivers and Taxi Rank Owners

Taxi driving is broadly divided into two business areas, Black or Hackney Cabs and private hire. Hackney Cabs have been historically regarded as the elite of the cab trade, as they carry the name of the original Hackney Carriages, the precursors to the modern day taxi. On a more practical level they can legally pick up customers off the street and in theory are able to generate more custom than private hire vehicles. Private hire cabs are legally forbidden to pick up customers off the street, all of their work must go through the taxi rank. However, the Hackney Cabs are subject to much tighter regulation from the local authority, which controls their licences and radios. There are also specific restrictions and separate rates depending on where the taxi stands in the town. Location by the bus and train station obviously generates more business than at a general stand and this is reflected in differential licensing. In contrast, private hire owners keep control of their own radios and therefore control the work that is given out.

In Oldham in 1994, there were twenty-three private taxi stands, of which seven were owned by Punjabi/Pakistani men and two by Mirpuri/(Azad) Kashmiris, with an additional one jointly owned by a Mirpuri and Bangladeshi. The majority of ranks are owned by white people, with seven to eight firms having only white taxi drivers. Of the remaining white owned firms the majority of drivers are white with a few African-Caribbean and South Asian drivers. This racialised division in the ownership and driver population of the town's taxi ranks is a result of the historical, restricted entry of South Asian drivers into the taxi market. Nawaz describes his experiences:

> People said that taxis was not such a good business because white people were violent, but I thought well, I have to do something. I still had a job. I just started working part time. So I would work six am to two pm in the mill, then work from about five pm to twelve midnight in the taxi. I started work with Dial-a-car on the basis of private hire. At that time the owners were white men, there were three to four directors. At that time there were ten Pakistanis out of twenty cars. They were the only firm that took on *kale* (Black people). The only reason that they took us on was because they were good people. Abdul Ghafoor was the first Pakistani with Dial a car and he is now working for 606060. Rana worked for Bluebird cars but he got a job when they first started and they only ever took on one of the Pakistani and that was his friend. These were the only two firms that took our people on.

I was told of many individual cases of *kakas* being refused work when approaching a rank. Ikram's case illustrates the widespread and endemic nature of racism.

> I had driven a taxi for two years at Dial-a car. It was owned by a Pakistani at the time. I saved enough money to buy my own car and get the licence. I went to Streamline cars, this was 1988, to see if they would take me on.

> The owner was a *gora,* his name was Neil Rogers, he was a local councillor. I asked him for a job, but he told me that he could not take me because I was a *kala* and his customers did not like been driven by Black people.

This situation only began to improve when Pakistani and (Azad) Kashmiri drivers began to take over director posts and ultimately to buy out complete ranks. Taking over a rank, parallels the way in which the night shift in the textile mills was slowly taken over, especially in those cases where an (Azad) Kashmiri was a foreman.

The first taxi rank to pass into Pakistani ownership in Oldham was Dial-a-car in 1986. From then on almost every year a taxi rank would pass into South Asian ownership. The main asset of private hire taxi ranks are the radios that are hired out to the drivers. Frequencies for the running of these radios are controlled and licensed by central government (The Department of Trade and Industry). This makes the process of setting up a new rank difficult. Rank premises tend to be rented and run-down and do not therefore contribute to the net worth of the business. Given the difficulties in establishing new companies, change of ownership was a regular feature of the taxi business in general and this was exaggerated amongst the Pakistani and (Azad) Kashmiris. Given the large sums of money involved, each rank was commonly owned by a partnership of four to five men.[1] Directors would frequently sell their shares or set up new companies. The rank generated a fixed income dependent on how many radios they had on hire to drivers. In that sense it was a relatively secure investment. I will return to the finances of ranks later in the chapter. The main point of concern here is that entry by Pakistanis and (Azad) Kashmiris into the private taxi business became firmly established after 1986 once ownership passed into their hands. Anwar relates how his brother went into cabbing:

> At that time we would all eat food together. It was flexible working as a taxi driver. They were all working in the mill. I told my younger brother to get a badge and see if he liked the trade. When I would come home to eat my *roti* at 5pm, he would go out and drive the cab for two to three hours and earn about twenty pounds. He got into driving taxis. He thought this was good work earning eighty to ninety pounds was good. So he stopped working at the mills. This was 1989. He was in Manor mill.

Leaving a secure job in the mills to work as a taxi driver was not a common occurrence in Oldham in the early 1980s. However, once ownership of a few ranks had passed into the hands of the Pakistani or (Azad) Kashmiri men, taxi driving became a realistic alternative to the diminishing mill work.

By taking control of taxi ranks in this way the Pakistani and (Azad) Kashmiri men were repeating the process that began on the night shift in the mills. White management was excluded which ensured access to employment for their own family and friends. However, the owners of the ranks I spoke to were significantly keen to emphasise how, unlike the white owned ranks, they were open in terms of recruitment practices:

> We take on *gore*, *kale* we don't care. As long as they do the job properly and we get no complaints from customers, we take on all people.

Despite this reasoning when pressed on the fact that there were not many white drivers in the ranks, one of the owners told me 'they wouldn't like to work for a Paki, they can't stand us here in the first place'. A segregated workforce in the mills was therefore followed by a segregated workforce in the taxi ranks.

As work in the mills began to become scarcer, a parallel process of entry into taxi driving took place. In the previous examples this shift was one based on seeing the potential opportunities in taxi driving and a few of those pioneer drivers ended up part-owning ranks. For the majority of the *kakas* entry into taxi driving was motivated by the necessity of income generation. Ikram began working as a taxi driver after being made redundant in 1989:

> Our men have come into taxis because they have no choice. If they could get a better job, they would not do taxis, because at the weekend we still get abused. If you had the choice you would not put your life at risk. Every time some man gets in the car you never know if he has a knife. You have to be very careful.

Facing discrimination in the wider labour market and for the other reasons outlined in the previous chapter, taxi driving was a niche in which the *kakas* knew there were other (Azad) Kashmiris and Pakistanis. In this sense, entry into taxi driving concurs with the findings of Ward et al (1984) who argue that one of the factors for the high levels of Asian self-employment is in response to racism in the labour market. By the late 1980s, taxis became established as a well worn route to income earning. The role of the first men who went into taxis was similar to that of those who first went to work in the mills facing the most hostility, but also paving the way for others to come.

In order to become a taxi driver in Oldham in 1995, one needs to be over the age of twenty-one and hold a driving license with no outstanding fines or endorsements. A license is required in order to become a driver, which is available from the City council. This is obtained upon passing a test and payment of a fee. The test involves an assessment of the applicant's knowledge of the locality in terms of the location of schools, hotels, night clubs etc. and the best routes from one place to another. The form of the test, written or spoken, varies from borough to borough. In Oldham it was an oral examination. The proposed introduction of compulsory written tests in Leicester in 1994 sparked off protests by Asian cabbies, who saw the move as a threat to their ability to become taxi drivers.[2] Once the license has been acquired there are a variety of options open to the potential taxi driver. The simplest is to work for a rank which provides the car, and therefore the insurance for a weekly rental. This is usually the first point of entry for many drivers as it involves the least amount of capital outlay. However, this route involves paying a high rent, for the car and the radio, to the owner of the rank. A more favoured option is to run the taxi of a relative or friend while they are resting. Therefore, one man will work on the day and the other on the night shift. In this way the car is fully utilised and the rent to the non-owner is lower. The next level up from this is for the taxi driver to use his own car. For a car to become a taxi it also has to be registered with the local authority and undergo rigorous tests to ensure its safety. This ordinarily costs between one hundred and fifty to two hundred pounds. With a registered car the potential taxi driver can then approach a rank and ask for his car to be put on to their company name. The rank rents a radio to the driver, for between thirty-five and forty-five pounds a week. Jobs are then passed on to the new driver from the rank. The amount of time they work, and therefore the amount they earn, is left entirely up to the driver. The only concern of the rank is that the weekly payment for the radio is made.[3]

Taxi ranks are normally set up as limited companies with assets ranging from between fifty to one hundred thousand pounds. Given this large capital outlay, they were almost always owned by groups of four taxi drivers or more. Conflict between the directors of the ranks was the most general cause of new ranks springing up and of the movements of drivers. The selling and buying of shares in taxi ranks and the general flexibility of the business was advantageous for their owners. It provided a relatively fluid source of investment as shares could be bought and sold relatively easily, unlike a shop or retail outlet which was a fixed asset. Flexibility of this sort was useful for the directors, but could involve the closure of a rank at short notice. This meant that taxi drivers were frequently left with no work. Mobility between ranks and insecurity of income was therefore characteristic of the work.

Owning a Black/Hackney Cab is considered to be the best job for a taxi driver because of the independence and security that this mode of taxi driving offers. Relying on the rank to offer work means that the private hire taxi driver is somewhere in between being self-employed and an employee, whereas a Hackney Cab driver is completely independent. Not having to rely on the rank for business also gives the Hackney driver protection from the opening and closing of ranks. Hackney Cab driving is also a potential source of income for the extended family, as the cabs can be run, by various male relatives, for twenty-four hours. However, the price for these advantages is quite steep. I was told that in the early eighties a Hackney Cab could cost up to thirty thousand pounds, for which the buyer would get a car, the plate and a licence for driving. During my conversations with groups of taxi drivers, a debate would often arise about the advantages of Hackney Cabs over private hire vehicles. Entry into the Hackney business is difficult compared to private hire as the number of Hackney Cabs is limited and controlled by the local authority. Any new people wishing to enter the trade have to buy a cab or plate off an existing driver. White drivers offered their cars to South Asian drivers at inflated prices. Afzal Khan was one of the first *kakas* to enter the Hackney business:

> I got a Hackney in 1987 off a *gora*, he offered it to me for £5000 more than it was worth. I said: 'Okay'. He was too shocked. Then he still told me he would wait and see. Next time I saw him, he told me I could have it. I offered him £3000 less and he took it.

Despite these difficulties, once the cab was bought it was owned in totality by the driver. It therefore had the advantages and disadvantages of a sole business. However, the initial capital required for a Hackney Cab was often beyond the means of *kakas* recently made redundant from the mills.

Whether as a private car driver or Hackney Cab owner or the director of a rank, all involved in the taxi business would be classified as self-employed. Generally, the receptionist at a rank is the only person classified as employed. This situation poses problems for any simple account of an 'ethnic' entrepreneur. Should a taxi driver, who is not a director of a rank, be seen in this way ? The taxi driving business opens up a series of questions about the meaning of self-employment amongst South Asians which were also raised by the take-away business in the previous chapter. For present purposes, the fact of self-employment in contrast to formal employment provides a useful way of looking at changes in work interaction and relationships at work.

Cabbing Work

By the late 1980s, taxis had become a major source of employment for all eligible (Azad) Kashmiri males. Given the criteria for entry, *kakas* were the most likely group to be involved in the trade. In a similar manner to the *babas* in the mills, working in taxis had its own rules, regulations and patterns of work. In contrast to mill work, relationships at work and the personal and financial risk involved in taxi driving is arguably a potent illustration of the shift from industrial to service sector work. In a similar manner to take-away work, but now on an individual level, the interactions that cabbies faced on a day to day level were markedly different from that of the mills. Even where interaction with other cabbies, often related by kin and friendship, took place, the nature of the work meant this would be fleeting.

Case Study:

> On a quiet Thursday night at about 10.30pm in the office of Dial-a-car in Oldham city centre, the drivers - all South Asian- cramp into the small waiting room, chatting and smoking between jobs. Anticipation fills the air, pubs are near to closing time, so work is about to pick up. Receptionists in these private hire ranks tend to be middle aged white women, who refer to the men in pseudonyms such as Prince and Captain. The names identify cars, rather than drivers, which I was told ensures no confusion amongst the plethora of Mohammeds and Tariqs and multiple use of the same car. Conversations in the rank tend to be fleeting, as the men are coming and going between jobs, exchanging stories of traffic jams, bad customers and sexist banter about young women passengers.

> The presence of a white woman receptionist in most of the ranks owned by (Azad) Kashmiris and Pakistanis in Oldham is a left-over from

the previous owners, where middle-aged women tended to answer the phone from customers and direct taxis to their destinations. In the early days, in white-owned ranks, these receptionists would often ensure that jobs would not go to South Asian drivers. Their presence also highlighted a sharp gender divide. In both the take-aways and taxi ranks, male workers were the only category of labour I came across. Indeed, even for younger South Asian women there was no possibility of entry into these arenas. The receptionist was also the only person that was formally salaried in the rank, and one of the directors of the ranks would often double up as receptionist in times of illness or holidays. Directors of ranks also tended to be taxi drivers, so hierarchical distinctions in the ranks only rested in the relationship between director and receptionist. There was little apparent hierarchical distinction between owners and drivers in the ranks I visited. Given the fact that the owners main concern was to get the money for the hire of the radio, there was a common interest to maximise customers.

Perhaps the greatest change from mill work was the daily interaction with white customers. Unlike take-away work, this new relationship was one marked by insecurity. In a take-away four to five males were present at any one time and could deal with any trouble. In the taxi, the customers usually outnumbered the driver. This is not to say that the majority of journeys in cabs did not pass without incident, but the fact that something could happen and the fact that so much has previously happened leads to a situation of anxiety. The deaths of Mohammed Sarwar and Sadiqque Dada in Manchester in 1992 not only highlight the endemic nature of racism in Britain but also focus attention on the dangers of taxi driving. [4] In contrast to the relative safety of the South Asian owned rank, the taxi driver is brought under threat every time a white passenger comes into the car. During my fieldwork period, three cabbies were brutally attacked in Oldham, such that they had to receive hospital treatment. [5] Explicitly violent reported events are only the thin end of a wedge of verbal and physical violence that the *kakas* face every night in towns up and down England. Indeed these nightly journeys mapped a geography that was sharply fragmented in terms of zones of safety and along divides of 'race'. The words of the taxi drivers are more articulate than any account of this situation can be:

> When I started driving in the early eighties there was a lot of violence at that time. When I first went to the pubs and would call for the customer, they would take the mickey and call me names. We were also patient because we knew when they saw a *kale* they would get pissed off. When

they've had something to drink they're not in their right mind (Nawaz Khan).

I don't do nights now. When I was younger it was okay, but it's too rough now. The *gore* treat us too badly. Friday, Saturday night they get drunk, they don't pay and they call you names. There is no respect (Abdul Ghaffoor).

The guy chased after the *gora* who had refused to pay him, but when he caught him the *gora* pulled out a knife and cut him up a few times. They say the white guy was member of the BNP (Hussain on Mohammed Sharif).

I dropped off this man outside a club in town. He met some of his friends and refused to pay. The guy smashed a bottle over my head. I had to have three stitches (Ali Mohammed).
About three months ago, a couple of guys did not pay and the *mangeter* ran after him. The *gore* beat him up and went back to his car, stole his money and then set fire to the car (Karim on a friend).

Last month I was driving and the passenger thumped me and I twisted my neck. The policemen caught the man and they are in court next week. But look at me, I feel tension expecting to be attacked any time. And all my time is being wasted going to court (Mohammed).

These quotes are only a small sample of the taxi drivers' expressions of insecurity, fear, anger and frustration at the treatment they received. In response to these problems, many of the ranks organised various means by which the drivers could protect themselves. For instance, an emergency code on the radio would alert drivers to the fact that one of their members was in trouble. Another rank went as far as having modified radios with an emergency button, which alerted all drivers that a particular cab was in trouble. The increasing numbers of *kaka* drivers in a particular company also aided the protection of the drivers. Ikram has been driving a taxi for fifteen years:

It has got much better now. The *gore* know there are quite a few of us, so they don't cause much trouble. But you still get a lot who don't pay. The young men get mad and run after them. But life is worth more than money.

Risk is the hallmark of any business, however this is often in relation to the generation of a regular income. For South Asian taxi drivers, the potential of violence is added to the indeterminate number of customers and insecure daily income as factors to be contended with when entering self-employment of this kind.

A comparison between the life of a taxi driver and that of a mill worker must inevitably begin with a consideration of financial changes. Akhtar has been driving a cab since 1981 and for him the monetary advantages of taxi driving far outweighed any other risks:

> I could make £500 a week. From eleven am to five pm and then seven pm to twelve am for Monday to Thursday. For Friday and Saturday, I would work until 3am. My take in was £500 for a week on average. In 1987-89, I took home £1300 a week, so much money. We didn't have time to sit down. There were queues of people, there was so much work. In one month I earned £2500. I still have it written in the books.

Akhtar's situation was mirrored by many of the men who had entered the taxi business in the early days. Even though they were working long hours compared to the mills, the business was relatively better. However, for those who joined in the late 1980s the market was saturated with ex-mill workers, and the financial equation was not as attractive. Mohammed Anwar is a Hackney Cab driver at the main rank in Oldham town centre, which is where the following interview took place.

> The busiest times are Friday/ Saturday night, that is when you make the money. You can get a job every ten to fifteen minutes. Otherwise it's tough. I've been sat here since 8.30am and it's now 3.15pm. In the last seven hours I've made £21 of which two were account jobs for which I'll get paid at the end of the month. I have to pay the council £25 a week insurance and then the radio rent is £140 a month. On top of which is petrol and car maintenance (Mohammed Anwar).

Anwar's story is one that is more often heard and reflects the contemporary difficulties with making ends meet in the taxi trade. All of the long term cabbies, those who had been driving for ten years or more that I talked to, seemed to agree that things were easier in the mid to late eighties. In the 1990s there was much more competition. As more men were unemployed, more saw taxi driving as a means of earning an income, while demand for taxis has remained relatively constant.

On the more general question as to whether life was better in the mills or as taxi drivers, the responses fell into two camps. There were those who felt they were happier being one's own boss in control of their own time and able to work according to their own schedule. For instance:

> Life as a taxi driver is better, you are self-employed - as much as you work that is as much as you get. I was unemployed for 6 months before I got this job and now I'm earning good money (Ishtiaq).

> I used to work in the mills then I worked for Blue Line, since the last 3 years, and now I have my own Hackney. Life as a taxi driver is good. It's much better than the mills. I'm my own boss, I work when I like. The money is better and I can spend more time with my kids (Tariq Khan).

In contrast there were those for whom a fixed salary was preferable to the risks of business:

> I worked for twenty years in lots of different mills with a fixed income, I knew if I work overtime I will get more money. Here I don't know whether I'm going to make £1 in an hour or £10, so life is harder (Aslam).

> Life in the mills was better at least you had a regular income. When I left I got £81 a week, which is not a lot of money, but at least its something. In taxis you have to run your own business and it's a headache. I have a loan on the car, then the radio rent. To make money you have to work for twelve to fourteen hours a day, seven days a week, then you can make ends meet, otherwise it's better to have lots of children and live on the dole (Mohammed).

> Life was better in the mills- we were all together. Even the *gore* were okay in the mills. It was more secure than being a taxi driver. Look at that poor boy who was stabbed last week (Shoaib).

These perspectives have been limited to the *kakas* that I interviewed as they provide a balance of opinion. The few *babas* working in the ranks were generally negative about their situation. Their positive opinions about mill life were tinged with rose tinted glasses resulting from a general perception that the past was a better place. [6] In contrast, the young lads working in taxi driving found the money they earned and the freedom that taxi driving offered more than compensated for the risk of violence. It would be too crude to relate these perceptions of risk to a narrative about generation differences. Rather, it is useful to go beyond the different opinions of the individual taxi driver to recognise considerable continuity between the experiences of life working in the mill and taxi driving, with one main disjuncture around the question of risk.

Risky Business

> The growing pressure of competition leads to an individualisation among equals i.e. precisely in areas of interaction and conduct which are characterized by a shared background (similar education, similar experience, similar knowledge). Especially where such a background still exists, *community is dissolved in the acid bath of competition*. In this sense competition undermines the equality of equals without, however, eliminating it. It causes the isolation of individuals within homogeneous social groups (Beck 1992: 94, my emphasis).

> You see, sardarji, *pyar kat giya* (the love between people has lessened). When we first came here and we lived and worked together. We had time for each other. Now even your brother is too busy to see you. We have lost our sense of duty to each other (Baba Razak).

This quote from Baba Razak, featured in Chapter Seven as part of his explanation for moral decay he perceives in the world around him. Perhaps a little surprisingly, it also shows many parallels with the quote from Beck which precedes it. Both are concerned with explaining changes in the world in which they live, one from a sociological perspective and the other from a social relations perspective. The concern with an increased sense of individualisation is common to both Beck and Razak. Indeed, one way of interpreting the change in relationships between people that Baba Razak and other *babas* were keen to point out is because of a lack of concern 'for each other'. Beck may be going too far when he dissolves the notion of community, but the fact that there has been a shift and change in social relations amongst the *babas* and *kakas* is undeniable. The nature of this change and its causalities are multiple, but as with the rest of this book, my concern is with the impact that changes in work patterns have made.

From the close knit life of working together in the mills, the *kakas* in present day Oldham work in those areas of the service sector that engender petty competition. As noted in the previous chapter, the take-aways are in competition with each other for customers and in similar manner taxi ranks and individual taxi drivers vie for the same customer. Rather than the immediate foreman or the mill manager being the natural source of antagonism, fellow workers are more the target of hostility.

Akhtar poignantly sums up the effects of the shift from textile mills to taxis ranks:

> Of course it was better in the mills. We were much more together. At the weekends we would meet to see a film or just hang out. We all worked together and helped each other out on the machines. Now there's never any time. Look at us now. My father works with me in this taxi rank. I am in competition with him for work. If he gets a job that means I don't. To eat, we have to take off each other's plates. How can we be together?

This element of competition was not restricted to taxi-driving and take-aways. Market trading, mobile phone sales, retail shops and practically all jobs in the self-employed service sector could pit one family member against another. In these situations the close co-operation and the family strength that the *biraderi* offered in the mill days was now a hindrance as these same people were potential competitors in the new market. [7]

The risks associated with migration, finding work and managing a hostile and new environment were shared by the *babas* who as was illustrated in Chapters Five, Six and Seven, relied on their kin and social networks to off-set the difficulties associated with these actions. Working in the mills often reinforced and helped to maintain these close associations. In contrast, the risk associated with contemporary self-employment is increasingly borne by individuals and any element of sharing is off-set by a strong competitive element in the working environment. As Beck (1992) proposes, workers are more likely to see each other as competitors rather than to oppose a boss or question the institution.

At the same time, there are new opportunities opened up by the processes outlined by Beck (1992). The competitive element of life in the taxi ranks and take-aways was, in some ways, balanced by the activities that the *kakas* could engage in because of the time flexibility these jobs offered. This allowed them to organise their days around activities of their choice. For instance, on Friday afternoons the Greengate Mosque in Glodwick resembled a taxi rank. A multitude of various private hire cars and black and white cabs would line the streets around the Mosque. This flexibility stretched to the other self-employed. Muslim owned shops in the inner areas of Oldham would bear signs: 'Gone to pray, back in half an hour'. This is not to say that all shops are closed and not all the taxi drivers are doing Friday prayer. But crucially working as a taxi-drivers, shop keepers, market traders and take-away owners/workers provides a certain flexibility which allows for a greater control over time which facilitates attendance at Friday prayer, at funerals and other family functions.

This ability to show an increased commitment to Islam and to family is not a phenomenon limited to the *babas*. For many of the *kakas*, one of the main advantages and attractions of the work in the taxi rank and take-away was the ability to fulfil duties to religion and extended family. The flexibility that these jobs offered in turn provided choices about lifestyle. The *kakas* could choose not to drive their cab on Friday and work on Sunday instead or to attend prayer at the Mosque by closing the shop for half an hour. These choices were not available to the *babas*. Even if they had wanted to do Friday *namaz*, they could not while working in the factory system of the mills. So while entry into these areas of self-employment may have initially been due to lack of choices in the labour market, the flexibility offered by this kind of work has meant that many of the *kakas* could justify the risks by reference to their ability to fulfil their family obligations. Indeed, for both the *kakas* and *babas*, though for different reasons the centrality of work has decreased since the mill time. For the *babas* long term unemployment and bleak employment prospects have meant a restructuring of their working day, as highlighted in Chapter Seven. Paradoxically for the *kakas*, the flexibility offered by low skilled service sector work has enabled them to lessen the ties of work through a greater commitment to family and faith.

It is clear that in the shift from textile mills to taxi ranks two major changes have occurred in the life of the *kakas*. The first is an increasing flexibility in working patterns and the second is a much higher level of risk, both personal and financial, in working practice. These two phenomena are not unique to the *kakas*. They are widespread throughout the British labour market (Featherstone 1990) However, the greater choice which has accompanied these changes has often been dismissed as a concept only applicable to those at the upper end of the economic ladder (Lash and Urry 1994) From this perspective, disenfranchised, poor people are more tied to societal structures. However, as this chapter has illustrated, the *kakas* are actively involved in decisions about their relationship to Islam and their families. Indeed, discussions about Muslims in Britain need to address debates about individual choice and consumer lifestyles rather than rehearsing tired arguments about primordial tradition, imposition of custom and re-created ethnicity.

From Taxi Ranks to .....?

In this and the previous chapter, the experiences of working in taxi ranks and take-aways were compared with work in the textile mills. Increased risk, both personal and financial, are the main areas of change that the *kakas* experienced in the change in occupation. At the same time, working long hours through the night for relatively little pay provides certain continuities with the mill life. In a similar manner to the control of the night shift, entry into taxi driving was facilitated once ownership of the ranks passed into (Azad) Kashmiri/Pakistani hands. However, the most important change was the individualisation and increasing competition of income generation, from working as a team in the mill to being an individual taxi driver or take-away worker. At the same time, increased flexibility in working hours and the ability, for some, to be self-employed also allowed the creation of a certain lifestyle, one which closely matched that of the *babas* outlined in the previous chapter and one of increased participation in religious and family affairs. [8]

Even though, Beck's (1992) outline of the 'Risk Society' does not take into account, or disregards, what he sees as traditional service sector employment, the shifts in the working patterns of the *kakas* certainly illustrate some of main features of Beck's proposal. In terms of the processes of individualisation and increased risk associated with the work environment taxi drivers certainly travel in a risk society. However, for the *kakas*, it is the aspect of Beck's work which concerns the blurring of the boundaries between work and non-work and the normal pattern of work becoming cyclical. When considering the career paths of the *kakas* in and out of taxi ranks, take-aways, unemployment, training and other forms of work, then the dominant normative pattern is cyclical, rather than linear. However, the aspect of the blurring of the lines between work and non-work perhaps needs to be rethought of in terms of a lack of commitment to the notion of work as determinant of life pattern. For Beck (1992) 'risk management' becomes the main focus of the worker in the 'risk society'. Indeed, the central focus of 'work' remains close to Beck's project. Here, I would argue that the *kakas* are able to replace the self-value found in formal work by a routine established by Islam and family commitments. Rather than a preoccupation with managing risk, other aspirations and fields of value are sought. The specificity of the *kakas* warrants mentioning here. For the lads, these processes are still being negotiated and a detachment from formal work does not necessarily mean an attachment to anything else (see Kalra et al 1999). Indeed, the substantially, almost radically, different labour market that the lads face when compared to the *babas* and *kakas* requires an understanding that is beyond the scope of this book, and this is the main reason why their experiences have not been considered in any great detail.

The working and non-working lives of the *babas* and *kakas* living in Oldham, over the last thirty years, have been detailed in this and the previous three chapters. This historical narrative has shown how changes in the economy have had a profound impact on the way in which life is organised by the *babas* and *kakas*. At the same time the shifts in lifestyle have been associated with increased commitment to religious and 'cultural' institutions. However, it is significant to note that the common thread that links the *babas* and *kakas* is the increased flexibility and choice in the utilisation of time. So, even though the *kakas* are engaged in full time work, they are still able to partially fulfil the social and religious responsibilities that are placed on them, in a way that the *babas* were unable to during the mill period.

---

[1] In 1994 a rank was sold for £75000.

[2] Eastern Eye 5/5/94 :6-7.

[3] Each rank had to apply for a licence from the Department of Trade and Industry in order to run the radios which were essential to run the business. Rent on the radios was used to offset this fee and provide an income to the directors.

[4] The death of these two drivers is the latest in a long line of attacks against Asian cabbies, beginning with Jagdeep Chaggar in Southall in 1976.

[5] See Oldham Chronicle 17/10/1994.

[6] See interviews at the end of Chapter Six for examples of this.

[7] I do not want to push this point too far, as the *biraderi* could also usefully act as a market for the new services being provided. The sale of mobile phones through this kind of family network is a good case in point.

[8] This perspective will hopefully complicate the all too simple 'inter-generational' or generation-led conflict models that have tended to dominate studies of diasporised South Asians.

10 Beyond Labour?

Introduction

> I also hope that my support for investigations of specific struggles in locales will encourage others to be wary of claims made on behalf of such unitary constituencies as Britain's 'Muslim' or 'Asian' community and *generalisations about the success or failure of ethnic minorities* (Eade 1996: 66, my emphasis).

John Eade's concerns resonate with those expressed by Thuyafel Ahmed in the extract from *Eastern Eye* which opened this book. In simple terms, Eade is wary of the 'stereotyping' that academia has engaged in when analysing the socio-economic position of Britain's South Asian minorities. In a similar vein, throughout this book, I have highlighted the complexity and specificity of the themes under consideration in order to avoid making 'generalisations about unitary constituencies'. In each of the descriptive chapters, I took care to locate the social and economic conditions in which the events under examination transpired. It is hoped that the reader will **not** be inclined to draw a singular, general conclusion from the narratives presented here, but rather is able to gain a partial understanding of the themes raised and to stimulate further study.

Alongside tying up some of the theoretical insights presented in each of the chapters, this conclusion is titled 'Beyond Work' to accommodate and incorporate contemporary notions of the changing role of work in people's lives. In the case of the (Azad) Kashmiris, this requires an examination of the role of Islam in determining and influencing working choices. The role of culture formed a significant pivot in the theoretical chapter that opened this book. However, in all of the literature on the labour market and racialised minorities the role of culture in terms of a religious ideology has made scant appearances. In contrast, a bludgeoning of literature about Muslims in Britain and Islam has emerged in academia in the last ten years. A conclusion is not the space to offer even a cursory review of this body of work. However, in each of the ethnographic chapters, the issue of an Islamic identity, world-view and life-style constantly re-appears, and it would be doing dis-service to this empirical constancy to ignore the role of Islam in these workers lives. At the same time, and indeed the reason why this issue was not forwarded in the first chapter, my intention was to provide material which would surreptitiously and meekly disrupt many emerging accounts of South Asian minorities which reduce them to a function of religious devotion and fundamentalism (Bhatt 1997; Said 1998). In between these two positions, of ignoring the role of Islam or centring it in an over-deterministic fashion, there is an emergent space in which critical analytical research can take place. This book endeavours to be constituent of as well as to occupy such a space.

Explanations

In Chapter One, for reasons of clarity, I divided the literature on the socio-economic position of racialised/ethnicised minorities in Britain into two broad groups; structuralists and culturalists. While this division was necessarily heuristic, it was a useful way to organise what is an extensive literature. Despite setting out to dislodge the divide between accounts which over-emphasise either structure or culture, this book has engaged in a to-ing and fro-ing rather than a collapsing of distinctions. Two areas of concern were identified in the literature review: the ahistorical nature of the analysis (Anthias 1992) and the fact that determinants for social action are reduced to a single factor, be it 'race', ethnicity, gender, migrant status or class. It is inaccurate and inadequate to reduce, for instance, employment and health issues to a function of 'community style' or 'religion and kinship'. At the same time, to explain the position of racialised groups only in terms of the structures of exclusion does not allow for agency. In this book the focus has been on the field of economic activity where specific narratives relating to a group of racialised male workers were analysed. The tools for this analysis were primarily borrowed and developed from the work of Brah (1993, 1996). Four features of the labour market, of the group under discussion and the local, national and global contexts were put under the spotlight. Brah provides a useful starting point to examine the labour market position of the (Azad) Kashmiri male workers without reducing their agency to the workings of the labour market or to that of structured capital.

Subsequently, several chapters took up particular theoretical issues and attempted to apply them to the particular case of the (Azad) Kashmiri workers. Attempting to bring the process of text construction closer to the fieldwork data, the Methodology chapter offered a broad ranging review of the ways in which racialised groups have been labelled in media, academic and policy discourses. In an attempt to be specific about the issues of gender, generation and time of migration a set of terminology was introduced to facilitate a non-essential, provisional labelling of the group of people under discussion. Ethno-national labels such as (Azad) Kashmiri, Pakistani etc. were found wanting because of their gender neutrality and collapsing of other relevant distinctions. However, these terms were still used throughout the book, where claims to a wider group were being made. My main point in developing the terms *babas, kakas* and *mangeters*, was to emphasise the provisional status of all such labels. It could be argued that these labels were themselves reductive and concealed as much as they revealed. But it is hoped that another project with a different research agenda may not find these appropriate to describe the same group of people. At the same time, these terms were able to provide a more richly descriptive account of my fieldwork.

Concerns with identity have come to dominate many recent studies of Britain's racialised minorities (see Modood et al 1996). Stooped in the influence of social psychology, identity has often been ascribed to the response given to the simple question 'who are you?'. This issue of self-definition is confronted quite forcefully in the Methodology chapter. It is not possible to posit a fixed identity across a range of different contexts. The interview process itself is just one of the many contexts in which identity can be elucidated. It is for this reason that there are many names and labels used in this book. The extensive review of the reasons behind the use of each label should hopefully provide a relatively transparent framework from which these labels could be further criticised and developed. It should also hopefully inspire those who wish to go beyond simple excuses of 'self-definition' to produce more nuanced accounts.

Retaining a sense of the theoretical and methodological chapters, Chapter Three contained an argument about the relative utility of various theories of migration. In effect I re-read the existing literature on migration from Mirpur and included new data from British India Office files. My intention was to question the central role give to the notion of 'chain migration' as described in Chapter One. At the same time, I was critical of those perspectives which denied any relevance of the migrant's region of origin to their becoming migrants. My main conclusion was that migration from Mirpur took place for reasons closely related to underdevelopment which arose due to the political and social history of the region. However, the process by which migration was *organised* is best described by the notion of 'chain migration'. Ongoing events, such as the building of the Mangla dam have an overwhelming impact on the process of migration despite existing links made through migrant chains. In this way it is a combination of structural constraints and the agency of the migrants which results in mass movement.

While there are certain specificities to the Mirpur case, there are also certain elements which can be applied to other migrations of South Asians. In particular, the historical connection between Britain and the sub-continent played a major role in migration from Jalandhar (East Panjab) to Britain. A distinction between these historical factors and the relative role of 'chain migration' would also form an interesting comparison with the Mirpur case. It is hoped that the detailed method presented in this book will inspire others to take up this mantle. Accounts of this type can help to provide a more sophisticated understanding of comparative migration from South Asia, an area which is under-researched.

The theme of migration also runs through Chapter Four. Here the focus is on Oldham. To some extent this is the other side of the migration story taken up in the previous chapter. However, it is also important to note how Oldham itself comes into being through rural-urban migration. Using migration as a trope for describing social change was useful in avoiding a static conception of Oldham. Too often the impact of migration is considered to be more profound on the sending area (in the Third World) rather than the receiving (in the West). A migratory history of the town also neatly fits with the rise of the textile industry. Rather than a focus on buildings and machinery, the rise and demise of the mills is viewed through the lens of labour. Chapter Four, specifically, attempts to draw continuities with what is called 'marginal labour'. This notion is underdeveloped in both the overall theorisation of the book and the chapter itself, but is worth flagging up as an area of potential further research. Black, Irish, white women and child labour were all produced in accounts of the mills as marginal workers, this despite their central role in sustaining the industry. Through a notion of 'nimble' fingers children, women and South Asians were constructed as 'good' workers for the industry. These continuities across ethnic and gender divides requires greater exploration as it relates to a particular perspective on the common role of labour and the common processes of class formation. It is not possible to draw conclusions from the limited nature of this research, but there is certainly scope for exploration across a range of other industries in which gender, age and ethnic divides were also prevalent.

Chapters Five to Seven are highly narrativised and primarily explored, the *babas'* lives in the mills. It is in these chapters that the emergence of the significance of Islam is most felt. Indeed, the way in which the *babas* accommodate long term unemployment is closely linked with the ability to re-organise their lives along Islamic principles. The impact on the *babas* of the shift from fields to textile mills to the 'dole office' in the space of one generation is difficult to gauge. It would be relatively easy to carry out research with a group of *babas* and not take into account these historical changes. Given their daily involvement with the Mosque and with their family, it would also be a simple task to assign this to a continuity with cultural norms and practices from 'back home'. Their experiences in the mills could be conveniently forgotten in the privileging of the present. A group of devout, elderly men with an overt pre-occupation with Islam could be readily forwarded in an account of this type. Indeed it could be argued that Islam is the main concern of these men, with an urgent worry about its transmission to a British born westernised youth. However, this would be missing out a critical aspect of the reconstruction of practice and renewal of commitments. The radical changes in environment that the *babas* experienced are sufficient cause to note that contemporary commitments to religion and family are not only a defensive posturing to a hostile host society but the result of an active engagement with their conditions. Obviously, employment and unemployment are not the only significant factors. But my intention was to draw attention to economic status as a consequential element in the process of reinvention of tradition.

Indeed, my central point and this is equally pertinent to the contemporary discussions of what is becoming known as 'Muslim' socio-economic status in Britain, is that we need to be careful not to associate this commitment to a religious identity as a clinging or longing for a past. [1] From the angle of employment, the *kakas* maintenance of religious and family commitment is made possible by flexible working conditions and therefore an ability to take control of their time. These choices equally reflect participation in an increasingly individualised, life-style led, fragmented British society, as they do participation in an economically marginalised diasporised Islamic grouping. This is precisely why the final ethnographic chapter of the book introduces Beck's notion of risk society.

Too often discussion of contemporary British or European societies fails to adequately account for the multiple constituencies which make up a multicultural nation state.[2] Indeed, this whole book could have been theorised in terms of debates about globalisation, or the shift to a post-Fordist, post-Industrial society. However, each of these areas of discourse require unpacking for their implicitly Eurocentric assumptions, a task beyond the humble scope of this project. Nonetheless, as an example of the kind of work that can be done, I took up a sliver of Beck's proposals about the development of risk society, particularly as it relates to the concept of individualisation and changing patterns of work. Taxi drivers and take-away workers are engaged in working practices which are increasingly risky when compared with working in the textile mills. Despite increased and often ruthless competition between the *kakas*, ties of kin, friendship and faith have buffered their sense of solidarity. This does not imply an unchanging sense of 'community' nor an unchanged set of social relations, as Chapter Nine clearly illustrates. Rather, it is to recognise the fact that social relations change through time and are deeply influenced by patterns of employment, even where other factors such as migration and minority status are present. Beck's work also allowed me to incorporate the presence of other influences and sources of identity other than work. A shift from the central role of industrial employment, to a position in which it is placed alongside other competing influences such as Islam and family are central to an understanding of the contemporary socio-economic status of (Azad) Kashmiris. It could also be argued that the *babas* and *kakas* always occupied a position 'after work' given their migratory and marginal status, a point which is best pursued through the stories presented in this book.

Narratives

> It is only in the last phase of British Imperialism that the labouring classes of the satellites and the labouring classes of the metropolis have confronted one another directly "on native ground." But their fates have long been indelibly intertwined......If their blood has not mingled extensively with yours, their labour power has long since entered your economic bloodstream. It is in the sugar you stir: it is in the sinews of the infamous British "sweet tooth": it is the tea leaves at the bottom of the "British cuppa".
> (Stuart Hall, cited in Gilroy, 1996: 223)

Hall's pertinent summarising of the impact of capitalist globalisation provides a useful frame in which to place the various narrative sub-strands that ran through this book. Indeed, there are few, if any, histories of the growth of the textile industry in Britain which have bothered to weave in the global story. Britain's industrial growth is usually reduced to the endeavours of individual great men and occasionally the labouring classes. This book placed colonial conquest and postcolonial migration into the same frame and constantly attempted to draw links from the past to the present. Beginning with the history of migration from Mirpur, I illustrated how that region of the world became a place which could not sustain its people. Political indeterminacy, poor agriculture and other structural factors were met by migration, initially to other parts of British India and ultimately abroad. This tide, once in place, continued into the post-partition era. In particular, the effect of large infra-structural projects such as the Mangla dam were considered to be influential in the migration process. Once in Britain, these workers took up jobs in the textile mills of the North West. The history of the textile industry returned us to the Indian sub-continent and another level of relationships instigated and maintained by colonialism. The South Asian workers came last into an industry which had previously employed Irish, women, and Europeans. A comparison with these workers contextualises their position in the history of the industry as well as in the ideologies of management representation.

In terms of the history of workers, as I argued in the opening chapter, the myth of Asian entrepreneurial success has all but wiped out the reality of South Asian industrial workers' experiences. As this book has illustrated, even to understand the present levels of self-employment amongst Mirpuris/Pakistanis requires an historical approach. Therefore, the processes by which men came to Oldham, the means by which they found work in the mills and their subsequent experiences therein play a part in the explanation of current high levels of unemployment and self-employment. Chapter Four detailed each of these issues and crucially related how the *babas* were changed by and effected change on the space of the mill. Focusing on two mills, the Aleck and the Adderton, I illustrated how hierarchical relationships in the mill were determined by the extent to which the *babas* could gain control of the night shift. Comparing two mills in this way offered up two general models of practices that were widespread throughout Oldham and the North West; one where the *babas* gained control over the work space and another where the management maintained control of this space.

Individual narratives play a major role in the descriptions of mill life presented here. Yet these function at the metonymic level rather than as case studies. In that sense their are very few biographies of individual, characters in the ethnographic chapters. This is regrettable, because it involves a smoothing out of the often humorous, occasionally tragic accounts of individual lives. At the same time the accounts presented here are limited to the individuals that were interviewed and the extent of my fieldwork. It is fairly mundane, but nonetheless necessary to point out that this is not meant to be a representative survey. However, the themes and issues touched upon should resonate with the experiences of those who have engaged in migration or worked in the lower ends of the industrial and service sector.

Central to my fieldwork experience were interviews with men who spent the best part of their lives working in the mills in Oldham. In one sense this book is a tribute to them, for the harsh conditions they endured and for showing an incredible resilience when put in new and adverse conditions. Redundancy from the mills and long term unemployment was, therefore, not something that was met by apathy. The many ways that the *babas* tried to earn a living, including returning to Mirpur to try and set up in business, is witness to their sense of purpose. The fact that long term unemployment was replaced by the ability of these men to reconstruct their lives by renewed commitment to family and religion again bears mark to their strength of character.

At the point where the *babas'* employment story comes to an end, the *kakas* take centre stage. Adding a new dimension to the growing literature on South Asian employment, my focus was on taxi ranks and take-aways rather than on retail outlets. These two sectors of the economy do not encompass the totality of the *kakas'* working lives, in a way that textile mills once did for the *babas*, but nevertheless they are a significant dimension in their labour market experiences. Indeed, working in taxi ranks and take-aways is synonymous with 'Pakistanis' in towns like Oldham. Rather than presenting a survey of the take-aways in Oldham, a case study of Maharaba sought to explain some of the key facets of this form of work. In the context of the prolific growth in consumption of 'Indian' food, the take-away sector has increased in its importance as an employer of *kakas,* though this is not to ignore the growing market of young muslims, who wish to engage in fast food burgers and pizza, served *halal* style. My main concern in this chapter and the next was to highlight continuities and differences with life in the mills. Working at night in semi-skilled occupations with relatively low levels of pay implies that the shift from industrial to service sector employment was not that great. A certain insecurity in relation to management could quite easily be compared to interactions with troublesome customers. The male camaraderie of the mills was also maintained, albeit on a much smaller scale in the taxis and take-aways. Putting these caveats to one side, the insecurity of income, the risk of intimidation and violence, the competitive environment between workers, rather than with management, all combined to produce significant difference between textile mills and taxis/takeaways. Whether this change was for the better was a subject that generated much debate, but was not just concerned with the shift in employment. For the *babas* in particular a general moral decline was in process, a feature common of many older peoples views of the present, whereas there was no conclusive attitude towards the shift out of mill work amongst the *kakas*.[3] While there is a considerable amount of overlap between working in a take-away and as a taxi driver, the status of employed and self-employed were brought into question in Chapter Eight and through this a general critique of the debate about South Asian entry into self-employment was also made. Whereas the focus of much of that literature has been on reasons for entry into self-employment taxi drivers are an uneasy group to quickly label self-employed with all its associated baggage of entrepreneurship.

Taxi drivers have a contradictory reputation, friendly but often sexist, rude but often helpful. The taxi driver *kakas* mirrored this general position and the patterns of employment, working long hours with small compensation are complaints that all taxi drivers make. But racialised differences mapped a different territory from white taxi drivers. Violence and intimidation marked the night shift on a taxi rank, in a way which makes the night shift in a mill look positively pleasant. On another level, the risk of not earning an income for the day was also never present. Risk functions not only as a theoretical tool but also as a useful description for the lives of the *kakas*.

A wide ground has been traversed in the stories told in this book. From the impact of migration on Mirpur to the difference between a good and bad menu in a take-away. A rather secure and hermetic narrative around the working lives of the *babas* and *kakas* has been presented. The all too easily described shift from the fields of Mirpur to the factories of Oldham and the Take-Aways of Union Street, can smooth over the many ruptures and cracks that mark a journey of this kind. It would be traditionally anthropological and too easy to argue that continuity through this text has been provided by the group of people being studied. An ethnography of a 'community' bounded by the confines of 'work' could, all too easily, be applied to a cursory reading of this book. This kind of perspective would be an antithesis to much of the theoretical territory laid out in the opening chapters and in particular the care with which the methodology was constructed. Nonetheless, it is hoped that this book will contribute to the debate about socio-economic status and minority groups in the British context.

Audiences

Ethnographic study of minorities in Britain has often stated that its primary reasons for knowledge production is in order to present the actors' frame of reference; to 'focus on the primary concerns of Pakistanis themselves' (Werbner 1990: iv). Other authors, in the same school, wish to 'dismantle stereotypes surrounding Pakistanis in Britain' (Shaw 1988: 8). In contrast, structuralist commentators have been more concerned with contributing to the 'fight against racism' by affecting policy-making institutions, more specifically the workings of local and central government. The laudable nature of these claims does not belie their implicit reliance both on academic credibility and avowal of 'true' representation. In both cases the implication is that an essential Mirpuri/Pakistani subject exists which can be represented in totality by the analyst. The anticipated audience is predominantly 'white' academe and in the long term, the wider intellectual debate -through the media and educational institutions- on race and immigrants in general. Unfortunately, too often, academic treatise have contributed to the:

> .....construction of 'authentic communities' which then become(s) the objects of public policy and legitimate representative ethnic spokesmen (Ranger 1996: 16).

Following from Eade (1996), this book does not claim to be an authentic representation. Nor are there any claims about the dismantling of stereotypes nor an attempt to set any record straight. Rather, the narrative presented here is a partial representation of the working lives of a section of the Mirpuri/(Azad) Kashmiri population in a small town in the North West of England. This book is therefore only one of a multiplicity of possible outcomes of fieldwork, and as such no grand claims should be made on its findings. If there is one broader intention, then this conversation with one of my respondents sums up my feelings perfectly:

> Anwar: Okay, *sardar ji*, why do you want to ask me all these questions?
> Virinder: I am studying at the University and this is part of my project. I am interested in your experiences of life in the mills, when you came to

work in Britain.

Anwar: But what for? Who is bothered to listen to us?

Virinder: Who would you like me to tell your story to?

Anwar: Tell it to all these young people who are fighting with each other and doing nothing with their lives. They know nothing about their history or where they come from. When I tell them how hard we worked for them to come to this country, they don't believe me. But will they read your book?

---

[1] Tariq Modood's work has been particularly associated with creating the concept of a 'muslim' underclass. The utility of this kind of notion remains to be seen.

[2] In a forthcoming paper titled 'Social exclusion: Who's Society and What is Excluded?', I pose the pertinent question about which society Asian Muslim young people are excluded from. The implicit assumption in this work is that Britain is a homogenous entity.

[3] This is in broad contrast to opinions by white mill workers who were by and large glad to see the back of the mill. For many the mill period was seen as the dark days of Oldham's industrial past (Millet 1995).

Appendix I

Profile Of Oldham's (Azad) Kashmiri/Pakistani Population

Population

Table AI.1 Population of Oldham by Ethnic Group: 1981, 1986 and 1991, 1995

Ethnic Group	NUMBERS				PERCENTAGES			
	1981	1986*	1991	1995	1981	1986*	1991	1995
White	210600	205200	200000	196800	95.1	93.3	91.3	89.1
Pakistani	5000	8200	9000	11500	2.3	3.7	4.1	5.2
All ethnic minorities	10800	14800	19100	24000	-	6.7	8.7	11
Total population	221400	220000	219000	220800	100.0	100.0	100.0	

Source: 1991Census and OMBC, Policy Unit

Figure AI.1 Relative Population of Minorities - Oldham, 1995

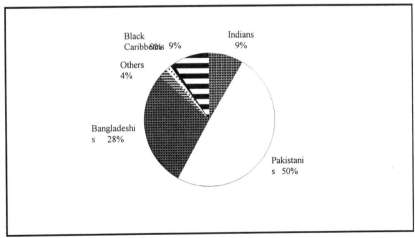

Source: OMBC, Policy Unit

Figure AI.2 South Asian Concentration by Ward - 1991

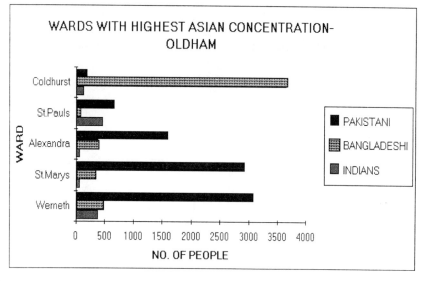

Source: 1991Census

Economic Activity

Table AI.2 Economic Status of Pakistani Population: Oldham 1991 - 1995

Economic Status	1991	1995
Employees F/T	19	17
Employees P/T	3	5
Self employed-employees	2	2
Self employed-no.employees	6	3
Govt scheme	1	1
Unemployed	16	15
students	8	11
Permanently sick	8	9
Retired	3	6
Other inactive	34	31

Note the 1995 figures are subject to a sampling error of +/- 3%
Source: 1991Census and OMBC, Policy Unit

Appendix I 209

Figure AI.3 Economic Activity of Pakistani and White Population in Oldham 1991

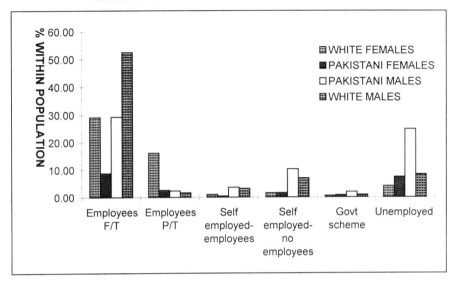

Source: 1991 Census

Figure AI.4 Economic Inactivity of Pakistani and White Population in Oldham 1991

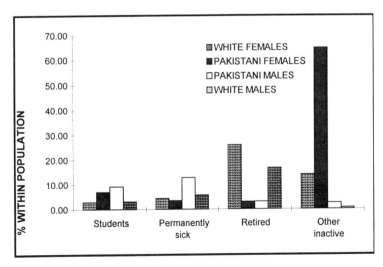

Source: 1991 Census

Unemployment Data - by Age

Figure AI.5 Unemployment by Age - Oldham 1991

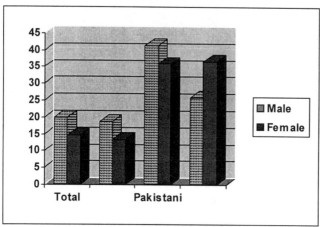

Source: 1991Census

Table AI.3 Unemployment by Age Range in Oldham's Pakistani Population 1992

1992

Age	% Pakistani Unemployed
18-24	37
25-34	27
35-44	24
45 +	13

Source: Employment Services, Oldham.

Sources:
Total population figures: Registrar General's Mid Year Estimates.

Percentage distributions by ethnic group:
1981 - Derived from 1981 Census population figures by country of birth.
1986 - OMBC 1986 Population Survey
1991 - 1991 Census
The numbers of people in each ethnic group are obtained by grossing up the percentage distributions to the population totals.
Notes:
These figures are subject to sampling error.

Economic Profile of Oldham

Table AI.4 Employment Change in the NorthWest 1971 - 1980

Employment change 1971-1980

	Total	Service	Manufacturing
North West	-54000	155000	-199000
1971-1977	-11000	123000	-126000
	1971	1977	
Textiles	151000	117000	-22.5
Transport	200	170	-15
Distributive trades	316	323	2.2
Misc Services	207	257	24.2

Source: Lloyd, P. and Reeve, D. (5: 1981) *Recession, Restructuring and Location*

Table AI.5 Employment Change in Oldham by Industry 1984 - 1993

Broad industry groups	Sep-84	Sep-87	Sep-89	Sep-91	Sep-93
Agriculture, forestry and fishing	150	200	0	0	0
Energy and water supply	1,047	1,000	800	700	500
Manufacturing industries	34,765	34,600	33,200	25,300	23,500
Construction	4,015	3,600	3,700	4,100	4,000
Distribution hotels/catering: repairs	17,126	17,300	18,000	15,800	17,400
Transport/communication banking, finance	2369	6,600	6,800	19,900	21,400
Public administration and defence, other service industries	11526	17,900	18,800	35,700	38,800

Source: Greater Manchester Research Unit - *Greater Manchester Industrial Profile 1984-1993*

Bibliography

Afshar, H. (1989) 'Gender Roles and the Moral Economy of Kin among Pakistani Women in West Yorkshire,' *New Community*, 15: 211-235.

Ahmed, A. (1991) 'Migration, Death and Martyrdom in Rural Pakistan' in H. Donnan and P. Werbner (eds.) *Economy and Culture in Pakistan*, London: Macmillan.

Akram, M. (1972) *Far Upon the Mountain*, London: Race Relations Unit of the British Council of Churches.

Aldrich, H. (1980) 'Asian Shopkeepers as a Middleman Minority: A Study of Small Business in Wandsworth' in P. Evens and D. Eversley (eds.) *The Inner City: Employment and Industry*, London: Heinemann.

Aldrich, H., Cater, C., Jones, T. and McEvoy, D. (1981) 'Business Development and Self-Segregation: Asian Enterprise in Three British Cities' in C. Peach, P. Robinson and S. Smith (eds.) *Ethnic Segregation in Cities*, London: Croom Helm.

Aldrich, H., Jones, T. and McEvoy, D. (1984) 'Ethnic Advantage and Minority Business Development' in R. Ward and R. Jenkins (eds.) *Ethnic Communities in Business: Strategies for Economic Survival*, Cambridge: Cambridge University Press.

Ali, A. (1993) *The Pakistani Community Centre: Oldham*, unpublished diploma thesis: Manchester: Manchester Metropolitan University.

Ali, N. Ellis, P. and Khan, Z. (1996) 'The 1990s: A Time to Separate British Punjabi and British Kashmiri Identity' in I. Talbot and G. Singh, *Punjabi Identity: Continuity and Change*, New Delhi: Manohar.

Ali, Y (1992) 'Muslim Women and the Politics of Ethnicity'in G. Sahgal and N. Yuval-Davis (eds.) *Refusing Holy Orders, Women and Fundamentalism in Britain*, London: Virago Press.

Allen, S. (1971) *New Minorities, Old Conflicts*, London: Random House.

Allen, S., Bentley, S. and Joanna, B. (1977) *Work, Race and Immigration*, Bradford: Bradford University School of Social Sciences.

Aloys, A. (1967) *The Indus Rivers: A Study of the Effects of Partition*, New Haven: Yale University Press.

Altorki and El Sohl (1988) *Arab Women in The Field: Studying Your Own Society*, New York: Syracuse University Press.

Amos, V. and Parmar, P. (1984) 'Challenging Imperial Feminism',

Feminist Review, 17: 3-19.
Anderson, B. (1983) *Imagined Communities*, London: Verso.
Ansari, A (1969) *The Disastrous Effects of the Mangla Dam Project*, Mirpur.
Anthias, F. (1992) *Ethnicity, Class, Gender and Migration: Greek-Cypriots in Britain*, Aldershot: Avebury.
Anthias, F. and Yuval-Davis, N.(1992) *Racialized Boundaries*, London: Routledge.
Anthias, F. and Yuval-Davis, N. (1984) 'Contextualising Feminism: Ethnic, Gender and Class Divisions', *Feminist Review*, 15: 62-74.
Anwar, M. (1979) *The Myth of Return: Pakistanis in Britain*, London: Heinemann.
Anwar, M. (1985) *Pakistanis in Britain: A Sociological Study*, London: New Century.
Anwar, M. (1986) *Race and Politics: Ethnic Minorities and the British Political System*, London: Tavistock.
Anwar, M. and Werbner, P. (eds.) (1991) *Black and Ethnic Leadership*, London: Routledge.
Anwar-un-musa (1984) *Village Mohra Bhatti, AJK*, Islamabad: unpublished Msc dissertation: Department of Social Anthropology, Quaid-e-Azam University.
Appadurai, A. (1990) 'Disjuncture and Difference in the Global Cultural Economy', in M. Featherstone (ed.) *Global Culture.*
Aronowitz, S. (1992) *Politics of Identity: Class, Culture and Social Movements*, London: Routledge.
Aspin, C. (1981) *The Cotton Industry*, Bucks: Shire Publications.
Auster, E. and Aldrich, H. (1984) 'Small Business Vulnerability, Ethnic Enclaves and Ethnic Enterprise' in R. Ward and R. Jenkins (eds.) *Ethnic Communities in Business: Strategies for Economic Survival*, Cambridge: Cambridge University Press.
Aziz, T. (1993) *Mirpuris in Birmingham*, Islamabad: unpublished M.Phil: Department of Social Anthropology, Quaid-e-Azam University.
Ballard, R. (1983) 'Emigration in a Wider Context: Jullundur and Mirpur Compared', *New Community*, 10: 117-36.
Ballard, R. (1985) 'The Context and Consequences of Emigration from Northern Pakistan', unpublished report on an ESRC research project.
Ballard, R. (1987) 'The Political Economy of Migration: Pakistan, Britain and the Middle East' in J. Eades (ed.) *Migrants, Workers and the Social Order*, London: Tavistock.
Ballard, R. (1989) 'The Effects of Labour Migration from Pakistan' in H.

Alavi and J. Harris (eds.) *The Sociology of Developing Societies: South Asia*, London: Macmillan.

Ballard, R. (1990) 'Migration and Kinship: The Differential Effect of Marriage Rules on the Process of Punjabi Migration to Britain' in C. Clarke, C. Peach and S. Vertovec (eds.) *South Asians Overseas*, Cambridge University Press: Cambridge.

Ballard, R. (1991) 'Kashmir Crisis; View from Mirpur', *Economic and Political Weekly* 26.

Ballard, R. (1992) 'New Clothes for the Emperor? The Conceptual Nakedness of the British Race Relations Industry', *New Community*, 18: 481 - 492.

Ballard, R. (1994) 'Introduction' in R. Ballard (ed.) *Desh Pardesh: The South Asian Presence in Britain*, London: Hurst and Co.

Ballard, R. and Kalra, V.(1994) *The Ethnic Dimensions of the 1991 Census: A Preliminary Report*, Manchester: Census Dissemination Unit, University of Manchester.

Banks, M. (1996) *Ethnicity: Anthropological Constructions*, London: Routledge.

Banton, M. (1983) *Racial and Ethnic Competition*, Cambridge: Cambridge University Press.

Banton, M. (1984) 'Ethnic Entrepreneurs: Strategies and Survival', *New Community*, 12: 196-198.

Baqi, L (1987) 'Talking about YTS: The Views of Black Young People' in M. Cross, and D. Smith (eds.) *Black Youth Futures - Ethnic Minorities and the Youth Training Scheme*, Leicester: National Youth Bureau.

Barth, F. (1969) Introduction in F. Barth (ed.) *Ethnic Groups and Boundaries*, Bergen: Universitetsforlaget.

Basu, A. (1995) 'Asian Small Businesses in Britain: An Exploration of Entrepreneurial Activity', (unpublished paper) Warwick University.

Bechhofer, F. and Elliot, B. (1976) 'Persistence and Change: The Petite Bourgeoisie in the Industrial Society', *European Journal of Sociology*, 17: 74-99.

Bechhofer, F. and Elliot, B. (1978) 'The Voice of Small Business and the Politics of Survival', *The Sociological Review*, 26(1) : 57-88.

Bechhofer, F., Elliott, B., Rushforth, M. and Bland, R. (1974) 'The Petite Bourgeois in the Class Structure: The Case of the Small Shopkeepers' in F. Parkin (ed.) *The Social Analysis of Class Structure*, London: Tavistock: 103-128.

Benson, S. (1996) 'Asians Have Culture, West Indians Have Problems: Discourses on Race Inside and Outside Anthropology', in T.O. Ranger Y. Samad and O.Stuart (eds.) *Culture, Identity and Politics*, Aldershot: Avebury Press.

Bentley, S. (1981) 'Industrial Conflict, Strikes and Black Workers: Problems of Research Methodology' in P. Braham, E. Rhodes, M. and M. Pearn (eds.) *Discrimination and Disadvantage in Employment: The Experience of Black Workers*, London: Harper and Row.

Bhabha, H. (1994) *The Location of Culture*, London: Routledge.

Bhachu, P. (1993) 'Identities Constructed and Reconstructed: Representation of Asian Women in Britain' in P. Bhachu and G. Buijs, (eds.) *Migrant Women, Crossing Boundaries and Changing Identities*, Berg: Oxford.

Bhat, A., Carr-Hill, R. and Ohri, S. (1988) *Britain's Black Population*, Aldershot: Gower.

Bhatt, C. (1997) *Liberation and Purity*, London: UCL Press.

Bilquees, H. and Hamid, M. (1981) *The Consequences of Migration to the Gulf on Villages in Gujjar Khan*, Islamabad: Pakistan Institute of Development Economics.

Bohning, W. (1972) *The Migration of Workers in the UK and the European Community*, London: Oxford University Press.

Bonacich, E. (1972) 'A Theory of Ethnic Antagonism: The Split Labour Market,' *American Sociological Review*, 37: 547-559.

Bosanquet, N. and Doeringer, P. (1973) 'Is There a Dual -Labour Market in Britain ?', *Economic Journal*, 83: 421-435.

Bourne, J. (1980) 'Cheerleaders and Ombudsmen: The Sociology of Race Relations in Britain', *Race and Class*, 21: 331-352.

Brah, A. (1986) 'Unemployment and Racism: Asian Youth on the Dole' in S. Allen et al (eds.) *The Experience of Unemployment*, London: Macmillan.

Brah, A. (1987) 'Women of South Asian Origin in Britain: Issues and Concerns,' *South Asia Research*, 7: 39-53.

Brah, A. (1993) "Race' and 'Culture' in the Gendering of Labour Markets: Young South Asian Muslim Women and the Labour Market, *New Community*, 19: 441-58.

Brah, A. (1996) "Race' and 'Culture' in the Gendering of Labour Markets: Young South Asian Muslim Women and the Labour Market' in A. Brah, *Cartographies of Diaspora*, London: Routledge.

Brah, A. and Shaw, S. (1992) *Working Choices: South Asian Young Muslim Women and the Labour Market*, Research Paper No.91:

London: Department of Employment.
Braverman, H. (1974) *Labor and Monopoly Capital: The Degradation of Work in the Twentieth Century*, New York:Monthly Review Press,1974
Brooks, D. (1975) *Race and Labour in London Transport*, London: Oxford University Press.
Brooks, D. and Singh, K. (1979) 'Pivots and Presents: Asian Brokers in British Foundries,' in S. Wallman (ed.) *Ethnicity At Work*, London: Macmillan.
Brown, C. (1984) *Black and White in Britain: The Third PSI Survey*, Policy Studies Institute: Heinemann Educational.
Brown, C. (1992) "Same Difference': The Persistence of Racial Disadvantage in the British Employment Market' in P. Braham, A. Rattansi and R. Skellington (eds.) *Racism and Antiracism*, London: Sage: 30-46.
Brown, C. and Gay, P. (1985) *Racial Discrimination: 17 Years After the Act*, London: Policy Studies Institute.
Burnett, J. (1994) *Idle Hands: The Experience of Unemployment 1790-1990*, London: Routledge.
Castles, S. and Kosack, G. (1973) *Immigrant Workers and Class Structure in Western Europe*, London: Oxford University Press.
Centre for Contemporary Cultural Studies (1982) *The Empire Strikes Back*, London: Hutchinson.
Chapman, C. (1904) *The Lancashire Cotton Industry*, Manchester: Manchester University Press.
Clairmonte, F. and Cavanagh, J. (1981) *The World in their Web: Dynamics of Textile Multinationals*, London: Zed Books.
Clairmonte, F. (1960) *Economic Liberalism and Underdevelopment*, Bombay: Asia Publishing House.
Clifford, J. and Marcus, G. (eds.) (1986) *Writing Culture*, Berkeley: University of California Press.
Clifford, J. (1988) *The Predicament of Culture*, Cambridge, Mass.: Harvard University Press.
Cohen, A.P. (1985) *The Symbolic Construction of Community*, London, Routledge.
Cohen, A.P. (1986) *Symbolizing Boundaries: Identity and Diversity in British Cultures*, Manchester: Manchester University Press.
Cohen, A. (1974) 'Introduction' in A. Cohen (ed.) *Urban* Ethnicity ASA 12, London: Tavistock.

Cohen, A. (1993) *Masquerade Politics: Explorations in the Structure of Urban Cultural Movements*, Oxford: Berg.
Cohen, S. (1984) *The Pakistani Army*, Berkeley: California University Press.
Collier, C. (1989) 'Textile Machinery' in D. Gurr and J. Hunt, *The Cotton Mills of Oldham*, Oldham: OMBC Leisure Services Department.
Cross, M., Wrench, J. and Barnett, S. with the assistance of Davies, H.(1988) *Ethnic Minorities and the Careers Service An Investigation into Processes of Assessment and Placement* ,A Report for the Department of Employment by the Centre for Research in Ethnic Relations, Warwick: University of Warwick.
Cross, M. (1992) 'Black Workers, Recession and Economic Restructuring in the West Midlands' in M. Cross (ed.) *Ethnic Minorities and Industrial Change in Europe and North* America, Cambridge: Cambridge University Press.
Cross, M. (1993) 'Ethnic Minority Youth in a Collapsing Labour Market: The UK Experience,' *New Community*, 19: 513-519.
Dahya, B. (1970) 'Pakistanis in Britain: Transients or Settlers', *Race* 14: 241-277.
Dahya, B. (1974) 'The Nature of Pakistani Ethnicity in Industrial Cities in Britain' in Cohen, A. (ed.) *Urban Ethnicity*, London: Tavistock.
Daniel, W. (1968) *Racial Discrimination in England*, London: Penguin.
Davis, G. (1991) *The Irish in Britain: 1815-1914*, Dublin: Gill and Macmillan.
Deakin, D. (1970) *Colour, Citizenship and British Society*, London: Panther Books.
Devons, J., Crossley, E. and Maunder, W. (1968) 'Wage Rate Indexes by Industry, 1948-1965', *Economica*, 35 : 392-423.
Dex, S. (1985) *The Sexual Division of Work*, London: Wheatsheaf.
Dicken, P. (1992) *Global Shift: The Internationalisation of Economic Activity*, London: Paul Chapman Publishing.
Docherty, C. (1983) *Steel and Steelworkers: The Sons of Vulcan*, London: Heinemann Educational.
Donald, J. and Rattansi, A.(eds.) (1992) *'Race', Culture and Difference*, London: Sage.
Duffield. M. (1985) 'Rationalisation and the Politics of Segregation: Indian Workers in Britain's Foundry Industry, 1945-62' in K. Lunn (ed.) in *Race and Labour in Twentieth Century Britain* , London: Frank Cass.
Duffield, M. (1988) *Black Radicalism and the Politics of Deindustrialisation: The Hidden History of Indian Foundry Workers*,

Avebury : Aldershot.
Eade, J. (1989) *The Politics of Community: The Bangladeshi Community in East* London: Tavistock.
Eade, J. (1996) 'Ethnicity and the Politics of Cultural Difference: An Agenda for the 1990s ?' in T.O.Ranger, Y. Samad, and O. Stuart (eds.) *Culture, Identity and Politics*, Aldershot: Avebury Press.
Eades J. (ed.) (1987) *Migrant Workers and the Social Order ASA 26*, London, Tavistock.
Eglar, Z. (1960) *A Punjabi Village in Pakistan*, New York: Columbia University Press.
Eriksen, T. (1993) *Ethnicity and Nationalism: Anthropological Perspectives*, London: Pluto.
Eversley, D. (1992) 'Urban Disadvantage and Racial Minorities in the UK' in M. Cross (ed.) *Ethnic Minorities and Industrial Change in Europe and North America*, Cambridge: Cambridge University Press.
Farnie, E. (1989) 'Cotton Mill Workers' in D. Gurr and J. Hunt, *The Cotton Mills of Oldham*, Oldham: OMBC Leisure Services Department.
Featherstone, M. (ed.) (1990) *Global Culture: Nationalism, Globalisation and Modernity*, London: Sage.
Fevre, R. (1984) *Cheap Labour and Racial Discrimination*, Aldershot: Gower.
Fielding, S. (1993) *Class and Ethnicity: Irish Catholics in England, 1880-1939*, Buckingham: Open University Press.
Fishcher, M. (1991) 'Marriage, Exchange and the Reproduction of Inequality' in H. Donnan and P. Werbner (eds.) *Economy and Culture in Pakistan*, London: Macmillan.
Frow, E. (1991) *Essays on the Irish in Manchester*, Lancashire: Community Press.
Geertz, C. (1973) *The Interpretation of Culture*, New York: Basic Books.
Geertz, C. (1983) *Local Knowledge*, New York: Basic Books.
Gell, S. (1996) 'The Gatekeepers of Multiculturalism: A Response to Pnina Werbner', *Critique of Anthropology*, 16: 325-335.
Gilroy, P. (1987) *There Ain't No Black in the Union Jack: The Cultural Politics of Race and Nation*, London: Hutchinson.
Gilroy, P. (1992) 'The End of Anti-Racism' in A. Rattansi and J. Donald (eds.) *'Race', Culture and Difference*, London: Sage.
Gilroy, P. (1993) *Small Acts*, London: Serpent's Tail.

Gilroy, P. (1996) 'British Cultural Studies and the Pitfalls of Identity' in H.A. Baker, M Diawara and R.H. Lindeborg, *Black British Cultural Studies, A Reader*, Chicago: Chicago University Press.

Goering, A. (1993) 'Reclothing the Emperor While Avoiding Ideological Polarisation: A Comment on Roger Ballard's Essay', *New Community*, 19: 336-47.

Goodall, J. (1968) *New Backgrounds*, IRR: London.

Grant, A. (1983) *Against the Clock*, London: Pluto.

Gupta, S. (1967) *Kashmir: A Study in Indian-Pakistani Relations*, New Delhi: Asia Publishers.

Gurr, D. and Hunt, J. (1989) *The Cotton Mills of Oldham*, Oldham:OMBC Leisure Services Department.

Hakim, S. (1992) 'Unemployment , Marginal Work and the Black Economy,' in W. Mc Laughlin (ed.) *Understanding Unemployment: New perspectives on Active Labour Market Policies*, London: Routledge.

Hall, S. (1980) 'Race, Articulation and Societies Structured in Dominance' in *Sociological Theories: Race and Colonialism*, Paris: UNESCO.

Hall, S. (1992) 'New Ethnicities' in J. Donald and A. Rattansi (Eds.) *'Race', Culture and Difference*, London: Sage Publications.

Harnetty, P. (1972) *Imperialism and Free Trade: Lancashire and India in The Mid-Nineteenth Century*, Manchester: Manchester University Press.

Harvey, D. (1990) *The Condition of Postmodernity*, Oxford: Basil Blackwell.

Heinrick, H. (1990) *A survey of the Irish in England: 1872*, London: Hambledon Press.

Hoggett, P (1994) 'The Politics of the Modernisation of the UK Welfare State' in R. Burrows and B. Loader (eds.) *Towards a Post Fordist Welfare State*, London: Routledge.

Honeyford, R. (1988) *Integration or Disintegration*, London: Claridge Press.

hooks, b. (1991) *Yearning, Race, Gender and Cultural Politics*, London: Turnaround.

Hopkins, E. (1995) *Working-Class Self-Help in Nineteenth-Century England*, London: UCL Press.

Hubbuck, J. and Carter, S. (1980) *Half a Chance? A Report on Job Discrimination Against Young Blacks in Nottingham*, London: CRE.

Hudson, R., Schech, S. and Hansen, L. (1992) *Jobs for the Girls? The New private Sector Economy of Derwentside Distict*, Occasional Publication

No. 28: Durham: University of Durham.

Iganski, P. and Payne, G. (1996) 'Declining Racial Disadvantage in the British Labour Market', *Ethnic and Racial Studies*, 19: 113-134.

Inden, R. (1992) *Imagining India*, London: Routledge.

Iqbal, M., Ara, S. and Van Riel, R. (1990) *Just for Five Years? Reminiscences of Pakistani Senior Citizens in Sheffield*, Sheffield: Sheffield City Libraries.

Isaac, J. (1954) *British Post War Migration*, Cambridge: Cambridge University Press.

Jackson, P. (1992) 'The Racialization of Labour in Post-War Bradford', *Journal of Historical Geography*, 12: 190-209.

Jahoda, M. (1979) ' The Impact of Unemployment in the 1930s and 1970s', *Bulletin of the British Psychological Society*, 32: 309-14.

Jefferey, P. 1976 *Migrants and Refugees: Muslim and Christian Pakistani Families in Bristol*, Cambridge: Cambridge University Press.

Jenkins, R. (1986) 'Social Anthropological Models of Inter-Ethnic Relations' in J. Rex and D. Mason (eds.) *Theories of Race and Ethnic Relations*, Cambridge: Cambridge University Press.

Jenkins, R. (1992) 'Black Workers in the Labour Market: The Price of Recession' in P. Braham, A. Rattansi and R. Skellington (eds.) *Racism and Antiracism*, London: Sage.

Jessop, P. (1994) 'The Transition to Post-Fordism and the Schumpeterian Workfare State' in R. Burrows and B. Loader (eds.) *Towards a Post Fordist Welfare State* London: Routledge.

Jobes, B. and Andrew, L. (1992) *Homo Northwestus- A Quest for the Species North-West Man*, Preston: Carnegie.

Joly, D. (1986) *The Opinions of Mirpuri Parents in Saltley*, Warwick: Centre for Research in Ethnic Relations.

Jones, T. (1993) *Britain's Ethnic Minorities: An Analysis of the Labour Force Survey*, London: Policy Studies Institute.

Jones, T., MCevoy, D., De Silva, P and Cater, J. (1989) *Ethnic Business and Community Needs*, London: CRE.

Joyce, P. (1980) *Work, Society and Politics: The Culture of the Factory in Late Victorian England*, London: Harvester Press.

Kaur, R. and Kalra, V. (1996) 'New Paths for South Asian Music and Identity' in S. Sharma. J. Hutnyk, and A. Sharma (eds.) *Dis-Orienting Rhythms: The Politics of the New Asian Dance Music*, London: Zed.

Khan, M., Sarwar, M. and Akram, M. (1982) *A Socio-economic Study of*

Farming Systems in Azad Jammu and Kashmir, Lahore: Punjab Economic Research Institute.
Khan, F. (1991) *A Geography of Pakistan: Environment, People and Economy*, Karachi: Oxford University Press.
Knight, E. (1895) *Where Three Empires Meet: A Narrative of Recent Travel in Kashmir*, London: Longmans.
Kulkani, V. (1979) *History of Indian Cotton Textile Industry*, Bombay: Millowners Association.
Lash, S. and Urry, J. (1994) *Economies Of Signs And Space*, London: Sage.
Lawrence, E. (1982) 'In The Abundance of Water the Fool is Thirsty: Sociology and Black Pathology' in Centre for Contemporary Cultural Studies, *The Empire Strikes Back*, London: Hutchinson.
Lawrence, W. (1895) *The Valley of Kashmir: Vol. 1*, London: Longmans.
Lewis, P. (1994) *Islamic Britain: Religion, Politics and Identity amongst British Muslims: Bradford in the 1990s*, London: I. B.Tauris.
Light, I. (1972) *Ethnic Enterprise in America: Business and Welfare among Chinese, Japanese and Blacks*, Berkeley: University of California Press.
Light, I. and Bhachu, P. (1993) *Immigration and Entrepreneurship, Culture, Capital and Ethnic Networks*, New Brunswick: Transaction.
Lloyd, P. and Reeve, D. (1981) *Recession, Restructuring and Location: A Study of Employment Trends in North West England, 1971-1977* Manchester: North West Industry Unit, Department of Geography, University of Manchester.
Lomas, G. and Monck, E. (1973) *The Coloured Population of Great Britain: Employment and Economic Activity 1971, Analyses of Special Census Tabulations*, London: Runnymede Trust.
Malik, R. and Gregory, S. (1991) *Living with Two Cultures*, Nottingham: Ujala Press.
Mars, G. and Ward, R. (1984) 'Ethnic Business Development in Britain Opportunities and Resource' in R. Ward and R. Jenkins (eds.) *Ethnic Communities in Business: Strategies for Economic Survival*, Cambridge : Cambridge University Press.
Martin, R. and Rowthorn, B. (1986) *The Geography of De-Industrialisation*, London: Macmillan.
Massey, D. (1988) 'Economic Development and International Migration in Comparative Perspective,' Population and Development Review, 14: 383-413.
Mc Laughlin, W. (ed.) (1992) *Understanding Unemployment: New perspectives on Active Labour Market Policies*, London: Routledge.

McEvoy, D. and Aldrich, H. (1986) 'Survival Rates of Asian and White Retailers', *International Small Business Journal*, 4: 28-37.

McEvoy, D., Jones, T., Cater, J. and Aldrich, H. (1982) 'Asian immigrant businesses in British cities,' Paper presented to the British Association for he Advancement of Science, Annual Meeting, September.

McLoughlin, S. (1997) *Breaking into Bounded Britain*, Manchester: unpublished PhD. Thesis, Department of Anthropology, University of Manchester.

McLoughlin, S. and Kalra, V. (1994) 'Mosque-Centre and Community-Mosque' Paper Presented at the ICCCR Conference' Multiculturalism, Identity, Politics, December 1994.

McPhillips, K. (1981) *Oldham: The Formative Years*, Oldham: OMBC Leisure Services.

Miles, R. (1982) *Racism and Migrant Labour: A Critical Text*, London: Routledge.

Miles, R. (1989) *Racism*, London: Routledge.

Miles, R. (1993) *Racism After 'Race Relations'*, London:Routledge.

Miles, R. and Phizacklea, A. (1980) *Labour and Racism*, London: Routledge.

Millet, F. (1995) *Oldham and Its People*, Oldham: OMBC Leisure Services.

Mitter, S. (1986) 'Industrial Restructuring and Manufacturing Homework: Women in the UK Clothing Industry', *Capital and Class*, 27: 123.

Mitter, S. (1988) *Common Fate, Common Bond: Women in the Global Economy*, London: Pluto Press.

Modood, T. (1992) 'Beyond Racial Dualism: The Case of the Indian Economic Success' in T. Modood (1992) *Not Easy Being British: Colour, Culture and Citizenship*, London: Trentham Books.

Modood, T., Beishon S. and Virdee S. (1994) *Changing Ethnic Identities*, London: Policy Studies Institute.

Modood, T., Virdee, S. and Metcalf, H. (1996) *Asian Self-employment in Britain the Interaction of Culture and Economics*, London: Policy Studies Institute.

Morkvasic, M. (1984) 'Birds of a Passage are also Women', *International Migration Review*, Vol 18 no 4.

Nowikowski, S. (1984) 'Snakes and Ladders: Asian Business in Britain' in R. Ward and R. Jenkins (eds.) *Ethnic Communities in Business: Strategies for Economic Survival*, Cambridge: Cambridge University

Press.
Ohri, S. and Faruqui, S. (1988) 'Racism, Employment and Unemployment' in A. Bhat, R. Carr-Hill, and S. Ohri, *Britain's Black Population*, Aldershot: Gower.
Owen, D. and Green, A. (1992) 'Labour Market Experience and Change among Ethnic Groups in Britain', *New Community*, 19: 126-139.
Pagnamenta, P. and Overy, R. (1984) *All Our Working Lives*, London: British Broadcasting Corporation.
Pahl, R. (1988) 'Introduction: Work in Context' in R. Pahl (ed.) *On Work: Historical, Comparative and Theoretical Approaches*, Oxford: Blackwell.
Pappas, G. (1989) *The Magic City - Unemployment in a Working Class Community*, New York: Cornell University Press.
Parker, D. (1995) *Through Different Eyes: The Cultural Identities of Young Chinese People in Britain*, Aldershot: Averbury.
Parkin, D. (1995) 'Latticed Knowledge: Eradication and Dispersal of the Unpalatable: Islam, Medicine and Anthropological Theory' in R. Fardon (ed.) *Counterworks: Managing the Diversity of Knowledge*, London: Routledge.
Parmar, P. (1982) 'Gender, Race and Class: Asian Women in Resistance' in Centre for Contemporary Cultural Studies, T*he Empire Strikes Back*, London: Hutchinson.
Patterson, S. (1963) *Dark Strangers*, London: Tavistock.
Patterson, S. (1968) *Immigrants in Industry*, London: Oxford University Press.
Peach, C. (1990) 'The Muslim Population of Great Britain', *Ethnic and Racial Studies*, 13: 415-419.
Peach, C. (ed.) (1996) *Ethnicity in the 1991 Census. - Vol.2 : The Ethnic Minority Populations of Great Britain*, London: HMSO.
Penn, R., Martin, A. and Scattergood, H. (1990a) *Employment Trajectories of Asian Migrants in Rochdale: An Integrated Analysis*, ESRC Social Change and Economic Life Research Initiative Working paper 14, Lancaster: Sociology Department, University of Lancaster.
Penn, R., Martin, A. and Scattergood, H. (1990b) *Gender Relations, Technology and Employment Change in the Contemporary Textile Industry: Integrated Analysis*, ESRC Social Change and Economic Life Research Initiative Working paper 20, Lancaster: Sociology Department, University of Lancaster.
Pennington, S. and Westover, B. (1989) *A Hidden Workforce, Homeworkers in England 1850-1985*, London: Macmillan Education.

Phizacklea, A. (1988) 'Entrepreunership, Ethnicity and Gender' in S. Westwood and P. Bhachu (eds.) *Enterprising Women: Ethnicity, Economy and Gender*, London: Routledge.

Phizacklea, A. (1990) *Unpacking the Fashion Industry*, London: Routledge.

Phizacklea, A. and Miles, R. (1992) 'The British Trade Union Movement and Racism' in P. Braham, A. Rattansi and R. Skellington (eds.) *Racism and Antiracism*, London: Routledge.

Pilcher, J. and Williamson, H. (1988) *A Guide to Young People's Experience in a Changing Labour Market. An Uphill Struggle*, London: Youth Aid.

Pinchbeck, I. (1969) *Women Workers and the Industrial Revolution: 1750-1850*, London: Frank Cass and Co.

Powell, J. (1976) *Work Study*, London: Arrow.

Powell, P. (1990) *Notes for UK Immigration Lawyers On Custom and Practice in the Indian Sub-continent*, London: Law Society Press.

Puri, B. (1993) *Kashmir; Towards Insurgency*, Sangam Press: London.

Rafiq, M. (1992) 'Ethnicity and Enterprise: A Comparison of Muslim and Non-Muslims', *New Community*, 19 : 43-60.

Rahim, K. (1995) *My Father: A Kashmiri Betrayed*, London: Volume II.

Ram, M. (1992) 'Coping with Racism: Asian Employers in the Inner-city', *Work, Employment and Society*, 6 : 601-618.

Ranger, T. (1996) 'Introduction' in T.O.Ranger, Y. Samad and O. Stuart (eds.) *Culture, Identity and Politics*, Aldershot: Avebury Press.

Renshaw, G. (1981) *Employment, Trade and North-South Co-operation*, Geneva: ILO.

Rex, J. (1973) *Race, Colonialism and the City*, London: Oxford.

Rex, J. (1983) *Race Relations in Sociological Theory*, London: Routledge.

Rex, J. (1986) *Race and Ethnicity*, Milton Keynes: Open University Press.

Rex, J. and Moore, R. (1967) *Race, Community and Conflict*, London: Oxford University Press.

Rex J. and Tomlinson S.(1979) *Colonial Immigrants in a British City: A Class Analysis*, London: Routledge.

Rex, J. and Mason, D. (eds.) (1986) *Theories of Race and Ethnic Relations*, Cambridge: Cambridge University Press.

Rex, J. and Drury, B. (eds) (1994) *Ethnic Mobilisation in a Multi-Cultural Europe*, Aldershot: Avebury.

Rimmer, M. (1972) *Race and Industrial Conflict*, London: Heinmann.

Rose (1911) *Glossary of Tribes and castes of Punjab and NWFP*, Lahore: Asian Book Company.
Rose, E. et al (1969) *Colour and Citizenship: A Report on British Race Relations,* London: Oxford University Press.
Rowbotham, S. and Mitter, S. (eds.) (1994) *Dignity and Daily Bread*, London: Routledge.
Sachdeva, S. (1993) *The Primary Purpose Rule in British Immigration Law*, Trentham Books and SOAS: London.
Sachs, W. (ed.) (1992) *The Development Dictionary: A Guide to Knowledge as Power*, London: Zed.
Said, E. (1978) *Orientalism*, London: Penguin.
Saifullah Khan V.(1974) *Pakistani Villagers in a British City*, unpublished Ph.D. thesis, University of Bradford.
Saifullah Khan, V. (1976a) 'Purdah in the British Situation', in D.L Barker and S Allen(eds.) *Dependence and Exploitation in Work and Marriage*, London: Longman.
Saifullah Khan, V. (1976b) 'Pakistanis in Britain: Perceptions of a Population', *New Community*, 5: 222-9.
Saifullah Khan, V (1977) 'The Pakistanis' in J.L. Watson (ed.) *Between Two Cultures* Oxford: Basil Blackwell.
Samad, Y. (1994) 'Kashmir and the Imagining of Pakistan' forthcoming in G. Rizvi and A. Matto (eds) *Kashmir.*
Samad, Y. (1996) 'The Politics of Islamic Identity among Bangladeshis and Pakistanis in Britain', in T.O.Ranger, Y. Samad and O. Stuart (eds.) *Culture, Identity and Politics*, Aldershot: Avebury Press.
Sastry, K. (1984) *The Cotton Mill Industry of India*, Delhi: Manohar.
Sayyid, B. (1997) *TheFundamental Fear*, London: Zed.
Shams, M. (1993) 'Religiosity as a Predictor of Well-Being and Moderator of the Psychological Impact of Unemployment', *Journal of Psychological Medicine*, 66: 341-352.
Sharma, S. Hutnyk. J. and Sharma, A. (eds.) (1996) *Dis-Orienting Rhythms: The Politics of the New Asian Dance Music*, London: Zed.
Shaw A. (1988) *A Pakistani Community in Britain*, Oxford: Basil Blackwell.
Shaw, A. (1994) 'The Pakistani Community in Oxford' in R. Ballard (ed.) *Desh Pardesh*, London: Hurst
Short, S. (1984) *Lancashire United? Black Workers and the Trade Union Movement in Lancashire*, Report for Conference of the Lancashire Association of Trades Councils, Lancashire: Lancashire Association of Trades Councils.

Simpson, S. (1995) *Issues in Local Demography with an Ethnic Group Dimension, and Policy Applications in Bradford City Council*, Paper presented to the British Society for Population Studies Conference, Brighton August 30 - September 1, 1995.

Singleton, J. (1991) *Lancashire On The Scrapheap The Cotton Industry 1945 - 1970*, Oxford: Pasold.

Sivanandan, A. (1981) 'From Resistance to Rebellion: Asian and Afro-Caribbean Struggles in Britain', *Race and Class*, 23: 111-51.

Sivanandan, A. (1982) *A Different Hunger*, London: Pluto Press.

Sly, F. (1996) 'Ethnic Minority Participation in the Labour Market: Trends from the Labour Force Survey 1984-1995' in *Labour Force Trends*, ONS: HMSO.

Smith, D. (1977) *Racial Disadvantage in Britain: The PEP Report*, Harmondsworth: Penguin.

Smith, D. (1977) *Unemployment and Racial Minorities*, London: Policy Studies Institute.

Smith, V. (1958) *The Oxford History of India*, Oxford: Clarendon Press.

Solomos, J.(1989) *Race and Racism in Contemporary Britain*, London: Macmillan.

Solomos, J. (1992) 'The Politics of Immigration since 1945' in P. Braham, A. Rattansi and R. Skellington (eds.) *Racism and Antiracism*, London: Sage.

Soni, S., Tricker, M. and Ward, R. *(*1987) *Ethnic Minority Business in Leicestershire:A Report to Leicester City Council*, Birmingham: Aston University Management Centre.

Srinivasan, S. (1992) 'The Class Position of the Asian Petty Bourgeoisie', *New Community*, 19: 61-74.

Srinivasan, S. (1995) *The South Asian Petty Bourgeoisie in Britain: An Oxford Case Study*, Aldershot: Avebury.

Tate, J. (1994) 'Homework in West Yorkshire' in S. Rowbotham and S. Mitter (eds.) (*Dignity and Daily Bread*, London: Routledge.

Thompson, E.P. (1978) 'Eighteenth-century English Society: Class Struggle without Class?', *Social History*, 3: 133-65.

Tonkin, E., McDonald, M. and Chapman, M.(eds.) (1989) *History and Ethnicity*, London: Routledge.

Turner, H. (1962) *Trade Union Growth, Structure And Policy: A Comparative Study Of The Cotton Unions in England*, London: Allen and Unwin.

Index

(Azad) Kashmir 55-73, 119-122
  Mirpur, 55-73, 103, 121, 150, 168, 184
Anwar, Mohammed,
  Myth of Return 9, 18, 19, 20, 22,
  Migration 38, 44, 53, 65
  Textiles in Rochdale 120, 122-132, 139-145

baba,
  terminology 39-50
  in mills 119- 145
  redundant 145-156
Ballard, Roger, 3, 4, 6, 9, 20- 24, 33, 54, 58-69
Bangladeshi, 33, 166, 169, 177
Black, 122, 139
  terminology 32, 33, 34, 35, 36, 38, 49
Brah, Avtar, 5, 10, 25, 26, 27, 28, 29, 31, 36, 193, 210

Class, 4, 5, 8, 10, 11, 13, 14, 15, 16, 21-39, 43, 72, 89, 94, 95, 98, 101, 115, 126-139, 161-163

Eade, John, 1, 26, 32, 196, 201, 2
Ethnicity, 16-18, 11-22, 26, 33-39

Indian, 12, 27, 34, 36, 37,

kaka,
  terminology 39, 40, 43, 47, 49,
  migration 103-107

Labour
  theory, 2, 3, 5, 7, 8, 10, 11, 13, 14, 15, 17, 18, 20, 25, 26, 27, 28, 29, 161-163, 191-194
  Unemployment, 131, 139-145

Mangla Dam, 52, 62, 63, 64, 65, 66, 67, 68, 69, 71, 73, 194, 197, 208
Media, 1, 86, 133, 152, 155, 190, 192, 223
Migrant Labour, 1, 2, 4, 5, 8, 10, 11, 13, 15, 18, 19, 20, 21, 24, 25, 27, 29, 69-73, 92-98
Migration, 18, 19, 22, 51, 52-76
  theory, 53-55
Mirpuri, 32, 33, 34, 35, 37, 38, 39, 40, 41, 44, 47, 50, 56, 61, 64, 66, 71, 111, 125, 138, 161, 162, 176, 198, 208
Modood, Tariq, 7, 22, 30, 34, 49, 100, 159, 173, 194, 201, 217
Muslim, 10, 25, 26, 27, 154-157
  terminology, 39-50

Oldham
  Labour history, 88-92
  Glodwick, 144, 153, 188
  Textile history, 77-88, 103,122,
  Werneth, 161

Pakistani
  terminology, 32-50

Racism, 5, 8, 10, 11, 12, 13, 15, 24, 26, 30, 34, 43, 49, 98, 120, 122, 127, 158, 176, 177, 179, 183, 193, 200
Rex, John, 4, 8, 11, 13, 14, 15, 22, 30, 39, 73, 93, 100, 215, 219, 221

NEWSPAPERS AND MAGAZINES

Eastern Eye 5/5/94 :6-7 'Cabbies Protest Council ruling'.
Friends Newspaper July 1994.
Oldham Chronicle 17/10/1994 'Taxi Driver Brutally Attacked'.
Pakistan and Gulf Economist Editorial of December 2-8 1995 Vol XIV No. 48.
Shiloh News Issue No.12 May 1984
The Islamic Times (Stockport) June 1994: 4).
The Observer Alibhai, Y. 'Home Truths' (Colour Supplement) 19/11/92, 46-49.

Westwood, S. and Bhachu, P. (1988) *Enterprising Women: Ethnicity, Economy and Gender Relations*, London: Routledge.
Willis, P. (1977) *Learning to Labour*, Farnborough: Saxon House.
Wilson, A. (1978) *Finding a Voice*, London: Virago.
Worsley, P. (1976) 'Proletarians, Sub-Proletarians and Urban Proletarians, Marginalidados, Migrants, Urban Peasants and Urban Poor', *Sociology*, 10: 223-245.
Wright, P. (1968) *The Coloured Worker in British Industry*, London: Oxford University Press.
Yiannis, G. (1988) *Working lives in Catering*, London: Gabriel Routledge.

REPORTS

A Survey of Homeworking in Calderdale, Bradford(1991). Yorkshire and Humberside Low Pay Unit.
ATWU Year Book 1972, Associated and Textile Workers Union, Lancashire.
Bradford Heritage Recording Unit (1994)
Employment Gazette March 1991 : table 1.2: p.198.
Employment Trends (1984-1992) Greater Manchester Research Unit, Oldham.
*Employment Trends Bulletin (*1990-1995) Greater Manchester Research Unit.
Fact File For (1991) Oldham Economic Development Unit Oldham: OMBC.
*Greater Manchester Industrial Profile (*1985), Greater Manchester Research Unit, Oldham.
Lancashire Industrial Language Training Unit (1987) *In Search of Employment and Training, Experiences and Perceptions of Redundant Asian Textile Workers in Lancashire*, London: CRE
Oldham Social Survey 1995 (1996) Policy Unit, OMBC.
Quarterly Statistical Review (Mar 1958).Cotton Board No. 49
Runnymede Commission (1997) *Islamophobia: Its Features and Dangers*
Social Focus on Ethnic Minorities, (1996) ONS London: HMSO.
The Textile Industry of Lancashire, (1992) Bolton Education Dept, Bolton MBC.

Wallman, S. (1979) 'Introduction: The Scope for Ethnicity' in S.Wallman (ed.) *Ethnicity at Work*, London: Macmillan.
Wallman, S. (1986) 'Ethnicity and the Boundary Process in Context', in J. Rex and D. Mason (eds.) *Theories of Race and Ethnic Relations*, Cambridge: Cambridge University Press.
Walton, J. (1990) *Lancashire A Social History 1558-1939*, Manchester: Manchester University Press.
Ward, R. (1990) *Ethnic Entrepreneurs*, London: Sage.
Ward, R. and Jenkins, R. (eds.) (1984) *Ethnic Communities in Business: Strategies for Economic Survival*, Cambridge: Cambridge University Press.
Warwick, D. (1992) *Coal, Capital and Culture: A Sociological Analysis of Mining Communities in West Yorkshire*, London: Routledge.
Watson, J. (1977) 'Introduction: Immigration, Ethnicity and Class in Britain' in J. Watson, *Between Two Cultures: Migrants and Minorities in Britain*, Oxford: Basil Blackwell.
Weber, M. (1976) *The Protestant Ethic and the Spirit of Capitalism*, translated by P. Talcott, London: Allen and Unwin.
Werbner, P. (1984) 'Business on Trust: Pakistani Entrepreneurship in the Manchester Garment Trade' in R. Ward and R. Jenkins (eds) *Ethnic Communities in Business: Strategies for Economic Survival*, Cambridge: Cambridge University Press: 166-188.
Werbner, P. (1987) 'Barefoot in Britain in *New Community*, 14: 182-189.
Werbner, P. (1990) *The Migration Process* Oxford: Berg.
Werbner, P. (1991a) 'Black And Ethnic Leadership in Britain - A Theoretical Overview' in M. Anwar and P. Werbner *Black and Ethnic Leaderships*, London: Routledge.
Werbner, P. (1991b) 'The Fiction of Unity in Ethnic Politics' in M. Anwar and P. Werbner (eds.) *Black and Ethnic Leaderships*, London: Routledge.
Werbner, P.(1991c) 'Factionalism and Violence in British Pakistani Communal Politics' in H. Donnan and P. Werbner (eds.) *Economy and Culture in Pakistan*, London: Macmillan.
Werbner, P. (1995) 'Critique of Caricature? A Response to Wilcken and Gell', *Critique of Anthropology*, 15: 425-32.
West, C. (1993) 'The New Cultural Politics of Difference', in S. During (ed.) *The Cultural Studies Reader*, London: Routledge.
West, C. (1994) *Race Matters*, New York: Vintage.
Westwood, S. (1984) *All Day Everyday: Factory and Family in The Making of Womens' Lives*, London: Pluto.